Bill Gates

1993

JUMP START

JUMP START

Japan Comes to the Heartland

DAVID GELSANLITER

Kodansha International
New York · Tokyo · London

Kodansha America, Inc.,
114 Fifth Avenue, New York, New York 10011, U.S.A.

Kodansha International Ltd.,
17–14 Otowa 1-chome, Bunkyo-ku, Tokyo 112, Japan

Published in 1992 by Kodansha America, Inc.
by arrangement with Farrar, Straus & Giroux.

Printed in the United States of America

92   93   94   95   6   5   4   3   2   1

Library of Congress Cataloging-in-Publication Data
Gelsanliter, David.
Jump start : Japan comes to the heartland / David Gelsanliter.
p.   cm.
Originally published: New York : Farrar, Straus & Giroux, c1990.
Includes bibliographical references and index.
ISBN 4-7700-1713-8
1. Automobile industry and trade—United States.   2. Corporations,
Japanese—United States.   3. Automobile industry workers—United
States—Attitudes.   I. Title.
HD9710.U52G357   1992   338.8'87292'0973—dc20
92-16919   CIP

Printed and bound by Arcata Graphics, Fairfield, Pennsylvania

For my father,
Who would never drive a foreign-made car

Home folks think I'm big in Detroit City,
From the letters that I write, they think I'm fine.
But by day I make the cars,
by night I make the bars;
if only they could read between the lines.
I wanna go home, I wanna go home;
Oh, Lord, I wanna go home.

—"Detroit City," words and music
by Danny Dill and Mel Tillis

Contents

Preface

Since *Jump Start* was first published in the summer of 1990, one of the best-kept secrets of the 1980s has exploded into headlines. Honda, Toyota, and Nissan have shown that American workers in the lower Midwest and upper South can build cars with quality standards as high or higher than those in Japan.

The Japanese now account for nearly a third of car sales in the United States, with an ever-increasing share built here at home. The threat posed to Detroit and the American Big Three has risen dramatically, and American companies are finally taking steps to respond.

In 1991, General Motors posted a $4.5 billion loss, the largest in U.S. corporate history, and announced the gradual closing of twenty-one plants, which translates to 74,000 lost jobs. In the same year the American car industry as a whole posted an $8 billion loss, and both Honda and Toyota surpassed Chrysler in U.S. car sales. For the third year in a row, the Honda Accord was America's best-selling car. Toyota and Nissan are doubling their manufacturing capacity in Kentucky and Tennessee. And in two recent twists, Lee Iacocca was forced out as Chrysler's CEO and GM's board of directors has asserted control over operational decisions.

American manufacturers, and not just those in the car industry, are eliminating unnecessary levels of management, but nowhere are current economic weaknesses being confronted with more intensity than the car industry. Executives are immersing themselves in the nitty-gritty of plant floor supervision, something ignored until recently. Chrysler is launching its first totally new cars since 1991. Future GM models will have fewer basic platform chassis and more interchangeable parts. Detroit's Big Three have started pooling research efforts. And, the failure of the United Auto Workers to organize either Honda or Nissan, explored later in this book, has emboldened General Motors to seek greater flexibility by clipping the union's wings.

If anything, Honda, Toyota, and Nissan have been too successful for their own good.

Until recently, we hadn't worried about losing the TV or VCR or even the steel industry because we had full employment, thanks to our enormous defense industry. Now, with the end of the cold war, the breakup of the Soviet Union, and the greatly diminished threat of worldwide communism, the focus of alarm has shifted to a new adversary. The Japanese government, fearful that we need a new enemy in order to rediscover our national purpose, has told its auto makers to jack up their car prices, reduce car exports from Japan to the United States, and concentrate on profitability rather than market share gains. The objective is to give the American Big Three a chance to recoup, if they can.

In this new strategy Toyota has taken the lead. Toyota has repudiated, at least for now, its goal of recapturing 10 percent of the world vehicle market by the year 2000. It has postponed plans to challenge Detroit's most profitable market segment with a full-size pickup truck, and appears ready to lessen the competitive pressure by keeping its most popular models on the market for five or more years.

The Japanese can't afford to be perceived as having blood on their hands. They don't want to be seen as having destroyed Chrysler or further crippled General Motors. If Chrysler is to go under or merge with another auto maker, and if GM is to lose further market share, the American public needs to understand that these companies did it to themselves. The Japanese don't want Congress to pass legislation that would limit or jeopardize their access to what is still the world's largest auto market. They need the U.S. government to say that cars built by the Japanese in America for export to Europe are as American as red, white, and blue.

For the American Big Three, this breathing spell may well be temporary. One determinant will be whether, in a quest for short-term profits over market share gains, American manufacturers again raise their prices to match those of the Japanese.

Jump Start tells the story of how Honda, Nissan, and Toyota transferred a large and still growing part of Japan's most important industry to our lower Midwest and upper South, why they picked the sites they did, who they chose to hire and promote, and how they won the loyalty of small-town America in the process. This refined and updated edition also explores how three giant Japanese auto companies worked overtime to do what they wanted without being disliked by the Americans, upon whom they depend for support. A crucial question for the remainder of the decade is whether we need a scapegoat to excuse our industrial deficiencies or whether we can blend what the Japanese have to offer with what we do best, so that one and one add up to Three.

JUMP START

Introduction

If the new Jefferson plant just limps along, bleeding
Chrysler with low productivity, I can just about
guarantee you it will be the last state-of-the-art
automotive plant ever built in inner city America.
—Chrysler vice-chairman Gerald Green-
wald in the Detroit *News*, May 1989

On a flat piece of land that was once a cornfield, in one
long, low, beige-colored building set behind towering oak
trees, more automobiles were being built than in any other
plant, in any single location, anywhere in America. They
were being built by three thousand high-school graduates
straight off the farm, by former waitresses, barbers, and
store clerks, almost all of whom had never worked on an
assembly line before. Their average age was twenty-eight,
all lived within thirty miles of the plant, and only four of
them were active union members.

Al Kinzer, a forty-four-year-old Virginian, was address-
ing a group of new recruits. Most were wearing jeans, freshly
pressed cotton shirts, and running shoes. There were seventeen men and four women. They had had three separate
interviews, conducted by three mostly different batteries of
interviewers. The qualities, besides mechanical ability, that
their interviewers were looking for were flexibility, open-
mindedness, a willingness to work overtime, and an eagerness
to learn more than one skill. Close family ties, attention to

detail, and a respectful, unemotional demeanor were equally prized.

"You're now in the automobile business," Kinzer says. "So let me read you a few recent headlines: Ford lays off 1,450; American Motors is idle for two weeks. At Chrysler they've got eighty-nine days' inventory; at GM, eighty-five; at Ford, fifty-eight." He pauses for effect. "Here we've got an inventory of only eight days."

Inside the plant, no one is running, but no one is exactly walking, either. An automated guided vehicle, which looks like a miniature railroad car, glides silently across the plant floor carrying car seats to the assembly line. As it approaches the workers, called associates here, it issues a warning—not a blaring siren but a lilting melody that has been programmed into its computer memory.

The melody is one clue that this is a Japanese, not an American, automobile plant. Another is that there are no private offices, only a few meeting rooms. All executives occupy one central work space, their laminated wood-grain desktops piled high with papers and bare of photographs or personal belongings of any kind. Everyone, even the executives, wears the same eggshell-white uniform with first name stenciled in red above the right breast pocket. *The Wall Street Journal*, in a tiny but nonetheless front-page story, called this plant "the darling of U.S. auto factories."

The time was the mid-1980s; the place, Honda's first auto plant, located eight miles west of Marysville, Ohio. The Big Three had weathered the recession of 1980–82 and were said to be on their way to matching the Japanese in quality and productivity. The Midwest and Upper South were still the two parts of the country where the fewest import cars were sold. No one really believed the Japanese could motivate the American worker better than an American company could, or that the Japanese could build cars of the same quality here as in Japan. The Big Three were awash in black ink. American managers were collecting record bonuses again. Honda, a maverick company formed after World War II, seemed scarcely a threat. The name Honda, like the name Sony, sounded hardly Japanese.

That was then and this is now. Now the Japanese appear to be on the verge of taking over the American auto industry.

At a time when polls show that many Americans consider Japan's economic muscle to be the single greatest threat to national security, it seems hard to believe that west-central Ohio, northern Kentucky, and middle Tennessee may one day replace Detroit as the center of the American automobile industry. But it is no longer inconceivable. Stranger things have been happening.

Twenty years ago Akron was the capital of the world's tire industry. Today it makes scarcely any tires at all. Twenty years ago the United Auto Workers was America's preeminent union, with more than a million and a half members. Today its membership is less than 900,000, and its very existence—like that of the American independent auto parts industry—is in jeopardy. Twenty years ago Americans were saying that a Japanese car was a cheap piece of junk. Drive one, and if a truck passed, the airflow would push you to the right, then pull you ahead momentarily. Today managers at American car companies scale twenty-foot walls and "visualize greatness" so they can become more like the Japanese. In the last fourteen years, the Big Three's share of the American market has dropped 18 points, to less than 64 percent, and it seems likely there will be further erosion. Suddenly the Japanese, of all people, are better able than American management to motivate the American blue-collar worker. Americans who had become estranged from the product they made were taking pride in craftsmanship again. A great deal had happened in a short space of time. Consider that:

After Nissan defeated the United Auto Workers by a

vote of two to one, workers at its Tennessee plant last year
waved American flags and wore T-shirts proclaiming "Union
Free and Proud of It."

At Toyota's Kentucky plant, workers start their day with
shoulder rolls, neck rolls, and bends at the waist to get ready
for the "most physical job" most of them have ever had.

In the heartland, the Japanese simplify their names—
Massy for Masyuki, Hiro for Hirano, Mac for Makoto—to
better blend in.

Until recently, too, the Japanese had begun to speak
out. American managers are good at communicating with
people in their own departments, but not so good at communicating with other departments. Americans bury problems and seek solutions on an isolated case-by-case basis
rather than bringing them to the surface so all resources of
the company can be brought to bear. Americans are too
proud. Japanese managers manage best and learn most by
being close to problems, not sitting behind a desk.

As recession hit the American auto industry, it was Big
Three, not the newer Japanese auto plants, that were being
forced to lay off and shut down. All of a sudden, it seemed
too late to reverse the trend.

In 1950 Japan made fewer than 32,000 cars and trucks and
the United States 8 million, but by 1980 Japan had passed
the United States as the world's leading vehicle producer.
Between 1970 and the early 1980s, the eight largest Ohio
cities—ethnically diverse and highly unionized—lost nearly
400,000 people. Vigorous import competition and a dramatic
shift in consumer preference to smaller, fuel-efficient cars
combined to make 1980 and 1981 two of the most difficult
years in American automotive history. General Motors, Ford,
Chrysler, and American Motors lost more than $5 billion.
Ohio and the Upper Midwest became the rust belt. The Big
Three began manufacturing small cars and small engines
overseas.

It was into this void that Honda came, building first motorcycles, in 1979, and then automobiles, in 1982, the one plant next to the other on farmland thirty-eight miles northwest of Columbus, Ohio. Honda came, not to one of the depressed cities, but to farm country, where the most characteristic sight is a nest of grain elevators, where small-town newspapers print the names of traffic-law offenders every day and noodles are not pasta but noodles still.

Honda set the standard, and other Japanese auto makers soon followed: Nissan in 1983 with a truck plant (soon expanded to include a car plant) in Smyrna, Tennessee; Honda in 1986 with another car plant in Alliston, Ontario; Mazda and Ford in 1987 with a car plant in Flat Rock, Michigan; Toyota in 1988 with a car plant in Georgetown, Kentucky; Mitsubishi and Chrysler (called Diamond-Star) in 1988 with another in Normal, Illinois; Toyota in 1988 with a second car plant in Cambridge, Ontario; Subaru-Isuzu in 1989 with a car plant in Lafayette, Indiana; and, also in 1989, General Motors and Suzuki with another in Ingersoll, Ontario. By 1990 nearly three hundred Japanese auto parts companies had also built plants in these six states and Canada. The heartland had taken the lead in building product again, but it was the Japanese who were leading the way.

Of the six Japanese auto makers, Honda, Toyota, and Nissan are the pacesetters, the ones least likely to suffer as U.S. overproduction of autos intensifies, the three most likely to remain nonunion. Their stunning quality and productivity records have made their new plants in Ohio, Kentucky, and Tennessee the most likely to flourish in the century ahead. The lesser Japanese auto makers could stumble here, but it seems unlikely that Honda, Toyota, or Nissan will. Toyota and Nissan control 60 percent of the car market in Japan. Honda, with a less than 10 percent share there, has staked its future in North America.

After Honda, Nissan, and Toyota come Mazda, Mitsubishi, and Subaru-Isuzu. The Mazda-Ford and the Mitsubishi-

Chrysler joint ventures are both unionized, both attempts by second-tier Japanese auto makers to gain access to the American market in a politically acceptable way. These two are modeled after the most successful of the joint ventures—the Toyota–General Motors plant in Fremont, California, thirty-five miles southeast of San Francisco.

Most observers had expected the Fremont plant, called NUMMI (New United Motor Manufacturing, Inc.), to set the pattern in labor relations for other Japanese auto makers in the United States. Until Nissan defeated the UAW in July 1989, it had been assumed that the Japanese would eventually adapt their philosophies to ours. *Fortune* magazine had said that "as a cooperative endeavor between a symbol of Japanese efficiency and a powerful U.S. union, New United Motor is the most important labor relations experiment in the U.S. today." As late as April 1989, Labor Secretary Elizabeth Dole said "NUMMI's joint venture between GM *and* Toyota has come to be considered the ideal labor-management partnership, a marriage said to be a *landmark* in America."

NUMMI began production in 1984 with a UAW work force. Union members had worked in the same plant when it was plagued by low productivity and wildcat strikes, and GM had shut it down. With most of these same workers and even union officials, however, NUMMI, managed by Toyota, became a remarkable success. Supervisors weren't called managers now but group leaders, workers not employees but team members. Everyone ate in the same cafeteria, parked in the same lot, and wore the same clothes. If a team member found that he or she could not complete a job, or that the quality of the job did not meet specifications, that person could pull a cord to stop the assembly line, an act that would result in disciplinary action in most other assembly plants. A plant wall was plastered with sheets of brightly colored paper containing handwritten before-and-after stories detailing improvements the workers had made. Above the display was the single word *Kaizen*, meaning "continual improvement." Under *kaizen*, workers find flaws in the manufacturing process, suggest improvements, and criticize their own performance.

In an era when American auto executives were blaming either imports, the American worker, or the UAW for their problems—and putting their faith in automated equipment instead—NUMMI's success with a low-tech plant and a UAW work force was evidence that the fault must lie elsewhere.

The NUMMI example, coupled with Honda's even more dramatic successes in Ohio with a nonunion work force, were clear indications that a new day was at hand.

In the 1970s Detroit suffered through two oil crises. Rising gasoline prices called into question the Big Three's ability to make cheap, fuel-efficient cars and, if they did, to make them of the quality attained by the Japanese. In 1970 Japanese car imports accounted for 12 percent of the U.S. market. Ten years later their share had more than doubled.

Detroit panicked. In 1979 Chrysler, near bankruptcy, had to be bailed out by the federal government. In 1980 and 1981 scarcely a week went by that Ford or General Motors didn't announce a cutback or plant closing. More than a quarter-million auto workers were unemployed. Protesters bashed Japanese cars with sledgehammers, and owners of Japanese cars were barred from using Big Three and UAW parking lots. In Detroit in 1982, a Chinese-American by the name of Vincent Chin was mistaken for Japanese and bludgeoned to death with a baseball bat by a former auto plant foreman at Chrysler. A Wayne County judge sentenced his assailant to only three years' probation and a fine of $3,790. It wasn't until two years later that a federal judge raised the sentence to twenty-five years in prison.

Douglas Fraser, the president of the UAW, went to

Japan and chastised Toyota and Nissan for exporting un-
employment. He noted that Honda had announced it would
build cars in the United States, and he urged Toyota and
Nissan to do likewise. Toyota gave him little satisfaction, and
Nissan said that if it were to come to the United States, it
wanted nothing to do with the union. Returning home,
Fraser, with others, began lobbying for protective legislation.
As a result, the Japanese became alarmed and agreed to
restrict their car exports to existing levels. In the meantime,
Nissan announced it would build a truck plant in Tennessee,
and, at GM's urging, Toyota negotiated the NUMMI joint
venture in California.

For a time then, after revaluation of the dollar against
the yen raised the price of Japanese exports, the threat from
Japanese auto makers seemed to recede. The Japanese were
portrayed as opportunists who had gotten lucky during an
oil crisis. GM and Chrysler began to relax. But the Japanese
kept the prices on the vehicles they sent to the United States
well below what appreciation of the yen could have justified.
They also launched a massive drive to cut costs and protect
market share. Then came the announcements of the Mazda-
Ford plant in Michigan, the Toyota plant in Kentucky, the
Mitsubishi-Chrysler plant in Illinois, and the Subaru-Isuzu
plant in Indiana. The export restraint pact, by forcing the
Japanese to invest in the United States, ensured that Detroit
would confront a new, more dangerous rival, this time on
American soil. In the last ten years GM saw its share of the
U.S. car market drop from 46 to 35 percent. The UAW has
been hurt as much as management by the Japanese influx.

In 1985 the union tried to organize Honda, but at the
last minute called off the election to avoid certain defeat. In
1989 the UAW tried again, this time at Nissan, long thought
the most vulnerable. There the union was defeated by a
margin of two to one, in a blitz of national news coverage.
For years the UAW had been losing thousands of members
as American auto parts companies built small nonunion

plants in the Lower Midwest and Upper South. But not until the Nissan defeat did it penetrate the national consciousness that a large and ever-growing segment of the automotive industry was likely to remain nonunion. Soon strikes would be disastrous, since in the event of work stoppages at Big Three or Big Three supplier plants, the Japanese would be able to pick up the slack.

It obviously is no longer a level playing field if the Big Three (and most of their suppliers) are unionized and the three leading Japanese companies (and their suppliers) remain not. The Japanese already have too many other advantages. Their U.S. plants are new and have younger, better-educated, and more carefully selected work forces. The Japanese have had nothing to pay out in pensions yet and far less in medical benefits. And since none of the Japanese plants have laid anyone off—and all seem determined not to—their employees are more adaptable and less threatened by change.

The American approach to auto making has been to narrowly define the job and then fill it with a low-skilled worker. U.S. plants have carried large parts inventories so that disruptions caused by worker error or defective supplies could quickly be remedied. Auto workers were and are hired or (more commonly) laid off in response to fluctuations in market demand.

The Japanese approach seems to be just the opposite. Jobs are rotated and the emphasis is on training and long-term employment. The worker on the assembly line has real authority. Frequent meetings, the absence of worker reserves, and an emphasis on teamwork generate peer pressure which, while stressful, reinforces a sense of common purpose. Just-in-time delivery and smaller buffer stocks save money and force suppliers to get it right the first time. Emphasis is on market-share gains rather than quarterly profits improvement. When times are bad, layoffs are a last, not first, resort.

An American at Toyota's Kentucky plant told me recently about the culture shock he experienced at one of his
first staff meetings. The Americans, when called upon, ticked
off all their successes; the Japanese, all their failures.

"Gary-*san*," his boss said, "I know you are a good
manager. I assume that every day you have many successes.
This is a given. But I must know the bad news. Once you
admit you have a problem, you can get it fixed. If we don't
know you have a problem, there is no way we can help you."

The man told me further that the wives of the American
executives there had formed a support group. Because their
husbands now had to be so patient at work, they were less
so at home.

My book has been written to explore whether Japan's
coming to the American heartland is enabling American
workers to recapture core values that many had believed
lost: the work ethic, a sense of community, a respect for
craftsmanship. Until the Japanese came, our brightest young
people, if they chose to work in industry at all, rarely
volunteered for production jobs. They usually preferred
marketing, finance, or design work instead.

I found little of the mistrust of Japanese economic
strength that I expected when I visited towns where they
have built assembly or auto parts plants. Kentuckians fearful
of change still say "Tie-Yota" for "Toyota," but more often
I heard people there and elsewhere say that before the
Japanese came, the top half of the high-school graduating
class kept moving away.

I wanted to find out how Americans in Ohio, Kentucky,
and Tennessee reacted to working with former enemies on
their home turf—which towns in the heartland welcomed
the Japanese, which not, and why. I wanted to discover
which of the Japanese auto companies was likely to be the
most successful.

Honda, Nissan, and Toyota compete fiercely with one
another and are all very different. Yet each watches, learns

from, and often copies the others. Honda has been the biggest risk taker, but though its image is the most American, it still has hundreds of Japanese managers and technicians in its Ohio plants. It also has the most restricted product line. Nissan, on the other hand, has had an American management team from the start, but until recently has been plagued by unexciting car models and may have hurt itself by being too obviously strident in its anti-unionism. Toyota, the largest, most cautious, and most Japanese of the three, has the deepest pockets as well as arguably the best production system.

Will a people who believe in racial purity, a nation of engineers adept at incremental change but not known for their creativity, ultimately be able to succeed in a nation of cultural and ethnic diversity such as ours?

Are the Japanese still likely to be punished for building their plants where there are so few members of the minority population?

Will Honda be able to Americanize its management and engineering staff fast enough? And in an era of "global economy," will it matter if it doesn't?

Will the Japanese auto makers in the United States ultimately be forced to buy many more complicated parts from "traditional U.S. suppliers" rather than from the Japanese suppliers they have encouraged to build plants in the United States?

Until now, the inability of Detroit to stem the Japanese advance has raised unsettling questions about America's ability to compete in the world economy. Yet I wonder whether the Japanese, by coming to our heartland in the way that they have, aren't saving the American auto industry from itself, restoring our faith in the American worker, and showing us, by example, a better way to manage.

This book has been written to try to find answers to these questions.

1

Journey without Maps

> They could have had damned near anything they
> wanted, but they didn't choose to do business that
> way.
> —Former Ohio Governor James A. Rhodes

Honda nurtures its image as a rebel willing to set trends in
a society more comfortable with following them. Because it
has few friends at home and less money to spend than its
rivals, it has had to run faster and learn to do almost
everything well.

Started with twenty employees in 1948, the company
had by 1960 become the world's leading motorcycle maker,
a position it retains. Not until 1963, however, did it build
its first car, and then over the opposition of the Japanese
Ministry of International Trade and Industry (MITI). MITI
wanted to restrict automobile production to companies already in the field, primarily Toyota and Nissan. Had MITI
had its way, Honda would not be making cars today.

When Honda built its first plant in the United States,
no other Japanese car companies were here. Its margin for
error was very thin, but its timing was superb. Protectionist
sentiment against Japanese car imports had yet to peak; thus
Honda would be anticipating rather than following the trend.
Nimble and gutsy, this youngest of the Japanese car companies gambled that it could do better in the United States
(and Canada) than back home in Japan. There land prices

had skyrocketed, the government was still unfriendly, and Toyota and Nissan had a monopoly on the best sales outlets.

The way Shige Yoshida remembers it, what Ohio Governor James Rhodes said was " 'I will give you the land free,' and the people from Honda responded, 'No, no, Governor, thank you very much, but we want to pay a reasonable price.' "

The slight, unpretentious Yoshida had witnessed the bidding war in 1976 between Pennsylvania and other states for the giant Volkswagen plant—Volkswagen being the first foreign auto maker to locate in this country. He wanted no part of it. He feared that if foreign companies were given more incentives to build plants than American companies, there would be no end of problems. Honda didn't want to attract undue attention to itself.

Yoshida's background was in purchasing. He had come to the United States in 1972 on temporary assignment as a buying agent. His job was to see if American companies could make parts for certain Honda products. He collected samples for research purposes. "It was a small job, but someone had to do it," he says. Eventually, he did well enough that Tokyo headquarters told him to stay in the United States and not come back.

Yoshida had seen the headlines on the front page of *The Wall Street Journal:* "A German Invasion: Residents Around Site of New Volkswagen Plant Have Mixed Emotions." And he had seen a certain Jack Wilkinson, "avid sportsman and owner of 1,000 acres of local farmland," quoted:

> I know this is progress, and I hope we can peacefully coexist with it. But what I see coming are traffic, sewage, pollution, and racial problems. If I wanted to live in Detroit, I would have moved there.

The multimillion-dollar incentive package that Pennsylvania had put together for Volkswagen at New Stanton, southeast of Pittsburgh, included purchase of an assembly plant that had been built in the late 1960s by Chrysler but never used. The state leased the plant back to VW, built new highway and rail connections, and threw in various tax breaks and training programs. It helped VW sift through the forty thousand job applications that flooded in.

But the selection process sparked complaints from civil rights activists. The new railroad line brought an outcry from store owners who saw their parking lots disappear. The new highway crossed deer paths in an area where more than a thousand deer had been killed by motorists the year before.

Prior to meeting with Governor Rhodes, Yoshida had consulted Americans at Du Pont in Circleville, Kenworth Truck in Chillicothe, and Rubbermaid in Wooster. He asked for advice and was told that "when a big industry comes to a small town and starts hiring, outsiders move in. The small town suddenly gets big. Serious problems with housing and crime occur. Mom and Dad get very nervous."

Yoshida and his people determined that whatever Honda did, it must do it differently from the way Volkswagen had.

"We had many discussions about site location," Toshi Amino, Yoshida's successor, remembers. "Our president, Mr. Kiyoshi Kawashima, said, 'Let's try not to be disliked by the community. Let's first make sure of that. Later, we can think how to be accepted. We do not want to bring drastic change to a quiet, peaceful farming area."

In 1976 Rhodes and his tall, silver-haired development director, James Duerk, had traveled to Japan, where they called on Honda, Toyota, and Nissan. Their trip was inspired by a brief wire story, datelined Tokyo, that appeared in the Columbus *Citizen-Journal*. It said an unnamed Japanese auto company was conducting a study to determine the feasibility of building a plant in the United States. Duerk clipped the story and showed it to Rhodes.

"Maybe," he said, "we should go to Japan within the next couple of weeks and check this out."

Rhodes looked at the story. "Good idea," he said. "Let's go tomorrow."

Next morning, Rhodes, Duerk, and a state highway patrol bodyguard in street clothes flew to Chicago. There they were met at the airport by a Japanese consular officer who gave them visas. After a twenty-hour flight, with a stopover in Alaska, they arrived in Japan. They slept the first day. The next day was the Emperor's birthday, when most offices were closed, except at Toyota. So after an early morning tour of the Tokyo fish market, which Rhodes insisted they see, the three boarded the bullet train to Toyota City, where they met with Toyota's executive vice-president. Next day they met Nissan's chairman and the president of Honda.

Rhodes pitched Ohio, and Duerk distributed a packet of inducements, which showed why, if anybody was to build an auto plant, Ohio was the place to be. The state was the transportation center of America, after all, within five hundred miles of two thirds of the U.S. and Canadian populations. It had low taxes and a skilled work force and had been among the first states to complete a network of interstate highways.

Rhodes suspected Honda of having commissioned the feasibility study. Toyota sold a lot of cars in the United States, but its sales here were only a fraction of its sales in Japan. The same was true of Nissan. Honda, still discriminated against at home, had the most reason to want to grow overseas.

As Tetsuo Sakiya relates in the official company biography, *Honda Motor: The Men, the Management, the Machines*, Soichiro Honda, the founder, battled against this discrimination from the start. When in 1963 MITI tried to restrict car production to companies already in the field, Honda fought back through the media. "Are the bureaucrats trying to block our plants to build cars?" he asked. "Democracy is meant to make individuals happy. I have fostered my own business, made profits, and paid taxes. Why is it that a private enterprise such as mine has to be sacrificed for the sake of the nation?"

As a result, Honda became a different kind of company: fresher and more original, more maverick than traditional, first and foremost an engine rather than just a car company. From the start, it had an antinepotism policy. Sons and daughters of employees—and even of board members— were barred from entering the company. By 1988 Honda had manufacturing facilities in forty-two countries, and more than half its employees were working overseas. Had it not been able to grow beyond Japan, the company could well have withered and died.

In 1971 consumer advocate Ralph Nader went to Japan and tried to talk with executives at Toyota, Nissan, and Honda about safety concerns. Only Soichiro Honda agreed to meet with him. The two discussed differences in specifications between cars for export and cars for the domestic market. Nader asked Honda if he would publicly urge all motorcycle riders to wear helmets, and Honda deflected the request by saying his company's advertisements already showed motorcycle riders wearing helmets.

Nader liked Honda for his openness and quick wit, however. He remembers asking Honda what a typical workday was like. Honda's two interpreters broke into peals of laughter. They said it was impossible to keep the old man in his office. He was always out in the plant stirring things up. Honda told Nader he feared that after he retired, the company would be taken over by faceless bureaucrats. (When Honda did retire, it was because he had lost sexual interest in women, it is said: no one should design cars after he has lost interest in women.)

In 1973, the year of the first oil crisis, Honda exported its first subcompact, the Civic, to the United States. From

1974 through 1977 the Civic was rated America's most fuel-efficient car. In 1975, with American car manufacturers still contending it couldn't be done, Honda then became the first auto maker to meet stringent emission standards under the U.S. Clean Air Act. Between 1970 and 1975 Honda's sales in the United States jumped from fewer than 2,000 to more than 100,000 cars a year. "We were faced with the challenge imposed by the Clean Air Act," Shoichiro Irimajiri remembers. "I was a member of the 'all or nothing' engine development team. It was called that because we knew we had the future of Honda in our hands."

America's opinion leaders were impressed. So were ecology-minded students, who later bought Honda model cars. Honda won for itself a halo effect that would persist into the next decade and beyond—despite problems with the UAW, unsafe all-terrain vehicles, and the Equal Employment Opportunity Commission.

Jim Rhodes had visited Japan twice in the 1960s, first in a group of governors, then as head of a trade mission. There he met and played golf with Soichiro Honda. He discovered that the two had much in common. Both were street-smart and had their idiosyncrasies. Rhodes had a sensitive stomach and when he traveled carried with him a supply of peanut butter and crackers. Honda had a penchant for red and pink suits.

Rhodes had been born in Coalton, a tiny town in southern Ohio. His father was a small-time mine manager and Republican precinct committeeman who died when his son was nine. As a teenager, Rhodes was a self-promoter and scrappy athlete who was kicked out of high school for talking back to (or throwing a punch at) his coach. Thanks to his mother, he later went back and got his diploma when he was twenty-one. He attended Ohio State University, but didn't graduate, and soon ran for office as a Columbus ward committeeman.

Honda's father was a village blacksmith, earning scarcely

enough to provide for his wife and nine children. From the time he was old enough to walk, Honda was never far from his father's shop. Always the tinkerer, he became an apprentice auto mechanic, opened his own car repair shop, then built and designed racing cars.

Rhodes had a similar love for politics. Author of the slogan "Profit is not a dirty word in Ohio," he was governor of Ohio for sixteen years (1963–71, 1975–83), longer than anyone else has been. Although considered by many rash and irresponsible for labeling antiwar protesters "terrorists, brown shirts, and communists," and for then permitting the National Guard to fire on (and kill four) students protesting the Vietnam War at Kent State University in 1970, he went on to win two more terms as governor. He considers the wooing of Honda his supreme industrial accomplishment.

After Rhodes and Duerk returned from Japan, they didn't hear anything for almost a year. Honda, meanwhile, asked two American consulting firms, Fantus and the Stanford Research Institute, to recommend states where they might build a motorcycle plant and, if that proved successful, an auto plant. The consultants recommended Ohio, Tennessee, Kentucky, Indiana, Michigan, and Illinois, not necessarily in that order. The choice eventually came down to Ohio or Tennessee. Tennessee was ruled out, Yoshida says, because the state then didn't have enough potential parts suppliers, and because the available land was too rocky for stamping operations—not cushiony enough for the repeated hard, jarring pounding. Others contend that Honda wanted a site far enough south to be out of union country, yet far enough north to be out of the South. German-Americans in Ohio were thought to be better workers than the Scots-Irish in Tennessee (or Kentucky).

On the face of it, Ohio seemed an unlikely choice. It had lost hundreds of thousands of tire, steel, and automotive jobs—in part, many felt, because of unfair competition from the Japanese. Its northern tier was (and still is) highly unionized. Midwesterners bought fewer Japanese cars than other Americans. And yet Ohio was also the bellwether state, the state presidential candidates say they must carry if they are to win. Ohio is part industrial, part agricultural, with affinities to both North and South. Lake Erie, the Ohio River, and the great railroad trunk lines had ensured a constant influx of new people and ideas.

Jim Duerk remembers that when he first met the Honda people they were very cautious. At these early meetings, Yoshida was exceedingly polite, but also very searching in the questions he asked. "I would bring everything I thought he could possibly need," Duerk says, "but invariably I would have to get on the phone and ask for more details." Duerk remembers, too, that "there was always an extra Japanese at the table. I finally figured out that his job was to read us Americans nonverbally—to notice who spoke loud or soft and on which subjects, to see who looked away when eyes met, who hesitated before speaking, and when."

Yoshida, for his part, remembers that Duerk proposed a number of sites, none of them satisfactory, before fixing on a half dozen that more or less met Honda's criteria: availability of large numbers of people who liked to come to work every day, enough land for expansion if need be, close but not too close to a major city, within an hour of a commercial airport, and below the snow belt.

Flying from a possible site near Delaware to another near Lima, Ohio, Yoshida looked out the window and saw for the first time, he says, the 7,500-acre Ohio Transportation Research Center, with its seven-and-a-half-mile test track and small landing strip. The TRC is between Marysville and Bellefontaine (pronounced "bell fountain") and had been proposed by Rhodes during his first term as governor. He had wanted it to become a magnet for expansion of Ohio's automobile industry.

Ohio was and is the second most important automobile manufacturing state (after Michigan), with some three dozen

General Motors, Ford, and Chrysler plants. Yet, although the federal government and several companies were using the TRC's testing facilities, it had failed to meet Rhodes's expectations. Farmers whose land had been seized were resentful, and most Ohioans saw the TRC as a white elephant.

Yoshida looked down and asked if there might be land available nearby. Duerk said he thought so. Yoshida asked if they could go down and take a look. The plane set down on a skid pad, and the people from Honda immediately started asking about zoning, water, and sewer availability.

"I have suspected, although I don't know for sure," says Duerk, who continues to work with Rhodes in his consulting business, "that they knew there was land zoned industrial there, and knew exactly where it was. I suspect they had people over here looking independently."

Rhodes contends that proximity to the TRC, with its test track and state-of-the-art research facilities, was the key factor in Honda's decision to locate where it did. Yoshida says it was an important factor, but not the primary one, the primary factors being the availability of a quality work force, plus plenty of land for expansion. Otherwise, Honda would have picked a site farther south, below Interstate 70, because of the TRC's closeness to the snow belt. The snow belt covers the northern third of the state, stopping roughly where the glaciers did in ancient times. In the snow belt, the land is flatter and the precipitation heavier. The TRC, though south of the snow belt, was not far enough south to suit some of the Japanese. Yoshida had originally told Duerk he wanted a site in the southwestern quadrant of the state.

Nonetheless, Honda built its motorcycle plant seven miles west of Marysville, on land adjacent to the TRC, then later its first auto plant next to the motorcycle plant. The second auto plant was completed in 1989 at East Liberty, five miles farther to the west, also on TRC land, and various phases of its engine plant twenty-four miles west of Belle-fontaine, at Anna, in the mid- and late 1980s. Although

Marysville is designated corporate headquarters, Bellefontaine has since become Honda's geographic hub.

Kinko Ito describes the region well.

She is a young Japanese who taught sociology at Wittenberg University in Springfield, Ohio, in 1987/88 because she didn't want to go home to an arranged marriage, she told me. For her doctoral dissertation at Ohio State, she obtained permission to study four Japanese companies that had built plants in Ohio. All, though unidentified, are obviously part of the Honda family. In her dissertation she writes:

> Company A is in a rather isolated agricultural area along an interstate highway. The town has a population of several thousand people, many of whom are descendants of German and British immigrants who first settled the region between 120 and 130 years ago. The majority have [been farmers] for generations and social mobility is extremely low. The area is racially homogeneous; Caucasians comprise 97 per cent of the population . . .
>
> As the farm economy in the region declined, several American factories opened seeking cheaper, surplus labor. These factories eventually closed, however, and the unemployment rate reached 13 per cent, one of the highest in the state. Thus, when the several Japanese companies arrived, they were well received.

Ito emphasizes the importance of the region's having what she calls a high-context culture. Residents share a common ancestry, common values, and a close-knit network of family and friends. They listen closely to one another and understand tacit messages. It is rude for a listener to ask for exact information, since cues for understanding are already embedded in the context. She notes that in a diverse, low-context culture, on the other hand (places such as Cleveland or Youngstown, Toledo or Canton, perhaps), the population is characterized by diverse values, different norms, and a varied ancestry. There communication is distinguished by "point-blank and elaborated messages; everything has to be spelled out in detail." Obviously, in a low-context culture, it would be more difficult for a Japanese company to succeed.

Honda's impact on the towns in west-central Ohio was at first minimal, since the company started out so modestly. Its initial investment was only $35 million (as contrasted with later initial investments of $550 million by Nissan in Tennessee and $800 million by Toyota in Kentucky). Yoshida wanted it that way. With a small operation, it would be easier to find and train top-quality people. And given the growing national hysteria over Japanese car imports, producing motorcycles was a prudent way to start. Americans were already accustomed to seeing magazine ads showing an attractive couple riding a motorbike under the slogan "You meet the nicest people on a Honda."

The land purchase had been easy. The 217 acres needed belonged to Ralph Stolle, a friend of Governor Rhodes, and the slim, dapper Stolle agreed to sell for what he had paid— $467 an acre, plus taxes. Rhodes then gave Honda an option to buy an additional 260 acres of TRC land from the state.

Even so, there were problems. Rhodes was not liked in Marysville. Although the county was Republican, the town's newspaper publisher and several members of its chamber of commerce were Democrats. Duerk had won agreement in principle from the county commissioners for a tax abatement, and from the mayor for extension of Marysville's sewer line. But he hadn't told anyone it was an auto maker that was coming—nor that the auto maker was Japanese. Neither Marysville's *Journal-Tribune* nor its chamber of commerce had participated in any of the discussions.

Rhodes made his announcement on October 11, 1977. At one end of the long oak table in his cabinet room sat state legislators and a half-dozen Honda people; at the other, two dozen media representatives. Seated against the wall were the Union County commissioners, Marysville's mayor and city councilmen, and a few members of its chamber of commerce. Nearly one hundred people were crammed into a room designed to hold no more than fifty.

Yoshida had asked that the expectations of each party be committed to writing. Rhodes agreed, although the practice was new to him. Honda's lawyer typed up the agreement, and Yoshida brought it with him to the announcement meeting in a large white envelope. Rhodes, in his euphoria, predicted that as a result of Honda's coming to Union County, Marysville's population would explode (from fewer than 8,000 to 50,000 people one day).

The problem was, Marysville didn't favor rapid growth. The town was then, and remains now, a county seat of fewer than 10,000 people, thirty-one miles northwest of Columbus. It has no parking meters, and its pharmacy on Main Street still sells coffee for five cents a cup. Except for a landmark white grain elevator, few of its other buildings are taller than one story. The town has long been dominated by the O. M. Scott lawn feed company. Scott has built a park there, and the YMCA is dedicated to one former Scott president, the mental health center to another. Scott commercials on national television give townspeople a reason to feel proud. Marysville gets feature billing, as in: "This spring in Marysville, something incredible happened." The something incredible is likely to be crabgrass at the Stevens place, followed by the tag line: "When all there is to do is watch the grass grow, you really get to know grass." By 1977 Marysville was in danger of becoming a bedroom community of Columbus as the capital's suburbs and office parks advanced to the north.

Conscious of Marysville's resistance to change, Honda moved ahead with great care and deliberation in these early years. It drilled its own water wells and built its motorcycle and first auto plant with union construction workers. It didn't complain when Rhodes had to renege on his promise to widen Route 33 to the plant site. Special attention was devoted to hiring.

"Birth is easier than resurrection," Al Kinzer often says when talking about the kinds of people Honda likes to hire. Kinzer was Yoshida's first American hire and would become Honda's first personnel manager. A motorcycle enthusiast, he had once been the part-time mayor of Radford, Virginia, before doing personnel work for White Motor and Perkins Diesel.

It was while working for Perkins in Canton, Ohio, that he had come across a Honda ad in *The Wall Street Journal*. Honda was looking for someone with personnel experience for its motorcycle plant. The ad seemed to be very carefully worded. Kinzer read it through several times.

By then he had become disillusioned with the way most American companies do business. He thought success should be determined by something more than short-term results. "Too much hinged on how quickly and by how much we could make a profit. There was no dream, no vision," Kinzer told me. He liked to go out on the shop floor and talk with the workers. He often felt frustrated when suggestions passed through him to upper management weren't heeded. He had heard that Japanese companies were different, and that of the Japanese companies, Honda was the most different of all.

And so he responded to the ad with a handwritten letter. In his letter he said: "If what you mean is ———, then what I can offer is ———." He used this same phrase several times, each time with examples. It was an attempt to merge goals he perceived to be Honda's with his own. Finally he wrote: "If I have misjudged what you were saying, please disregard this letter." He was almost immediately hired.

Kinzer wears rimless glasses and appears slight, almost frail, until you listen to what he says.

"It's easier to take a man and teach him something new than to force him to have to relearn. The way to find out if a person has potential is to take someone with one job skill and have him do something totally different."

For its assembly-line jobs, Honda restricted its hiring to one person per family, to high-school graduates (the younger the better), and to people with preferably no manufacturing—and almost certainly no automobile manufacturing—experience. "Fresh blotting paper," Kinzer called them. Honda hired from a radius of twenty miles, later expanded to thirty, with the formula for developing managers much the same. Most of the first hundred hires have been promoted three and four times.

The people living within Honda's initial hiring radius were predominantly German-Americans. In Logan County to the north and west, there were enclaves of Mennonites and Amish whose forefathers had left Europe in the eighteenth century. Most of the others had come in the nineteenth century. Mental-health professionals say German-Americans often have difficulty expressing feelings of anger or affection. They tend to be pragmatic, open to what works, and suspicious of idealogies. Their children are rewarded for good manners and expected to do well in school. Like the Japanese, German-Americans are hard workers, with a respect for craftsmanship.

"Farm kids, kids who have grown up in a farm environment, tend to be your best workers," Kinzer told me in the cafeteria of the engine plant where he since has been promoted to plant manager (under a Japanese counterpart). "They know how to outsmart nature. They're accustomed to change. They have this philosophy 'If there's a better way, let's try it.' They repair their equipment in bad weather so they can make the best use of it in good. It's a little like car manufacturing."

"Farmers are modest people, never boastful. They are dependent on too many things out of their control," others would say.

Yoshida agreed.

"In the beginning, there was one applicant to two or three Honda representatives," he told me. "Always three interviews. First we talked about the Honda way and observed reactions. Then we encouraged talk about themselves. Finally we stressed that Honda is not free-lance. Every job has a standard, both written and in photos. An associate can improve on the standard, but he must have approval before he does."

Few who were hired seem sure of the qualities they possessed that others, less fortunate, did not. There were no written tests. Interviewers seemed to care less about high-school grade averages than about whether applicants had often been absent or tardy. It didn't matter if they said that, if hired, they still hoped to farm on the weekends.

The interviewers didn't pry. They didn't ask "why" questions. They seemed as interested in what an applicant would volunteer as in what he or she might say in response to a question. And persistence paid off. One man told me of photocopying several dozen copies of his application letter. He sent the company a fresh copy each week. After six months they called him in.

Some of the questions interviewers did ask were:

Why do you want to work for Honda?

What are you looking for in an employer?

Do you do your own car repairs?

If you were working on the assembly line and couldn't keep up, what would you do?

If you were working on the assembly line and somebody kept passing you a bad part, what would you do?

Would long hours pose a problem for your family?

Often the same questions were asked again and again, by different interviewers, in different ways. Candidates who couldn't identify any "weak points," or who had to keep selling themselves, didn't do well. Nor did those who saw the world in absolutes, who didn't understand nuance. Those who had played team sports had an advantage.

"We don't need any prizefighters," Kinzer says. "Prize-fighters don't depend on anyone but themselves. But the third baseman who backs up the shortstop who misses the ground ball, these two are people we can build upon."

Honda has a policy of hiring only one person per immediate family. In this way, the benefits of the company's presence are spread and the appearance of favoritism is avoided. Spouses and siblings are often hired by one of Honda's Japanese supplier companies, however.

In Japan, Honda guarantees its employees jobs for life. In Ohio, the company makes no such promises, but does give its associates assurances of job security. Potential hires must agree to move from job to job at management's discretion, since such flexibility will minimize the chances of layoff. The company also has several hundred temporary workers doing menial, less critical work. These people are paid considerably less and, in the event of a deep recession, would be laid off first.

"We're not looking for superstars," says Kinzer. "We want a bunch of .290 hitters. If you have a bunch of guys consistently hitting .290, I can guarantee you'll be a winner."

In November 1979, two years after Governor Rhodes announced that the motorcycle plant would be built, and a scant two months after it started production, Shige Yoshida received a telephone call from Tokyo. He had been expecting to hear. He was concerned because thus far production in the motorcycle plant had been anything but smooth. He expected a reprimand. Instead, he was told to prepare the announcement that Honda would build an automobile plant next door.

The decision seemed risky. Volkswagen was the only foreign auto company making cars in the United States, and it hadn't had outstanding success. The yen-dollar ratio was still such that it was much less expensive to build cars in Japan.

"Despite all that, we wanted to begin automobile production in the United States," Tetsuo Chino, president of Honda North America, remembers.

"If you really want something, you can dress up the figures a bit, I can now confess . . . I know Mr. Kawashima spent some sleepless nights before the meeting at which we presented our feasibility study . . .

"He has since said that if the decision had been a 'simple binary yes or no,' the decision would have been no. But decision making at Honda is not so simple. Mr. Kawashima used a Buddhist dictum that postulates four decisions:

"Yes.

"No and yet yes.

"Neither yes nor no.

"And finally no.

"The decision on the Ohio project was no and yet yes.

"When, after hours of discussion, Mr. Kawashima said simply, 'Go ahead anyway,' we had all made up our minds to turn the no factors into yes."

The announcement came at a propitious time. Pressures were already building to limit the importation of Japanese cars. Honda's action seemed prophetic.

Still, Yoshida was careful, careful not to attract too much attention. Once the new auto plant was up and running, when the first Accord rolled off the assembly line in November 1981, he invited neither community leaders nor media representatives to witness the event. A few Japanese flew in from Tokyo and Sayama to celebrate, but the official ceremony wasn't held until spring. By then the flowers were in bloom. By then the production flow in the plant had smoothed out.

2

Referendum

One of the most unsettling misconceptions of the 1980s is that American business can be globally competitive only if it is located on the East or West Coast. Fortunately, Ohio has overcome this bicoastal bias.

—Ohio Governor Richard Celeste, February 1988

Ten years after Shige Yoshida and Governor James Rhodes shook hands on the deal that would bring Honda to Ohio, residents there got the chance to evaluate the company's performance. The place was Perry Township's birch-paneled community room in tiny East Liberty, Ohio; the date, December 22, 1987; the topic for discussion, Honda's request for a zoning change from agricultural to industrial for the 7,500-acre Transportation Research Center. The company hoped to buy the TRC for future expansion.

Speaking for Honda was Susan Insley—born, raised, and graduated from high school in Bellefontaine, fourteen miles up the road. Her father had owned and managed the local pharmacy and been chairman of the Republican Party there. Insley herself had been with Honda less than three years, but as vice-president of corporate planning was its highest-placed woman and already among the top-ranking women in the world automotive industry.

"This is kind of a big night for our company and I'm a little nervous," she said.

She stood facing an audience of mostly men, some fifty of them, a few in bib overalls and John Deere tractor caps, all attentive to what she was about to say. Insley is slim and attractive, has dark hair, and wears glasses with clear plastic rims. In the dress she had chosen to wear, she looked a little like the history teacher she was for a year before going to law school. She spoke in a calm, level voice.

"Thanks to all of you for coming out on a kinda snowy night. As I said, this is very important to us. Much of what we hope to do begins right in this room, right here with you, in the public hearing process."

Approval of the zoning change by the five townships with land in the TRC would enable Honda to build a second auto plant and, in related moves, double the company's Ohio investment from $800 million to $1.7 billion. Included in the strategy was a $600 million expansion of the engine plant in Anna, a tripling of research and development personnel from 180 to 500, a quadrupling of engineers from 50 to 200, and a pledge to purchase 75 percent of needed parts and supplies domestically by 1991, up from the current 60 percent. Most of the new people would locate in Ohio.

The request was sensitive and could easily become controversial. Some of these same farmers had had their land seized when Governor Rhodes starting building the TRC back in 1971. Honda needed unanimous approval because since the initial request had been made, a month earlier, some objections had been raised and modifications made. Without unanimous approval, the process would have to start all over again. Should that happen, who could tell what might happen. In other parts of the country, the Not in My Back Yard movement was already a force. Near Nova, Ohio, a battle royal had recently erupted when a company tried to put a huge garbage incinerator a thousand feet from a plot of farmland whose owner had hoped his boys would be the sixth generation to farm. Despite the care Honda had taken not to be disliked, the company's reception in Marysville and the southern part of Union County hadn't been all it might have hoped. And two of the five townships represented were from Union County.

The zoning change was necessary because Richard Celeste, the Democrat who succeeded Jim Rhodes as governor in 1982, had surprised Honda by offering to sell the company the 7,500-acre TRC.

Richard Celeste and Jim Rhodes couldn't be less alike. Rhodes is short in stature, plain-spoken, and often profane. Celeste is six foot four, a former Rhodes scholar, and oozes charm. His wife is Viennese; two of his six children were born in India, where he was an aide to U.S. ambassador Chester Bowles; and he had been director of the Peace Corps under President Jimmy Carter. Rhodes has made his entire career in Ohio. Yet both men reached out to Honda. Celeste's surprise offer to sell the TRC was a case in point.

Celeste had been fearful that Honda's next expansion would be not in Ohio but in Canada or Indiana instead. He was right to be concerned. By the time Celeste offered to sell the TRC, Honda's Scott Whitlock was looking elsewhere for a site upon which to build a second auto plant. The engine plant at Anna is near Ohio's western border, and Whitlock had been looking in eastern Indiana.

Whitlock had been a partner in the Columbus law firm of Vorys, Sater, Seymour, and Pease. A cherubic-looking man with curly white hair and pink cheeks, he now was manager of the first, Marysville, auto plant as well as something of a corporate troubleshooter. A specialist in commercial real estate, contract disputes, and public-utilities law, he had been asked in 1982 to serve as Honda's legal counsel. When, two years later, Robert Watson, Honda's first American auto plant manager, died suddenly of an aneurysm, Whitlock volunteered to take a sabbatical to help pick up the pieces, then was named to succeed Watson. The two had been friends and had worked together when Watson was executive vice-president of Ranco, a Columbus-based auto parts supplier.

Celeste had been elected with union and black support. Honda, on the other hand, had successfully derailed a UAW organizing drive, wasn't buying many parts from companies with a UAW connection, and was currently under investigation by the Equal Employment Opportunity Commission for alleged racial and sexual discrimination.

Celeste might have philosophical problems with Honda, but Ohio was still losing tens of thousands of jobs and he had been elected to stop this hemorrhaging. Honda had already created more new jobs in Ohio than anyone else, and every few months seemed to launch another expansion. Before one expansion was completed, another was begun. Celeste and his people had been meeting every few months with the Honda people to review where they had been, where they wanted to go, and how the state could help. At one of these meetings, Celeste said to Tetsuo Chino, president of Honda North America, that if Honda was going to be building so many engines, it might have to build a second auto plant.

Chino smiled and said yes, this was so.

After the meeting, Celeste had his people prepare a list of twenty-six possible sites.

"But then I said to myself," Celeste told me, "if all a state does is say, 'Here are twenty-six possible site locations; see what you can find there that might be of interest to you,' we aren't helping them make a positive decision for Ohio. We need something with hook to it, a real attraction. And the TRC was right there cheek by jowl with their first assembly plant. They were already a major user.

"My background is in real estate. I saw that the TRC was an asset to the state of modest proportions. The way it was being used, it had an operational value but not an investment value. It would best serve us only if it brought in major new investment."

Three months later, when Honda asked for another meeting, Celeste thought it wanted to talk about a second auto plant. Instead, the company wanted to discuss further expansion of its engine plant. Those present were Shoichiro Irimajiri, president of Honda of America Manufacturing; Shige Yoshida; Whitlock; and Susan Insley. Celeste brought up the subject of the second auto plant.

Early on, at the beginning of the lunch, there was some general discussion of Honda's future plans, Celeste remembers, at which point he said, " 'You ought to give some thought to the possibility of using the TRC as a site for your expansion.'

"Nobody said a word. Nobody picked up on it. It was a typical Japanese response. But at the end of the luncheon, as people were leaving, one of the senior Japanese took me aside and said, 'Were you serious about the Transportation Research Center?'

" 'Absolutely,' I told him."

Two months later, Scott Whitlock called and asked if they could talk further about the TRC. A year of relatively leisurely meetings followed. Then, in early August 1987, Celeste learned that Irimajiri was about to leave for Japan, where a decision was about to be made on the location of the second auto plant. Sites in Canada, Indiana, and Ohio were under consideration.

Celeste called Irimajiri and suggested they meet. He said he wasn't sure Honda had heard Ohio's best pitch. Irimajiri said he didn't think another meeting was necessary. He had just one question: Was the governor still willing to consider a transfer of the TRC? Celeste again said absolutely. There had been no discussion of price.

A month later, Celeste and the Honda people met for lunch again. Celeste expected more preliminary discussions.

Instead, the Honda people brought along a slide projector and threw on a screen details of their new global strategy. It had Ohio as its focus. The second auto plant would be built on the TRC. The company offered to pay $16 million for the land and facilities, a little more than $2,000 an acre. Celeste huddled with his aides and came back with a price of $31 million. The Honda people seemed pleased. The deal was struck.

The company had said nothing about what Indiana or Canada might be offering. Celeste had said nothing about Honda's need to do a better job of hiring minorities or of buying from American (and unionized) suppliers. He told me he didn't think he needed to. He had faith that Honda would do what needed to be done.

The agreement was announced fourteen days later, but one obstacle remained. As always, Honda wanted to move ahead very quickly. The second auto plant must be ready to build cars for the 1990 model year, but the property was still zoned for agricultural use. Its purchase was contingent on the company's being able to negotiate a zoning change. When Governor Rhodes expropriated the land, the state, because it was the state, hadn't needed to change the zoning classification. The necessary public hearings would amount to a referendum on Honda's ten-year performance in Ohio. Irimajiri asked Susan Insley to handle these hearings.

Insley, like Whitlock, had joined Honda from the Columbus law firm of Vorys, Sater, Seymour, and Pease. She had done a lot of zoning work and some of it for Honda. In 1983 she went to Japan as a member of a trade mission led by Governor Celeste, and there had helped to convince AP Technoglass, a joint venture of Asahi Glass and Pittsburgh Plate, to build a plant in her hometown of Bellefontaine. Yoshida had seen Insley in action, been impressed with her, and hired her to be Honda's vice-president of corporate planning.

"I've met people who were smarter, flashier, perhaps

better organized," says Bruce Henke, a colleague from Vorys, Sater who still works with her on zoning cases. "But I've never met anybody who could put it all together the way Susan can. She can take something complex and put it in such simple, understandable language. She is always pre-pared, but she can also shoot from the hip when need be."

Henke, from Sidney, Ohio, also worked with Insley when the two of them were assistants to Ohio Congressman Clarence "Bud" Brown. In Washington, Insley helped Brown meet the needs of constituents who now live within Honda's hiring radius.

A person of great stamina, Insley not only works a twelve-to-fourteen-hour day, but still finds time to play golf, tennis, and sometimes even basketball. While at Vorys, Sater, she played in the Columbus city league. She was in her late thirties then, and the other players were younger, but as she tells it, she did okay.

"I shot one team out of a zone [defense] into a man-to-man. We came down the floor four times, and four times I got the ball, four times I put it in. Anywhere from twelve to sixteen feet, I'm a dead shot. It's the truth. I came off the bench when Coach needed a score. There were a lot of red faces, sure. We didn't have a fast break. We played like North Carolina, only slower."

She suspects some of the Japanese don't know quite what to make of her. She speaks up. She has opinions. She is not submissive. But she doesn't give it much thought anymore. For Insley, being a pioneer is nothing new. She tells of an encounter she had with an older Japanese. She was still a lawyer and he was the president of one of Honda's supplier companies. She had solved a problem for him and over lunch he wondered if he could ask her some questions.

"Are you married?"

"No."

"Do you have a house?"

"Yes, I have a condominium."

"Do you cook?"

"Yes, and I'm a good cook."

"Do you sew?"

"No, I don't like to sew. Sewing makes me nervous."

"But you're a lawyer," he said. "A professional person. In Japan, you would have to have a wife to do all this."

In a commencement address at Ohio Northern University, where she earned her law degree (and where, as her father was, she is a member of the board of trustees), Insley recently told graduates:

"When I graduated from high school, the commencement speaker concluded by saying, 'So God bless you, have an interesting life, and don't get married too soon.' I think I can say I have followed his advice. I have the feeling his advice has haunted my parents. I hope my comments today will not disturb your parents so much. But let's not forget . . . it is your life we are talking about and not your parents' life . . .

"For most of you may be perceived as I was, a university graduate from a reasonably average background. But the fact that your background may be perceived as average doesn't mean that you have to follow an ordinary path . . . What I have learned is that you can achieve above-average results on an average day by committing yourself—really, by overcommitting yourself."

Insley's rise in the Honda hierarchy reached public notice in 1987. At a news conference to announce a $450 million expansion of the engine plant at Anna, she had been scurrying about, acting as traffic cop, making sure everyone knew everyone else. Tetsuo Chino gazed out at the rows of reporters. Among them were some of the top auto writers in the country. Chino speaks flawless English and was scheduled to speak next. Instead, he leaned over to Insley and whispered, "You answer all the questions." She did and, as they say in show business, a star was born.

                                        *   *   *

"I can't stand here and tell you that if we buy the site, current employees at the TRC will have a job forever," she was telling a questioner at the zoning hearing. "I don't know if *I'll* have a job forever. I don't manufacture anything. I may be the first to go. But what I can say is that they'll have a job for two years. And we would hope for a good many years thereafter as well."

Insley had been answering questions for almost an hour. She had been explaining to the men in bib overalls and John Deere tractor caps what Honda would do if it got its zoning change. She passed a few questions along to Bruce Henke, who had dressed down for the occasion (from a three-piece suit to corduroy pants and sport coat), but she answered most of them herself. There were other Honda executives in the room, but they left the talking to her.

And why not.

Insley was a Logan County native, and Perry Township, where the meeting was being held, is in Logan County. Honda had said that though a final decision had yet to be made, its preference was to build its new plant in Logan County, not Union, this time. It wanted to spread the wealth. The Benjamin Logan school district there had just passed a $6.8 million bond issue for a new high school, although earlier proposals had always been voted down. The bond issue passed this time thanks to voter belief (discreetly encouraged by Insley) that once it got its zoning change, Honda would help pay for the school. The second auto plant would generate millions of dollars in new tax revenues.

Insley was good at putting out fires.

"I understand there have been questions about fencing," she had said at the first zoning hearing. "There are a lot of deer, or a number of deer, on the TRC site. Sometimes they jump over the eight-foot fence and get on the test track. That's why we're proposing a fifteen-foot fence. We have been told deer can't jump over a fence that high . . .

"I can't stand here and tell you we won't sell any of this acreage. I can't tell you that in twenty or thirty years that would never happen. I can't do that and I won't do that. But I can tell you we have no plans to do so today."

She had answered a question about water-table depletion by citing the experience of the first auto plant. There the plant uses 600,000 gallons of water a day, and the company had drilled its own wells. Farmers complained that the water table was being drawn down, so Honda hired engineers from Columbus to find out for sure. They discovered that yes, within a half-mile radius, the company was at fault. Farther out, it was possible, though not likely. The company felt, however, that whether it was at fault or not, the perception was that it was. So Honda drilled fifteen new wells for farmers within a two-mile radius.

Finally, in response to questions implying that the company might be withholding information, Insley said, "So there will be no misunderstanding, so that if anybody thinks we intend to put up multiple housing units or office buildings or a residential park or something, I guess the clearest way to say that we don't is to take the vagueness out of our request, just simply to take it out, eliminate it."

Honda's Al Kinzer then asked to be recognized.

"I remember, ten years ago, some of these same questions being asked," he said. "Questions about what kind of neighbor we would be. You've seen us develop 865 acres of land. We've planted more trees than farmers in the area, I think. You've seen the environment we've tried to create. We regard our place as a campus . . . We're running on our record."

The more abrasive questions had been asked at the first zoning hearing, a month earlier. At this second hearing, the atmosphere was less tense.

Finally there were no more questions and it was almost time to vote. The township chairpersons left the room to consult with their legal counsels. Insley and Henke were optimistic. And yet, because the yes vote had now to be unanimous, they were anxious, too. They were worried about what Larry Ream might do.

Ream was chairman of the Allen Township board of trustees, one of the two townships in Union County. And Ream was the one trustee who had voiced opposition to the zoning change. He is a prematurely white-bearded man given to wearing bib overalls. His farm sits across Route 33 from the first auto plant, and some of his relatives had had their land expropriated by the state. Until Honda made changes in its proposal, he had been encouraging other trustees to vote the proposal down.

"I was afraid they'd build a city in there," he told me later. "Not Honda necessarily, Honda has done all right by us, but some company Honda might sell out to. I was afraid they would build a city cut off from the rest of us by a fifteen-foot fence. Build dormitories and fly in workers from some foreign country. There already have been so many changes here."

While the township trustees talked with their legal counsels, Insley and Henke consulted with Carmen Scott. Scott had been the regional planning director here for twenty-one years, and was also from Bellefontaine. He had found the Japanese easy to deal with.

"They don't argue," he told me. "You explain your regulations to them and they listen and take notes. They don't say, 'Why, that's ridiculous, why do I have to do that?' like so many Americans do. They may come back later and ask for a waiver. But before they do, they will have done their homework."

Scott suggested that Ream be asked to vote, not first or last, but third, so he would feel less conspicuous.

When the trustees came back into the room, they all, including Ream, voted yes for the zoning change. Bess McMillian later explained why.

She is the chairperson for Perry Township, where the

new plant would be built. She had turned down repeated invitations to eat lunch at the headquarters plant until after the vote for fear her constituents would think she'd sold out. Her husband was a World War II veteran, and she didn't have any family working at Honda. She thought it was all right for Ream to have been the devil's advocate. She praised him for having the guts to ask the questions he did. She, too, had been nervous about having to decide so quickly. Ordinarily, a decision of such magnitude would have taken months, not weeks. But like Scott, she, too, had found the Japanese easy to deal with.

"They pay such attention to the little things. There's a man on the TRC who taps trees for maple syrup, and a college professor who collects a rare kind of butterfly. Honda is going to let them both stay. Thanks to Honda, people who never could have afforded to send their kids through college now will be able to."

No one at the hearings had mentioned that in the past five years American-owned plants in the area had laid off 2,400 workers, nor that Honda had more than picked up the slack. In 1982 Ohio had ranked next to last among the fifty states in job growth; by 1989 it was fourth.

"By their vote tonight, these people sent a message to the state legislature, perhaps to the nation," Carmen Scott said. Twenty-one days later the Ohio Senate, by a vote of 33–1, agreed to let Honda buy the TRC.

Shoichiro Irimajiri had said he hoped one day to see Honda in Ohio do everything that Honda in Japan had been able to do.

"When I joined Honda in 1963, the company had only six thousand associates," he said. "Now we have forty-five thousand. In the United States, Honda employs six thousand now. My dream is to see Honda grow in the U.S. as it has in Japan."

3

Doing It the American Way

American workers are stronger. They can pick
things up faster. If the Japanese run into a problem, they go back to the cookbook or hold a
committee meeting. Our people were able to learn
the Japanese way of doing things a lot faster than
the Japanese thought they could.

—Emil Hassan, vice-president of engineering, Nissan Motor Manufacturing,
U.S., Smyrna, Tennessee

There were similarities between the way Nissan and Honda
began manufacturing vehicles in the United States. Both
started simply: Nissan with trucks, Honda with motorcycles.
Both were careful not to ask too much of state or local
governments. Both were skillful in creating an early favorable
image of themselves. But the differences are far more
striking.

Honda came in quietly; Nissan, with a splash. Honda
was medium-tech; Nissan, robotics. Honda seemed unsure
of how to deal with the UAW and in perhaps typical Japanese
fashion kept its options open; Nissan announced itself anti-
union from the start. Honda brought along scores of Japanese managers and technicians (and has since added more);
Nissan soon sent all but a few of its Japanese home. Honda's
president is Japanese, as are the key decision makers in every
department. Nissan portrays itself as an American company

and, in most respects, is. The key difference, however, is that Honda's future as an auto maker depends on what it does in Ohio; Nissan's future does not depend as much on what it does in Tennessee.

At each company you read or hear certain phrases repeated. At Honda these have a vague, collegial air: "The answer was no and yet yes." "There is a relationship—almost a human relationship—between the automobile and the people who use it." "Our get-together was a little like a town meeting." At Nissan the phrases are more incisive: "We seek to minimize the negative impact of outside interference on all internal aspects." "We strive to create an environment where each individual can be a valuable contributor." " 'Seniority' is a UAW word."

Some of these differences relate to timing, others to geography. By 1981, when Nissan broke ground for its truck plant, Honda was already producing motorcycles and had a car plant under construction. Chrysler, nearly bankrupt, had had to be bailed out by the federal government. Ford and General Motors were announcing massive cutbacks. Protectionist sentiment was at a fever pitch, and Nissan had come to a state from which so many men had gone to war that it was called the Volunteer State.

David Halberstam reports in *The Reckoning* that Nissan's president, Takashi Ishihara, saw the United States as a nation of customers, not workers. He had visited American factories and found the employees there indifferent, "always seeming to be taking a break." He was wary of building cars in the United States for fear that the Big Three would put their house in order, produce cars of excellence again, and leave Nissan stranded. He determined that if Nissan must build vehicles in the United States, he would minimize the risks: start with trucks because they were the simplest and easiest to build (and Nissan's weakest-selling item), ensure that the plant was highly automated, and locate it in a part of the country where the chances of its ever becoming unionized would be minimal.

Nissan was the first Japanese auto maker. It started in 1933, making small cars that didn't compete with American imports, then built trucks for the Japanese military. It was an early borrower of American technology and mass-production techniques and was the first to set up a quality control program. From World War II until the mid-1950s, Nissan was Japan's leading car manufacturer. It was then passed by Toyota, but remained a strong number two. Like Toyota, it concentrated on several basic models retained year after year and improved incrementally, rather than adapting the American practice of annual model changes.

In 1953 Nissan broke a strike by Japan's nascent industry-wide auto makers' union. The union had thought if it could crack Nissan, other Japanese auto companies would fall into line. Nissan, rather than Toyota, was targeted because it was located in and around Tokyo and Toyota was in distant Aichi Prefecture.

Nissan's success had huge consequences. Docile company unions—rather than an aggressive industry-wide union like the UAW—soon became the norm. The absence of an industry-wide union made it possible for a pyramid of lower-cost parts suppliers with sharply *declining* wage scales to form.

As Michael Cusumano notes in *The Japanese Automobile Industry: Technology and Management at Nissan and Toyota*, the early decision by Nissan and Toyota to subcontract components, rather than expand in-house capacity to meet new demand, was the most significant departure from American practice. The shift of parts manufacture and even portions of final assembly to outsiders with lower wage scales reduced personnel expenses, fixed-investment requirements, and inventory carrying costs.

Nissan's strikebreaking left a legacy of bitterness, however. Its own company union was affected. Nissan was

therefore not able to implement as many cost efficien-
cies as Toyota and Honda could. This was another reason
why Ishihara—once he decided to manufacture in the
United States—was determined that his plant there remain
nonunion.

When Nissan came to the United States, it came with two
disadvantages: it was about to change the nameplate of its
models from Datsun to Nissan, a less appealing signature.
(America was the one country where Nissans were still sold
under the Datsun name, and Tokyo wanted to standardize.
Datsun meant "son of fast rabbit"; Nissan represented the
first letters of Nihon Sangyo, the holding company of which
Nissan was a part. The changeover took longer than expected
and caused confusion.)

The company was also then in a phase of dull car
designs. Its models were known as "boxes on wheels." As a
result, profits were affected and Smyrna, in its early years,
was not able to expand as rapidly as it might otherwise have
done.

Nissan's announcement that it would build a plant in
the United States generated a wealth of excitement, however.
Twenty-four state governors bid for the plant site, although
it soon became apparent (to Tennesseans at least) that
Tennessee had the inside track.

"Teams of eight, ten, fifteen Japanese were coming to
see us every couple of weeks, each of them asking the same
questions in different ways," said James Cotham, the state's
commerce secretary. Many months before Nissan announced
where it would locate, Republican Governor Lamar Alexander charged a task force of thirty people with doing
whatever it took to make Tennessee the logical choice. "We
hadn't won the site yet, but it was ours to lose," Cotham
told me.

By the time Alexander was elected governor in 1978,
Tennessee already had a fair amount of Japanese investment.

Toshiba had its biggest American plant in Lebanon and Sharp its largest in Memphis, both making TV sets and microwave ovens. Like Ohio, Tennessee was crisscrossed with interstate highways and close to the nation's population center. Unlike Ohio, it was a right-to-work state. This meant that unions, even if they won the right to represent workers in a company, couldn't force them to become members or pay dues.

By February 1980, before Nissan even announced it was looking, its representatives found an ideal tract of land south of Nashville. The site was a 433-acre dairy farm, flat as a tabletop, that once had been part of a cotton plantation. The problem was it wasn't for sale.

Alexander called on its owner, a Mrs. Maymee Miller Cantrell, and without saying why Tennessee needed her land exactly, convinced her to grant him an option to buy. Two months later, he made a similar call on Richard and Kathryne McClary, who owned an adjoining 200 acres. They agreed to give him an option, as well.

By then Alexander and two of his assistants, Joe Davis and Fred Harris, were highly optimistic. "But how can I justify spending taxpayers' money on this?" Harris remembers Alexander asking. Harris is a tall, relaxed-seeming man, now development director for the Nashville Chamber of Commerce.

"We fiddled with this, fiddled with that, and finally agreed we couldn't spend money on the site. We didn't think that could be justified. On the other hand, if we built a road, the road would be for Tennessee workers to drive to and from work. So that was no problem. And if it was a question of utilities up to the property line, we could handle that, too. We would do that for an American company. The same with training. We could spend money for Tennesseans being trained for jobs. The total came to about $20 million.

"The governor then proposed he invite the entire leadership of Rutherford County (some sixty to eighty people) to the mansion—not to his office, because then it would be a public meeting, but to the mansion—for a briefing.

"The idea would be to tell them in confidence everything that was going on. And this is what he did. The radio guy said can I tape this, and the governor said no, you can't turn anything on and the newspaper guys can't take any notes either. You're here to be backgrounded, to help us make some decisions.

"The governor told them everything. He talked for thirty minutes. Tennessee is still at the back of the line economically, Nissan pays high wages, is environmentally clean. This is the kind of plant that will encourage Tennesseans to come back home again, be a magnet for other industry. That's the deal, guys, he told them. It's an opportunity that may never come again. What I need to know is: Do you want it or not want it? I can't wait to find out. I need to know right now."

Harris says that naturally he and Joe Davis had a couple of guys salted away in the back of the room who quickly jumped up to say, "Ah, hell, Governor, of course we're for this thing."

Nissan announced on October 30, 1980, that its plant would be built in Smyrna, Tennessee, rather than in McDonough or Cartersville, Georgia, the two alternative sites. There were no news leaks until a day or two before the announcement, and by then it didn't matter. The announcement came six days before Ronald Reagan's landslide victory over Georgia's Jimmy Carter in the Presidential race. Nissan officials had previously met with Tennessee's U.S. Senate Majority Leader, Howard Baker.

Governor Alexander was ecstatic.

"We Tennesseans have much in common with the Japanese," he would say in his book *Friends*.

Our maples change colors at about the same time as theirs and our dogwoods and their cherry trees bloom at about the same time too. Their most popular flower, the iris, is our state flower. When I was driving in their mountains, I was reminded of our Smokies . . .

During a first visit, everyone notices how different Japanese and Tennesseans look. But after a few days, you think instead about how much people in either place look the same. Living on islands that for one thousand years have never been invaded and which for years banned foreign visitors, the Japanese have become one of the world's largest, most homogeneous populations. Many of us have lived in our small coves and valleys and small towns for seven generations. In both Japan and Tennessee there is the same homogeneity which causes people to grow independent, self-sufficient, and skeptical of strangers.

Smyrna, where the new plant would be located, is twenty miles south of Nashville and two miles east of Interstate 24. It had but one traffic light and was a notorious speed trap. Like most of middle Tennessee, it had been founded by Scots-Irish settlers who came over the mountains from Virginia and the Carolinas. It had served as a way station on the Nashville and Chattanooga Railroad for cotton planters in the region. And its Stewart Air Base, named for a pilot shot down in the Pacific, had served as a training site for bomber crews during World War II. Until Nissan arrived, it had been best known for the restored plantation of Sam Davis, a Confederate hero (and spy) hanged in 1863 for refusing to divulge intelligence to Union soldiers.

Smyrna's mayor, Sam Ridley, claimed to be the most decorated World War II veteran in the county, but had been for Nissan from the start. In 1981 he had been mayor for thirty-two years already, and was to remain in office for six more, proud that in all that time he had never raised property taxes. Though forced to resign in 1987, for violating conflict-of-interest laws (he did thousands of dollars' worth of city business with his own Ridley Chevrolet agency), he was

succeeded in office by his identical twin, Knox. Both men
have since made small fortunes in land development. Sam
Ridley says the first time "I looked out from the overpass
and saw Nissan's new plant glistening white in the sun, I felt
like Moses looking down on the promised land."

Unlike Honda and also Toyota, which would come to Kentucky later, Nissan hired an American to build and run its
plant. He would make most of the major decisions.

"Most Japanese companies with American subsidiaries
have relied on Japanese managers to run those enterprises,"
explained Masahiko Zaitsu, Nissan's project director. "We
decided to try a different way: we would hire the most
experienced American we could find, and give him a free
hand to build an American company with American leadership and American workers."

Nissan's choice was Marvin Runyon. Incisive, charismatic, with a mane of silver hair, he and the men from Ford
he would bring with him are very different from the Americans I found at Honda and Toyota. There the Americans
are lower-key, softer-spoken, more like their Japanese counterparts. Fewer of them have had previous automotive
experience. They appear to have smaller egos.

Runyon had gone to work for Ford in its Dallas, Texas,
assembly plant in 1943 and, with the exception of two war
years in the Air Force, had stayed with the company until
1980. He earned a graduate degree in engineering from
Texas A & M, then began his progression through the ranks
of management. In 1957, at the age of thirty-three, he
helped to build an assembly plant in Lorain, Ohio. Eight
years later he was manager of the company's Norfolk,
Virginia, plant. When he retired, at fifty-six, he was Ford's
vice-president for body and assembly.

At Ford, Runyon hadn't been able to rise high enough,
he thought. Ford was then being run by finance men, bean
counters. Men from the factories felt a certain defeatism.

They weren't paid as well or promoted as fast. Runyon thought he would take a job teaching, but then he heard that Nissan was looking for an experienced American to run its first American plant.

He was intrigued. He had heard that plant managers at Nissan had more autonomy, manufacturing men more prestige. Ishihara's determination to keep the union out meshed with Runyon's own conviction that an organized plant would be a distinct liability. Runyon struck a deal whereby, if he took the job, Ishihara would be the only Nissan executive to whom he would report. Later, when Nissan's vice-presidents in Tokyo sent Runyon directives, he ignored them.

Meeting Runyon, I was struck by how youthful he looks. He has a health-club tan and, at sixty-three, thanks to a meatless diet and regimen of daily exercise, is pencil-thin. He is chairman of the Tennessee Valley Authority in Knoxville now, but his seven years at Nissan appear to have been the high point in his life. Knoxville is two hours from Smyrna, but his spirit still seems to hover over the plant there. At Nissan's Tokyo headquarters, the Japanese still refer to him as "the originator."

He pulls from the shelf a copy of *Nissan in Tennessee*, a book of lush photographs and vivid prose he had prepared, and wants to know if I've read it. I ask about his philosophy regarding American parts suppliers, and he wants to be remembered to Robert Drake, Nissan's purchasing vice-president. I mention how striking the Smyrna plant looks, and he notes that while most company headquarters have three flagpoles out front—for the American flag, the state flag, and the company flag—he made sure that the Smyrna plant would have just one, for an oversized American flag. He wanted to make sure that no overly zealous employee ever made the mistake of flying a Japanese flag there.

Runyon and Jerry Benefield, his successor, often talk about how un-Japanese the Smyrna plant is. Employees, called technicians, are offered a variety of company uniforms,

but none is mandatory. Some wear Nissan T-shirts, some
Nissan golf shirts, others windbreakers, still others just the
blue trousers with a shirt of their own. It's the same with
participation in a quality circle: involvement is encouraged,
but not compulsory. (Quality circles are small groups of
employees who band together temporarily to solve a particular problem.) In contrast to Honda, workers can have radios
at their work stations (with the decision on which station to
play determined by consensus). Vice-presidents have offices
(and department heads sit two to a cubicle) because Americans sometimes need privacy. As in Japan, however, where
frequent (Shinto) festivals provide some of the emotional
bonding necessary for smooth functioning, there are many
ceremonies.

"One thing that contributes to the wellness of a company
is its traditions," says Runyon. "Great companies have great
traditions, big events that employees can look forward to.
Every event in a company's history deserves an event to
remember it by. Whether you're producing job one or job
one million, whether the company is ten years old or a
hundred, it's important to observe these milestones."

Runyon had obviously given a lot of thought to examples that could serve as metaphors. In his speeches, he
would say:

"In the companies that are prepared for the future, the
supervisor's job is not to manage the process. The technicians
are experts at that. The supervisor's job is to manage the
people. It seems ironic. Yet it's true. High technology is
making companies more people-oriented."

Or:

"One of my first jobs was putting tires on truck axles at
the Ford assembly plant outside Atlanta. I'm not a big man,
but those tires were big, and the other men working with
me were all very big.

"The first day they got a real kick out of watching me
swing the tires into place for eight hours.

"That night on my way home, I stopped by the hardware store and bought a piece of plywood and some two-by-fours. And the next day I showed up at work with a little ramp. I used that ramp to roll the tires up to the truck hubs, rather than lift them up.

"All my co-workers thought that was the funniest thing they'd ever seen. They laughed at me for about an hour. Then they all asked me to build ramps for them, too."

When asked what it had been like working for him, Brenda Ballard, his secretary, told *Nissan News*:

> Don't ever go to him with a problem unless you have a solution in mind. When I tell him about a situation, the first thing he says is "Well, what are you going to do about it, Brenda?" He wants your opinion. He may not always agree, but he'll discuss it with you and either you'll win him over or he'll win you over. But most of the time, a decision is made right then.
>
> He carries a stack of note cards in his shirt pocket and anytime he thinks of something he wants done, he jots it down.
>
> We keep his schedule 16 weeks in advance, and every day we give him a new one with changes from the previous day.

Looking back, Runyon seems proudest of having done it the American way, of having brought with him a handful of former Ford executives to become the nucleus of his team, of having forced Nissan's Japanese parts suppliers to compete equally with American parts suppliers. Honda might appear to have a head start in America, but Honda is doing the job with Japanese, Runyon told me. Eventually, it would have to put Americans in charge. Nissan, having built with American managers and American parts suppliers from the start, will have the advantage then.

"No *keirtsu* at Nissan" is the phrase Runyon coined.

What it meant was that the Japanese companies that sold to Nissan in Japan could not expect to have the same cozy relationship with Nissan in Tennessee unless they were able to compete at least as effectively as American companies could. "We didn't want to become an assembler of foreign parts if we could help it," Runyon said.

It was not always easy. In the early years, Runyon rejected parts from U.S. suppliers at least twice as often as parts from Japanese companies. Sometimes when an American supplier couldn't deliver on time, he had to fly in parts from a Japanese supplier, and this was expensive. But, at some political cost to himself, Runyon remained true to his convictions.

He also remained true to his and Ishihara's conviction that Smyrna must remain nonunion. Runyon had left Ford when the UAW was still being blamed for most of the problems plaguing the American auto industry, before the era of "jointness" and company-union cooperation. Unlike Honda, Nissan didn't use union construction workers to build its plant. Instead, Runyon selected the Daniel Construction Company of Greenville, South Carolina, as general contractor. Daniel had no experience building vehicle assembly plants, but had a worldwide reputation. Runyon knew what he wanted, wanted it done quickly, and thought Daniel would do the job best.

The plant, designed by Albert Kahn Associates in Detroit, was the size of four football fields set side by side and had a spacious feel then unique in the auto industry. It was laid out like a reclining "E" with administration in the long spine, which also served as a walkway and parts-movement corridor. Stamping, paint, and trim and chassis operations were housed in each of the three wings, and each had a separate parking lot (the UAW would contend that the parking lots were kept separate to discourage off-duty employees from talking to one another). Basketball courts and Ping-Pong tables adjoined break areas, and in administration areas dividers broke the monotony of too much openness. Though criticized by at least one securities analyst as a "Taj Mahal," the plant was built in such a way that it could be doubled in size by fleshing out the skeletal arms of the "E."

Fearing a union demonstration at the groundbreaking, two of Governor Alexander's assistants—Fred Harris and James Cotham—urged that Nissan wait before announcing who the general contractor would be. Runyon said no.

"How can you have a groundbreaking ceremony and, when somebody asks, say you don't know who the contractor will be?" he told me he said.

On February 3, 1981, when the ceremony took place, several hundred union construction workers showed up to protest. An airplane flew overhead trailing a banner reading: "Boycott Datsun. Put America back to work." Big, burly men carried signs saying: "Quality projects with skilled UNION workers. Boycott Datsun," and cries of "Go home, Japs," drowned out the words of the speakers. When the driver of the snowplow truck that was supposed to break ground tried to move forward, he discovered that his tires had been slashed. Runyon himself then got in the truck and managed to move it forward a little, plowing up a small patch of turf.

"Problem was we couldn't restrict access to the site," Harris told me. "It was a public event. You couldn't ask someone if he was a union member and, if he said yes, say he couldn't attend.

"But in the end it turned out not so bad. The demonstration so shocked the community, and the national TV people, that they came down heavy on the union. The next day the legislature passed a resolution condemning the building trades union. Can you imagine any general assembly in these United States doing that? I couldn't. But they did. The union spent a lot of money saying how sorry they were. They ran full-page ads saying, 'Hey, we apologize. We didn't really mean it. Things got out of hand.' "

Runyon seemed to have wanted the demonstration. "In

the long run I think some good came out of it," he later
would say. "At the very least, it made our company and the
state of Tennessee more determined than ever to be successful in this venture."

The demonstration discredited trade unionism in middle Tennessee for years to come. When in 1988 the UAW
launched its organizing campaign, Nissan played on its in-
house video, *Nissan Network News*, the tape of construction
workers disrupting the groundbreaking ceremony. The clear
implication (unstated, but never proven) was that the UAW
had been involved.

4

After the Honeymoon

> Nissan sold itself to the community. Honda sold itself to its employees.
> —Jim Turner, UAW organizer, Smyrna, Tennessee, April 1988

For a long time it seemed as if Nissan and Marvin Runyon could do no wrong. Every story, article, or book about them praised one or the other as leaders the U.S. auto industry would be well advised to follow. The early reviews were all positive.

Smyrna's *Rutherford Courier*, Murfreesboro's *Daily News Journal*, and Nashville's *Tennessean* and *Banner* ran story after story lauding Nissan for donating seed money for this or that worthy cause. Runyon led the Middle Tennessee United Way to a record year. At Smyrna's milestone events—Job One, Sentra One, 500,000th vehicle, Family Days, Christmases—Runyon brought in the White Creek High School Handbell Choir to play or the Middle Tennessee State Chamber Choir to sing. And "Job One" at Nissan was a far splashier affair than "Accord One" at Honda had been. At Honda, neither local officials nor media people had been present. At Nissan, fist raised high, Runyon himself drove a gleaming white truck through a blue-and-white banner to the cheers of VIPs and technicians alike. This first truck was placed on permanent loan to the state museum in Nashville, a featured item in the "Made in Tennessee" exhibit.

Tokyo was pleased, even surprised, by the quality of trucks built in Smyrna, and Nissan president Ishihara gave Runyon approval to add a line of Sentra model cars. Although the Sentra was a subcompact—and Honda and Toyota were to start by building compacts—it was still a car, and Ishihara had been leery about building cars in the United States. In June 1983 Nissan became the first Japanese company to build trucks here, and in March 1985 the second to build cars, the first and (and still only) U.S. auto maker to build both on the same assembly line.

Runyon exuded confidence. He took the Big Three to task for bumping up their car prices after the yen rose in relation to the dollar. Had they been less greedy and kept prices down, they could have increased market share instead, and market share was now the name of the game.

In May 1984 *Fortune* magazine called Nissan one of the ten best-managed companies in America:

> There's no time clock and no union . . . Marvin Runyon walks around in a uniform reminiscent of a [super-clean] garage mechanic . . . Over 200 robots and other highly automated equipment make Smyrna one of the most technically advanced auto plants in the world.

For three straight years, Nissan was included in *The Best 100 Companies to Work For in America*, the only automobile manufacturer to be listed.

> A year after he started working for Nissan, Ken Herndon sold his '76 Chevy station wagon and started driving a brand new Stanza sedan. It was not just company loyalty that caused Herndon to switch. Any Nissan employee with 12 months' service qualifies for a leasing program. The $160 a month the company deducts from Herndon's paycheck also takes care of maintenance, tax license and insurance costs . . . At General Motors, Ford, and

> Chrysler, only top managers are entitled to such leasing deals . . .
>
> Nissan employees can best be described as having a love affair with the company . . . [Many] have been sent to the company's plants in Japan, where they worked on the line for at least six weeks to pick up the Japanese way first hand.

One of those sent was diminutive Gary Damesworth, a twenty-seven-year-old team leader, who had never been out of Tennessee or Kentucky before. When he returned, he got down on his knees and kissed the Tennessee dirt. In the summer of 1987 he shared some impressions with me.

"The Japanese can do things we can't do. They can do what needs to be done with their left hand as well as their right. They can get by on two hours' sleep a night. During work breaks, they lie flat on their backs and take a nap. At lunch, they eat in ten minutes, then go outside and play baseball. But one thing they never do is question instructions. They don't think for themselves. They've been told if they do the job the same way every time they won't screw up. If they drop something, however small, they always pick it up. They save everything, even things we wouldn't think were worth saving."

Damesworth was impressed, flattered that his company had sent him to Japan, gladder still to be back. Others, if only a small minority yet, were less content.

For by the summer of 1987 Nissan was beginning to get some bad press. Perhaps there had been too much publicity. After a honeymoon of six years, an article appeared in a liberal magazine, *The Progressive*, sharply critical of both Runyon and Nissan.

Founded by Senator Robert La Follette of Wisconsin, *The Progressive* had a circulation of scarcely 30,000. John Junkerman, the article's author, had gone to school in Japan, spoke Japanese, had an advanced degree from the University of Wisconsin, and had written for *The Progressive* before. But this time he made no attempt to write a balanced piece. He hadn't visited the plant, he hadn't attempted to talk with anyone in management, and most of his quotes were unattributed. No one thought such an article, in a little-known magazine, would cause such a stir. But its publication proved to be something of a turning point. It gave the UAW, until then seemingly ineffective, its first rallying cry.

Perhaps this was because the union had hired savvy Maxey Irwin to be its political adviser and public relations consultant. The Harvard-educated Irwin was from Sparta, Tennessee, had run political campaigns in Maryland and the Upper South, was a lobbyist on trade and environmental matters, and had once been a reporter for *The Washington Post*. He'd also been a disc jockey in Nashville, when his moniker was Johnny Shannon, as in "Scubby doo baby boppin' Johnny Shannon raisin' hell and boppin' on your bippy." Irwin put Junkerman in touch with disgruntled Nissan employees, obtained advance proofs of his article, and sent copies to various newspaper editors.

Or perhaps the article was a turning point because three years earlier Junkerman had helped produce a *Frontline* program for PBS on Nissan in Japan called "We Are Driven." It focused on Nissan's strikebreaking activities, and asked whether a leopard could change its spots.

Or perhaps it was none of these but, rather, a need felt to balance a story many considered too good to be true. This is Ralph Nader's view. He financed some of Junkerman's research. The Nashville *Tennessean* should be ashamed of itself for its fawning and uncritical coverage of the huge Nissan and Saturn projects, he told me. Runyon had made no secret of his hatred of unions. Given half a chance, reporters usually prefer to side with the underdog.

Candy McCampbell, business editor at the Nashville *Tennessean*, defends her decision to banner a story summarizing the Junkerman piece across her business front page headlined: "Overwork, Intimidation Claimed at Nissan," saying:

"It was one of the best stories we had that day or week. It became one of the most talked-about stories we'd run in months. The company was given ample opportunity to comment, and their comments were included in the story. Of course, it helped that we had an advance copy."

Junkerman contended (as the UAW's Owen Bieber would do later when kicking off the union's organizing drive) that innovative Japanese management had had little to do with Smyrna's success:

> It was achieved the old-fashioned way—through the speed-up. "Eight-hour aerobics" is how one employee describes it . . .
>
> The barber near the center of town tells people he can spot Nissan workers, even when they're not wearing their telltale blue uniforms, because they're the ones who fall asleep in the chair.
>
> Management has broken the work force down into small groups . . . the smaller the group the greater the peer pressure.
>
> If an employee falls behind in production or takes a sick day, the burden must be shouldered by others in the group. This pressure intensified after Nissan began . . . awarding merit points for accident-free production. Instead of reporting injuries . . . employees will work with injured wrists, hands and elbows.

Junkerman cited examples of safety violations and sexual harassment, but didn't identify many of his sources. He contended that the company's most recent annual employee survey revealed more disenchantment than any previous one, and said workers wet their pants rather than risk going to the bathroom. He concluded by saying:

The white-haired folksy Runyon addresses the work force every three months on a closed-circuit television system that extends throughout the plant. Favored employees are selected for inclusion in the studio audience, and that still has the capacity to thrill some.

But Runyon's charm has its limits. He wrapped up a recent address by saying, "I'm sure everyone is enjoying their job." The entire trim-and-chassis line reportedly burst into laughter. When the address was rebroadcast for the night shift, that line had been edited out.

Rather than ignore the article, Runyon fired off a four-page letter of protest to *The Progressive*'s publisher. He called the piece a "classic example of 'reporting' used to confirm preconceived attitudes."

Instead of requesting a visit to the company or otherwise investigating his allegations firsthand, the author chose to depend upon disaffected former employees and un-attributed sources for his one-sided portrayal. Any organization can be made to look bad by this kind of selective reporting. The magazine's gratuitous use of offensive illustrations smacks of sordid sensationalism, and it compounded Junkerman's biased report.

Runyon was particularly incensed that two people Junker-man did quote were *former* employees who were suing the company. A third was a woman who had alleged sexual harassment, had filed a lawsuit, but had been unable to prove her claim. Runyon noted that the woman had, at her request, been transferred to a new work station. "We are absolutely committed to providing an environment free from sexual harassment," he said. But Nissan also had "an obligation to protect the reputations of employees charged with harassment, a serious offense."

Runyon refused to let *The Progressive* print his letter, threatened to sue, but then decided not to. "We don't want to give continued life to the article through the judicial process," the company's legal counsel said.

But by then the damage was done. *Newsweek*, the Chicago *Sun-Times*, the Detroit *Free Press*, and even *Pravda* sent reporters to Smyrna—and a spate of anti-Nissan stories resulted. Ironically, most of these had ignored Junkerman's article, even after the story about it appeared in the *Tennessean*, until Maxey Irwin sent them copies of Runyon's letter of protest.

Runyon's ire rose again when the Nashville *Banner* ran a story headlined "UAW Disputes Nissan's Claim of Few Injuries." The union had obtained copies of workmen's compensation records that showed Nissan had had 102 accidents resulting in eight or more lost workdays in less than two years. The company responded that in the most recent years for which figures were available, Nissan had lost fewer workdays per 100 employees than the average for the U.S. auto industry or the average for all U.S. manufacturing.

Runyon visited the *Banner* and berated the editors for running the story and Cathy Schulze, its senior business writer, for reporting it. Schulze, unintimidated, soon became more aggressive in covering the union's side of the story.

Beside Jim Turner's desk there once hung a plaque with the inscription "God grant me patience—and I want it right now." On the facing wall was a painting of an Alaskan grizzly bear.

A fiery speaker when aroused, the bearded Turner was the UAW's chief organizer for ten southeastern states and part of Pennsylvania. He looked a little like an Alaskan grizzly and sometimes talked like one, his voice alternating between whisper and full-throated roar. In his organizing drive at Nissan, however, he had had to learn patience.

"In most campaigns, you have 30 percent with you, 30 percent against, and 40 percent undecided," he told me.

"You work to win over half that 40 percent, plus one. Here we have had to start from almost zero. Nissan workers act like 'the chosen.' "

The people Nissan had hired were older than those at Honda. They had more education, more work experience, and usually more technical skills, particularly in electronics. Some initially commuted from as far as a hundred miles away. Applicants were required to take 40 to 200 hours of unpaid preemployment training, which they could do at night or on weekends so they wouldn't have to take time off from other jobs. Trainers looked for manual dexterity, enthusiasm, and willingness to accept criticism. Applicants who expressed preference for only one kind of work were seldom hired. "In playing sports, should greater recognition be given to the individual or the team? Tell us how your most recent supervisor would describe you. How your co-workers would." These were some of the questions asked.

Two hundred thousand Tennesseans applied for the three thousand jobs, but because of lagging car and truck sales there had been few promotions. Many who had started on the night shift were still on it. The work force had shrunk thanks to productivity gains and attrition.

In the summer of 1987, in the wake of the fallout from the Junkerman article, Turner began marshaling his forces. By mid-July he had four full-time organizers working on the Nissan campaign and had rented a concrete-block warehouse on the New Nashville Highway two miles south of the plant. It had offices in the front and a large open space in the back, which Turner used as an assembly hall.

He was born in Dayton, Ohio, but as a boy had moved back and forth between Dayton and Crossville, Tennessee, where most of his relatives lived. His father was a union carpenter who had held jobs in Dayton and Oak Ridge, Tennessee. After graduating from high school, Turner worked first as a machinist in Dayton, then for Martin Marietta in Orlando, Florida. In Orlando, at the age of twenty-two, he was elected to his first union job. Ten years later he became a full-time organizer.

When, as part of its "southern strategy," General Motors built plants in the Southeast to take advantage of union weakness there, it was Turner who personally organized several of the factories. When plant managers tried to invalidate neutrality pacts worked out between the union and company headquarters in Detroit, Turner held their feet to the fire. For some in the UAW, organizing is the necessary purgatory one has to endure before ascending to the heaven of a nine-to-five staff job. Organizers must work nights and weekends, be willing to leave home and family for weeks at a time, and be optimistic when there is little to be optimistic about. But for Turner, organizing was not just a job, it was a mission.

He had worked since 1978 out of the UAW's regional headquarters in Brentwood, a suburb of Nashville. After the UAW failed to organize Honda, it was Turner who was asked to do a postmortem. He had been given special assignments before. Earlier, he had helped organize twenty thousand of Michigan's state office workers.

At first Jim acted like a "huff-and-puff macho kind of a guy," Ben Perkins, Turner's boss in Detroit, remembers. "At first he resisted our urgings that he use helium-filled balloons to carry the union message into the workplace. 'Balloons?' he spluttered. But Jim was capable of change. Before long, he was handing out carnations and wearing a T-shirt which said 'A woman's place is in the union.' "

The organizing drive at Honda had been a disaster, Turner told me. "Organizers held meetings every week whether they had anything to discuss or not. They used up their issues as they went along, rather than wait for the right moment. No city directories were used, no license plates videotaped. Workers signed cards just to get organizers off their backs. One was signed Jack Meoff, for Christ's sake."

Turner vowed that in Tennessee he wouldn't make the

same mistakes. He wouldn't attempt to organize Nissan until its workers, in significant numbers, started coming to him. This started happening in late 1986 and early 1987, he said. And this was when he started gearing up, first by borrowing the meeting hall of the United Rubber Workers at Bridgestone (another Japanese-owned company in nearby La Vergne), then by renting his own assembly hall. By the fall of 1987 he was meeting regularly with groups.

"I've never seen such fear," he would say, shaking his head. "They come to our rallies, but a lot of them won't get out of their cars. They sit in the dark and listen. They give me signed cards to put in my wallet, but not to turn in yet. We're taking it step by step. We're going real slow. We're not asking anyone to sign a card unless he's really sure. We're going to do all the things our people failed to do at Honda."

Turner was optimistic. For unlike Honda, Nissan had been outspokenly anti-union. It would be easier to provoke Nissan into doing something rash, he thought. Marvin Runyon had such a large ego.

But then the unexpected happened.

In November 1987 Turner went into the hospital for a routine checkup, and his doctor found he had cancer of the colon, liver, and bladder.

"You've got only a few months to live," his doctor said. "If there's anything you've wanted to do but haven't done yet, think about doing it now."

Turner said the only thing he wanted to do was organize Nissan. He started chemotherapy treatments, took a couple weeks of vacation, and returned to the job.

But then in December, President Reagan appointed Marvin Runyon chairman of the Tennessee Valley Authority. Six months earlier, Runyon had told *Automotive News* that, though sixty-three, he expected to be with Nissan for fifteen more years.

"You don't have to retire at sixty-five?" the reporter asked.

"Oh, no," Runyon said. "The chairman of our company is seventy-nine, and he hasn't retired yet. He's seventy-nine, I'm sixty-three—that's sixteen years. So maybe fifteen more years isn't a good number. Maybe it ought to be twenty."

Runyon knew he had no chance of becoming head of Nissan in the United States. He was a manufacturing man, and Nissan's problems at the time were in sales and design. Then, too, a different face might be advantageous in combating the UAW's organizing drive.

Jim Turner's next adversary would turn out to be a different kind of man.

5

Oh, What a Feeling

This may be the only place in the world where you can see people driving a Volvo with a gun rack in the back.

—Pamela Bradley, then of the Toyota
Planning Center, Georgetown, Kentucky

As you come in from the south, past horse farms with their distinctive white and black plank fences, and tree-lined drives leading to old Kentucky homes, Georgetown looks peaceful enough. Its Baptist college is known for the college presidents it counts among its alumni. It has more fine old houses, many of them Greek Revival, than most towns its size anywhere. And around the courthouse, utility wires are coming down, sidewalks being bricked, aluminum sidings removed to reveal the original façades underneath. Attracted by the fine old houses, a number of IBM families have settled here, since the giant IBM plant is located only ten miles away, on the outskirts of Lexington. Yet something seems amiss.

Too many big trucks are lumbering down Main Street. And a block behind City Hall, a red-and-white sign reads OSAKA HEALTH SPA. I drive farther north, through the villages of Stamping Ground and Great Crossing, on into the part of Scott County where Indians once hunted buffalo. The road narrows then. I see unpainted houses with iceboxes on

their porches and abandoned cars in their yards. I notice
that the direction signs have been taken down.

I am told that eighteen months after Toyota announced
it was coming here, the stack of lawsuits contesting the deal
was still two feet high.

Scott County, to which Toyota had come, is something of a
microcosm of Kentucky itself—a state that somehow super-
imposes old-money horse owners onto some of the most
individualistic tobacco farmers and coal miners to be found
anywhere. Scott, like most Kentucky counties, is dry and, as
a result, has its share of bootleggers. Trees, fence posts, and
telephone poles are smothered in political posters, and it's
not uncommon to find campaign workers pulling tacks from
old placards for use in anchoring the new. Kentucky governors can't succeed themselves, and until recently county
sheriffs couldn't, either. The political pot is always boiling.

Until Toyota and its parts suppliers arrived and began
creating a new middle class, Scott and some of its neighboring
counties resembled a Third World country with extremes of
wealth and poverty and little in between. One day you would
read in the newspaper that "ballroom fall can't stop socialite"
or that Britain's Queen Elizabeth was making her third visit
to the Blue Grass. The next, you would hear about satanism
in Shelbyville.

Toyota's announcement in December 1985 dwarfed all the
other Japanese auto plant announcements and triggered the
most controversy, then or since. Toyota is Japan's General
Motors, after all; Kentucky, the most turbulent of the states
to which the Japanese auto makers have come.

Founded in 1937 as a spin-off of the Toyoda Automatic
Loom Works, Toyota is still a family-owned company. Although it has grown to become the world's number-three
auto maker (after GM and Ford), it is still, as Michael
Cusumano notes in *The Japanese Automobile Industry*, regarded

as a "rural" company. Its factories and corporate headquarters are in Aichi Prefecture, two hundred miles southwest of Tokyo. It originally hired and trained malleable farm boys. Its assembly plant and suppliers are, for the most part, within bicycling distance of one another. The parent company changed its name from Toyoda to Toyota because in written Japanese "Toyota" looked aesthetically superior and because now the number of strokes needed was eight, a lucky number.

Toyota was no late-blooming maverick, like Honda, nor an early borrower of American technology and mass-production techniques, like Nissan. Instead, it had developed and perfected its own seemingly unsophisticated (and later much copied) production techniques, which were to make it the world's lowest-cost auto producer. Toyota had relied on local engineers and academics to design its early vehicles, and this experience enabled it to build vehicles which, if less flashy, were better adapted to the Japanese market than Nissan's more sophisticated models.

Such techniques would be hard to duplicate outside of Toyota City, however. This is an important reason why Toyota was the last of the major Japanese auto makers to come to the United States. It wasn't until Washington forced the Japanese government to "voluntarily" restrict car imports that it became obvious that if Toyota was to continue to increase its market share here, it would have to build a plant.

The company had already asked three consultants to suggest a strategy, but their report was not encouraging. They said it would be next to impossible for Toyota to achieve, on its own, the same quality, productivity, and favorable labor climate in the United States that it enjoyed in Japan.

And so Toyota proposed a joint venture in the United States with Ford, a company that the Toyoda family, who owned Toyota, had long admired. Toyota had tried before to work with Ford, but always unsuccessfully, and this attempt was to prove unsuccessful as well. Thus, when in March 1982 General Motors proposed a somewhat similar venture, a deal was struck. Called NUMMI, the plant would be located in Fremont, California.

As Maryann Keller writes in *Rude Awakening: The Rise, Fall, and Struggle for Recovery of General Motors,* Toyota was concerned about anti-Japanese sentiment in the United States and thought such a partnership could be politically advantageous. It also saw a joint venture as a way to discover how Americans handle labor problems before committing itself to build a separate plant of its own. The agreement was for ten years, after which either party could opt out.

NUMMI would build subcompacts (Toyota Corollas and Chevrolet Novas). General Motors would furnish the building and supervise marketing and relations with American parts suppliers. Toyota would manage the plant. In layout, the plant would be a clone of Toyota's Takaota plant in Japan. Its machinery was the same, and it was producing a model, the Corolla, that Toyota had been making for years. If there were technical problems, details of a problem could be faxed to Toyota City, and the solution received back within hours. The only imponderable was whether a racially mixed, culturally diverse, and unionized American work force could adapt to Toyota's management style. The fact that it did adapt—and brilliantly—was crucial to NUMMI's success.

Kiyoshi "Nate" Furata was Toyota's lead trainer at NUMMI (and later in Kentucky). A slight, energetic, surprisingly candid man, he told me that scores of veteran UAW members were sent to Toyota City, not for formal training, but rather "to clean their brains out," the idea being to show them the benefits of job rotation and let them experience firsthand a new style of supervisor-worker relations.

"They had been fed the rhetoric that Japan was ahead because of low wages and unfair labor practices. We wanted them to see for themselves. We wanted them to understand that the Japanese supervisor is an older brother, a part of the team, a truly hands-on kind of person. Not at all like the American supervisor, who doesn't know half what the worker knows about his machine, who just stands off to one side and says, 'Do it.' "

It wasn't only rank-and-file union members who were impressed.

"What was so great about the assembly line, where you do the same job every day? Was that paradise?" UAW president Owen Bieber would later ask in a speech to auto executives. "The opportunity to rotate jobs and learn new skills has been liberating."

NUMMI was not an immediate success—not that anyone expected it to be. Its first shift didn't reach full production for nearly a year. Parts were rejected and sent back to suppliers. A second shift wasn't added until Toyota was satisfied that vehicles built on the first shift were as near-perfect as possible. Finally, however, NUMMI succeeded beyond anyone's expectations, and Toyota gained enormous confidence from the experience. It learned it could build cars in the United States of as good a quality as in Japan and do it in a "worst-case" scenario. It learned who the best U.S. suppliers were. It learned from GM what not to do in marketing, since marketing the Chevrolet Nova proved to be NUMMI's one nemesis. Ironically, however, its success at NUMMI appears to have made Toyota overconfident.

For NUMMI was to be prologue; Kentucky, the main event. California was too far removed from the bulk of the American population, too distant from most American parts suppliers, too unlike Aichi Prefecture, too close to Japan.

By the time Toyota announced it was coming to Kentucky, Honda was already building cars in Ohio; Nissan, trucks and cars in Tennessee; Mazda had agreed to a joint venture with Ford in Michigan; and Mitsubishi, to another with Chrysler in Illinois. Each of them had a state to itself, and many thought the Japanese government planned it that way.

The Midwest and Upper South were where the Japanese auto makers wanted to be. Our national newspapers and news magazines might consider the so-called heartland "flyover country," might say that nothing of significance happened in America unless it started on the East or West Coast, might still see the auto industry through the lenses of their Detroit bureaus—but the Japanese saw homogeneous people, interstate highways, and all that empty land.

By the time Toyota got around to picking a state, only Indiana and Kentucky, among the prime candidates, remained untapped, however. Kentucky won out, it appears, because of the aggressive wooing of its governor, Martha Layne Collins. Fearful that Toyota would choose Fort Wayne, Indiana, reportedly its alternate site, she made a number of last-minute concessions that carried the day.

Martha Layne Collins was Kentucky's first woman governor. A 1959 graduate of the University of Kentucky with a degree in home economics, she had been a teacher in the Versailles (pronounced "ver sails") and Louisville public schools. She would later make education and economic development her twin priorities. She wanted to be remembered as the governor who gave Kentucky's backward school system a jump start, she says. Only the prospect of a dramatic increase in skilled jobs could free up the necessary moneys from a conservative rural legislature.

A former Miss Kentucky and 1984 chairman of the Democratic National Convention, Collins is still a beautiful woman. She wears the high heels and tailored suits that were her trademark as governor, and is cordial, but barely so, when asked about the incentive package she gave to Toyota. She has had to answer that question, she says, too many times before. Out of office now, she owns a small consulting firm, Martha Layne Collins & Associates, run inconspicuously from a Lexington office without a sign.

Collins was elected lieutenant governor in 1978, then governor in 1982, with little support from the business community. After Kentucky lost General Motors' giant Saturn plant to Tennessee, she heard mutterings to the effect that a woman didn't know how to close a deal.

The Saturn plant, when first announced, was to be America's answer to Japanese imports, a flashy new small-car plant aimed at beating the Japanese in both cost and quality. State of the art in every way, it would be a paperless operation with administrative tasks and most communications handled electronically. First preference in hiring would go to UAW members laid off elsewhere. The UAW, in return, had agreed to eliminate most job classifications and work rules.

The plant would be located thirty miles southwest of Smyrna, in part so that Nissan would be less able to resist union organizing pressures, knowledgeable observers say. Once Nissan was organized, it would be easier to organize Honda, the argument went.

But almost as soon as GM announced its plans, it began to scale back. At first 500,000 cars a year would be produced, then 250,000. At first 6,000 people would be hired, then 3,000. At first hailed as America's answer to the imported small car, the Saturn model gradually became larger, at last report a vehicle in the $9,000–$12,000 range. By the summer of 1989 *Automotive News* was reporting that Japanese, German, and joint-venture suppliers would provide the car's steel, brakes, windshields, windows, ashtrays, electrical motors, and air conditioners. The first car was still scheduled to be built in 1990.

While Collins was sorry to have lost Saturn, she saw Toyota as the bigger prize. And with Toyota she was determined not to fail. She made eight trips to Japan. The result: not only

did Toyota invest $1.1 billion and commit to 3,500 jobs while
she was governor, but several dozen Japanese auto-parts
companies later built plants in her state, as well.

But none of this came easily, and it was very controversial. A Pearl Harbor Day demonstration threat forced Toyota
to change its construction strategy. Ralph Nader almost
convinced the Kentucky supreme court to declare the Collins
incentive package unconstitutional. At one point there was
even scattered talk of her impeachment.

The problems were several: the size of the incentive
package, Toyota's insistence on getting the "best possible
deal," the refusal of Lexington and Louisville newspapers to
"play ball" (as newspapers in Ohio and Tennessee had done),
and Toyota's failure to understand that building a plant
nonunion in Kentucky was not the same as building a plant
nonunion in Tennessee. Tennessee was a right-to-work state;
Kentucky was not. In Kentucky, the United Mine Workers
had fought and won many a bloody battle in the hills to the
east.

First, the incentive package:

Fearful that Kentucky would lose Toyota, as it had lost
Saturn, Collins had her staff put together a flurry of last-
minute concessions, the largest being for training, site purchase, and site preparation. The package totaled $125 million
(not including interest payments) and was larger by far than
anything any state had given a foreign auto maker before,
far larger, too, than anything anyone could remember having
been given an American company.

Collins apparently had had no choice. As Ohio's governor Richard Celeste tells it, Toyota was bent on striking
an exceptionally hard deal:

"At the end of six or seven hours of meetings with ten
or twelve state departments, the Toyota people invited me
in to summarize our package and to talk about what I might
do to sweeten it.

"When I was through, the lead person for Toyota said,

in Japanese, and then it was interpreted, 'Governor, why haven't you said what every other governor has said, "Tell us what you want and we'll do it"?'

"I had already offered $105 million. It was as high as I could go, perhaps already higher than I should have gone. To have offered more couldn't have been justified to a comparable American company."

Toyota's site choice was also controversial. Scott County is in the so-called golden triangle between Lexington, Louisville, and Cincinnati, and the triangle in general and Scott County in particular had a lower unemployment rate than counties to the east and west. But the triangle is where the universities are, where the interstate highways intersect, where there was already a small pool of skilled labor.

Then, too, Collins was unable to obtain options to buy all the necessary land before word leaked out that the giant auto maker was coming. The Lexington *Herald-Leader* and the Louisville *Courier-Journal* were locked in a battle for dominance in northern Kentucky, with each afraid the other would print the story first. The *Herald-Leader* did and, in doing so, succeeded in raising land prices at the site 10 to 15 percent, Carroll Knicely, then Kentucky's commerce secretary, says. A few landowners made fortunes. A number of others, who did not, filed lawsuits.

Most serious, however, was the breakdown in communications between Frankfort, the state capital, and Scott County. The plant would be located a mile north of Georgetown's city limits, but city and county officials weren't given any details until the last minute. They were allowed no say in how to cushion the plant's impact. Money was promised but not allocated for a bypass road, nor was anything said about the extra police and fire protection that would be needed.

The banner headline in Georgetown's *News and Times* read: "Toyota, a Big Yes; Oh, What a Feeling." But the euphoria was short-lived. Toyota's problems were about to begin.

6

Toyota's Opposition Mobilizes

The only people against this project are Ralph
Nader and the unions.
> —Kentucky's commerce secretary
> Carroll Knicely, February 1986

Four persons, working independently of one another, were
responsible for raising opposition to Toyota to a fever pitch.
At first they seemed isolated, their opposition ineffective,
their arguments self-serving. Cartoonists depicted the most
capable of them as a redneck and Japan basher. But later,
it would become apparent that the four spoke for others too
inarticulate—or too fearful—to speak for themselves.

The first was Jerry Hammond, a former Air Force
intelligence analyst who had become secretary-treasurer of
the Kentucky Building Trades Council, its only full-time
paid employee. After leaving the Air Force, Hammond had
tried selling insurance and repossessing tractors before set-
tling down to become an ironworker. Twice in the 1980s he
had run for a seat in the U.S. Congress and been badly
defeated.

"You develop a unique philosophy when you go out
and struggle with iron every day," he says. "You can't talk it
into place. It teaches you patience."

A second opponent was James Musselman, twenty-eight

years old and one of Ralph Nader's assistants at the Center
for the Study of Responsive Law in Washington, D.C.
Musselman grew up in Allentown, Pennsylvania, in the
shadow of Bethlehem Steel, and developed an early aversion
to big-company politics. He remembers Bethlehem officials
saying, "If you don't do what we say, we'll close your plant
down."

A third was Jane Allen Offut, a wealthy ophthalmologist's
wife who lived in Lexington, but who with her husband
owned a farm in Scott County downstream from where
Toyota was building its plant. Under their farm was limestone
pockmarked with sinkholes, and Offut worried that effluent
from the plant might infiltrate and pollute the area's water
supply.

A fourth was Charlie Sutton, judge executive for Scott
County. Sutton's base of support was in the rural part of the
county, and the county was almost bankrupt. As will be
explained, Sutton got county officials to slap both a payroll
and net profits tax on Toyota before it could even break
ground.

These four—Hammond, Musselman, Offut, and Sutton—were responsible for the bulk of the lawsuits and most
of the grief that would plague Toyota and the Collins
Administration for two years to come. Several times, the
uproar reached such intensity that officials in Frankfort
feared the giant auto maker might pack its bags and go
home.

The way Jerry Hammond tells it, the trouble began even
before December 1985, when Toyota announced it was
coming to Kentucky. Hammond is six foot one and wears
glasses. He has the pallor of someone who now spends his
days on the telephone or looking at a computer screen. He
is good at telling his story, which he has neatly and chron-
ologically organized.

The trouble began on November 20, he says, when he

met with Lucky McClintock, president of the central division of the Building Trades Council. The two men discussed how the various craft unions that made up the council might benefit if the giant auto maker were to come. McClintock had heard that Ohbayashi, a Tokyo-based company, would supervise construction and wanted to meet with them. Rumor had it that Ohbayashi would hire 3,500 construction workers. Hammond and McClintock were anxious to do business.

The trade unionists soon discovered, however, that Ohbayashi wanted a "merit shop." This meant that—as at Nissan—the work would go to the subcontractor who submitted the lowest bid, regardless of whether he was unionized or not. Not wanting to jeopardize Kentucky's chances for landing the giant auto maker, the two made a counterproposal that kept the discussion alive until after Toyota made its announcement. Ohbayashi had hired Lewis Smoak of the Greenville, South Carolina, law firm of Ogletree, Deakins, Nash, Smoak, and Stewart to deal with the unions, the same law firm Nissan was using.

By 1985 nonunion labor accounted for three fourths of all construction work in Kentucky, up from only 30 percent ten years before. Union membership had dropped from 40,000 to 25,000 in the previous six years. Although large industrial projects represented the last union stronghold, Smoak had urged Ohbayashi to build nonunion. Nissan, after all, had done it.

But Kentucky was not Tennessee, Toyota was not Nissan, and Toyota, by coming last, had given trade unionists the chance to learn from others' mistakes. Hammond says he can remember the exact moment when he decided to dig in his heels. His eyes sparkle as he tells the story.

Though intense, Hammond does not look much like a tough guy. He lives in a modernized log-cabin house atop a bluff overlooking the Kentucky River near Versailles. He has a lot of books on his shelves. His wife has a master's degree in library science and is getting another in psychology.

He was eating breakfast, he said, when he picked up the *Herald-Leader* and saw on page one an interview with Dr. Shoichiro Toyoda, Toyota's president and chief executive officer.

The reporter had asked, "How do you account for the success of an auto firm like yours at a time when U.S. auto makers are beset with so much difficulty?"

Dr. Toyoda's response: "When Japan was making great efforts to rehabilitate and reconstruct after the defeat in the Second World War, we acquired the concept of quality control. This was introduced to Japan by [your] Edwards Deming. [The most revered American in postwar Japan after Douglas MacArthur, Deming had first tried unsuccessfully to introduce his quality control concepts to Big Three auto makers. His quest, to improve the quality of industrial products by applying statistical controls, evoked little interest, however. In America's booming postwar economy the use of systems to expand production, not the use of controls to improve quality, became the hot ticket.] This spirit of producing good products at low prices has prevailed in Japan in the thirty-five years since the concept was introduced. It is a very large factor in the success that Japan now enjoys."

Reporter: "Then you're beating us at our own game?"

Dr. Toyoda: "In the Japanese form of wrestling, the pupil expresses his gratitude . . . by becoming so strong and capable that he is able to defeat his teacher."

Next day, when Hammond met with his union brothers, they all agreed that Dr. Toyoda's philosophy was "so alien to our view of things, so different from our worldview, as to be a gross insult. In America, if a student slaps his teacher, the student gets expelled from school."

And so, with McClintock's blessing, Hammond told Smoak that merit shop was unfair. It would allow contractors to hold expenses down by paying low wages and tolerating poor working conditions. Kentuckians would be deprived of jobs. Cheap labor would be brought in from out of state.

According to Hammond, Smoak then tried to induce several of the brothers to break ranks by offering them golf trips to Hilton Head Island and tickets to the NCAA basketball tournament finals. When this tactic failed, Ohbayashi started hiring nonunion.

Negotiations continued, however, though Hammond and his people grew restless. Hammond videotaped the license plates of cars leaving the construction site and discovered that many were from out of state. There was talk of picketing, which Hammond says he recommended against. Were there to be an incident, and someone injured, he argued, the union would be blamed regardless of who was at fault.

Hammond is a voracious reader and has a satellite dish in his back yard. He had read and taped everything he could find about Japan and the Japanese. He had compiled fact sheets about the *zaibatsu* (cartels), about Shintoism and Buddhism, about the martial arts. He was particularly fascinated by the samurai, Japan's warrior class, noting that in the nineteenth century the samurai were transformed into bureaucrats and required to master administrative skills as well as military arts. He characterized Toyota as a samurai company, determined to win at any cost, as distinct from Honda, which he called a "commoner company" (Hammond rides a Honda Gold Wing motorcycle). He had read that when the Japanese are about to engage in mortal combat, they don a *hachimaki*, or headband.

And so in April 1986, during what he anticipated would be his final meeting with Smoak and Smoak's Japanese "observer," Hammond says that he said, " 'Now we are going to give you our answer in Japanese fashion, so there will be no mistake.'

"There were eleven union leaders present.

"On a prearranged signal, we nodded to each other and began undoing our neckties. Mr. Smoak looked scared. He started to get up from his chair. 'I don't believe I know what the hell is going on,' he said.

'We took off our neckties and tied them around our heads.

" 'I'm sure Mr. Suzuki knows,' I told Mr. Smoak.

"Mr. Suzuki, who had never said anything or shown emotion before, flushed beet-red. He then came over and shook each of our hands. We never saw Mr. Smoak again."

Shortly thereafter, Hammond went to Washington and won support from heads of the various building trades unions to raise the ante. Patrick Campbell of the carpenters' union, a World War II veteran who had read Russell Braddon's book *Japan Against the World, 1941–2041*, acted as Hammond's advocate. Braddon, in his book, says: "The Japanese have brought to post-war industry precisely that spirit of daring and devotion that yielded them such stunning victories in the Pacific in the first five months of 1942—then inspired them to suicidal feats of valor for three further years of war."

In Washington, the trade unionists hired a consulting firm, the Kamber Group, to analyze Toyota's vulnerabilities. Kamber recommended that lawsuits be filed contesting the incentive package and Kentucky's too liberal awarding of environmental permits. Hammond's contention was that Ohbayashi—and through Ohbayashi, Toyota—had gotten bad advice from its South Carolina law firm. The problem was one of communications. Lawsuits would force all relevant facts into the open. The more facts became known, the more support there would be for the union. In Washington, the trade unionists authorized more than a million dollars in legal fees.

By July 1986 subcontractors were pouring concrete for the plant's foundations. In such work, the land is normally cleared, leveled, and then allowed to settle for as long as a year. But Toyota couldn't wait. It needed to start building cars in 1988. Its plant had to be finished as soon as possible. And so, to speed the process, Ohbayashi hired engineers to study soil types, to find a way to skip the settling-in period.

What they came up with was a blend of crushed rock and dirt that would not shift after a heavy rain or with the weight of the building. But even as concrete was being poured, Toyota acknowledged that Hammond's flurry of lawsuits was slowing the job.

"Let's be truthful. Let's be candid. Hammond's goal is to prevent construction of the plant, not to protect the environment," one company lawyer said.

"Delay only costs Toyota money," said another.

By then, too, the lawsuits had brought into the open more disturbing facts about the incentive package. Seventy million dollars of the $125 million had been allotted for job training, $20 million for roads and sewers to the plant, and $35 million for purchase of the 1,600-acre site and improvements there. Already there had been cost overruns on buying and improving the site, a miscalculation of federal funds available for job training, and failure to include tax losses associated with the bond issue that had been floated. On July 2 a tight-lipped Governor Collins was forced to admit under oath that she hadn't known all of what was in her own incentive package. The details, she said, had been worked out by "several of my cabinet secretaries."

By then, too, Jim Musselman, representing Ralph Nader, was characterizing the incentive package as "corporate freeloading on the backs of taxpayers." A headline on the front page of the August 24 Lexington *Herald-Leader* read: "Toyota Deal: Did Kentucky Give Away Too Much?" On September 9 the newspaper reported that the cost to taxpayers, when interest on principal was added in, would be triple the $125 million that state officials had been quoting.

Finally, on November 12, the *Herald-Leader* reported that union leaders from across the country were planning a massive anti-Toyota rally to be held in Lexington on December 7. Hammond said both that he opposed the rally—"I don't want to condone anything that will detract from the larger issues. We don't want to be labeled as Japan bashers"—

and that pressures from his union brothers might be such
that he would have no choice but to participate. Later, he
would tell me, "The samurai warrior always carries two
swords. Two swords make him look twice as dangerous."

A week later, hundreds of construction workers demonstrated, first outside the Japanese embassy in Washington,
D.C., then in front of the Hotel Pierre in New York, where
the Japanese ambassador was meeting potential investors.
"Got a yen for fairness?" the placards read. "Forget Toyota.
Stop giveaways to corporations that don't respect American
habits."

"We'll do as many of these as we have to," national
building trades union president Robert Georgine told reporters. "These demonstrations aren't just to resolve the
Georgetown issue. They go to the whole question of whether
Japanese investors can come to this country and disregard
the standards we've worked for."

Three days later, it was all over. Smoak resigned as
Ohbayashi's representative. Ohbayashi agreed that two thousand future construction hires would be referred through
union hiring halls. Hammond agreed that the one thousand
workers already on the job could stay.

Shortly thereafter, Honda, which had built its motorcycle
and first auto plant with union construction workers, but
then started building its engine plant at Anna nonunion,
switched over to union construction workers at Anna, as
well. Robert Farrington, secretary-treasurer of the Ohio
Building and Construction Trades Union, had worked with
Hammond on strategies with which to confront Toyota.
Farrington had been a construction supervisor in Saudi
Arabia and claimed to be familiar with "Eastern mind games."
Honda, he says, told him it had warned Toyota not to build
such a large plant nonunion.

Once Ohbayashi agreed to hire union workers, Hammond
dropped his lawsuits; it was part of the deal. The furor over

the incentive package and environment continued, however. Musselman remained to lobby state supreme court justices, and Jane Allen Offut persisted in her crusade against water pollution.

"I think they assumed they were dealing with a nut and not a sensible person," she told me. "They acted as if a mere citizen needn't be taken into account."

A smallish woman in her early forties, Offut had grown up in Frankfort, where her father was minister of the First United Methodist Church. When she was ten, and the Louisville *Courier-Journal* ran an article mildly critical of her father, Jane Allen fired off a letter to the editor in which she called the newspaper "naïve." The editor saw fit to print her letter on page one, and a career in the public eye was launched.

In 1977, while living in Georgetown, she ran for the city council and won, then won again handily in 1979. In 1981 she raised her sights and ran for mayor, but was badly defeated. In a heated campaign, she was castigated for being a rich doctor's wife, guilty of driving a Mercedes, wearing fur coats, and sending her children to private school. Friends say the experience scarred her and may have had something to do with her later crusades.

"Toyota does not understand that the governor does not have the authority to sell the environment of the people who live here," she told *Bluegrass* magazine. "The governor can't say I have to accept hazardous waste in the creek running through my pretty little farm out there on the old Oxford Road, any more than I can say she has to accept it at the mansion."

Offut showed up at public hearings carrying pictures of Japanese disfigured by the Minamata pollution disaster. (Among industrial nations, Japan has one of the poorest records in pollution control. In the 1970s mercury waste from a chemical factory near Minamata caused a disease that crippled hundreds of people. *Life* magazine photographer

W. Eugene Smith documented the suffering.) To the horror
of the Japanese, when Offut didn't get her way, she would
spread the Minamata pictures out on the table in front of
her. Like Hammond, she took a certain delight in playing
hardball.

Her crusade led to tighter enforcement of water quality
standards. The state built a pipeline through her land that
releases the effluent at a point well beyond the sinkholes.

"Jane Allen was very effective in making her points,"
says Steve Mooney, then director of the state-funded Toyota
planning center. "She sensitized us all to the need for more
effective pollution controls."

Like Hammond and Musselman, Offut had said that
most people were against the incentive package but were
afraid to speak out. Eighteen months after Toyota announced it was coming, the University of Kentucky released
its first impact study. It said: "Only one in three people
surveyed in 41 north-central counties support the incentive
package, even though their towns will gain the most benefits
and jobs."

Governor Collins told me she had given Toyota as much
as she had because she sensed that after the auto plant was
built there would be lots more to come: an engine plant, a
truck plant, probably a North American headquarters, as
well. She had made eight trips to Japan, and several visits to
Toyota City. She knew that Toyota would also be bringing
dozens of its key suppliers along.

But none of this was in writing. These were things she
couldn't say publicly.

7

Honda Stumbles

If you have set your goals high enough, you will have many failures.
—Shoichiro Irimajiri, then president of
Honda of America Manufacturing

Honda never had to face the local opposition Toyota did, but that isn't to say it hasn't had problems.

The company broke ground for its second, East Liberty plant on March 20, 1988, doing so on a Sunday, when most of its associates and their families could attend. The ceremony was delayed forty-five minutes because of the traffic jam on Route 33 that resulted. Susan Insley presided and was given the honor of being the first American to scoop dirt (after Honda of Japan's president, Tadashi Kume, and Shoichiro Irimajiri).

Dignitaries were seated in the west cafeteria of the first auto plant, and the ceremony was seen via large-screen television in its three other cafeterias. The actual ground-breaking had taken place earlier that wintry morning, five miles to the west, and been videotaped. Dirt from the site was then hauled to the first auto plant and shoveled into specially constructed wooden boxes. Visitors found metal scoops and brown paper sacks beside each of the boxes. Following the ceremony, anyone who wanted a dirt sample could take one home, and, in fact, many did.

The East Liberty plant would have more robots than

the Marysville plant, but still not as many as some of the new Big Three plants. It would have a production capacity of 150,000 cars a year, but the same had been said of the first auto plant, and its capacity had since doubled. By now Honda had become the first Japanese auto maker to sell more cars in the United States than in Japan.

In the euphoria of the moment, Governor Celeste said he hoped Honda would transfer what was left of its California offices to Ohio, then one day put its world headquarters here. Later he would joke that he had reserved a corner in downtown Columbus for a Honda headquarters building. "It makes sense for all of us to be in the Eastern Time Zone," Susan Insley often says. "Wall Street and Washington are in the Eastern Time Zone. We're looking to export cars to Europe from here."

The day after the groundbreaking, a full-page advertisement appeared in *The Wall Street Journal.* Headlined "Quality for the World, Made in Ohio," it featured an accompanying map showing thirty-three Ohio locales in which a hundred companies had plants supplying Honda.

The next day, however, the news broke that Honda had resolved a long-standing federal discrimination complaint. The company would hand over $6 million in back pay to 377 employees, black and female (of both races). These were people who "were offered and have accepted positions . . . but were previously not hired at the time of their original applications," Al Kinzer explained in an internal memo to all employees. The timing of the announcement—after, not before, the groundbreaking—had obviously been part of the agreement.

The company, in agreeing to fork over $6 million, did not admit to any wrongdoing. It said, instead, that it was settling the issue to avoid the trouble and expense of further legal proceedings. The company's position was that the complaint had been brought by outsiders, not by anyone inside the plant. Honda's percentage of minority employees (then 2.8 percent) was typical of its hiring area. At least 25 percent of its associates were women, a higher percentage than in most auto plants.

"We have not been required to hire any additional people as a result of this agreement, and we have not hired anyone any earlier than required by our production needs," a spokesman said.

The company justified its restricted hiring radius of twenty (later thirty) miles, saying, "There was a fair amount of manufacturing in the area. In the early 1980s many plants were closing or laying off. Residents hoped we'd hire locally, and we were committed to deepening our ties with the local community."

Susan Insley added that a factor in Honda's locating and expanding where it did had to do with air-pollution controls. In a memo she showed me, written before the decision was made on where to locate the East Liberty plant, a company lawyer had written: "Since nearly all major urban areas now, and in the future, will fail to meet national ambient air quality standards for volatile organic compounds (which include paint fumes), the complications, costs, and risks . . . are almost certainly greater in metropolitan areas than rural."

So what was the problem?

The problem was Honda's restricted hiring radius excluded Columbus, thirty-eight miles to the southeast, and Columbus had central Ohio's largest black population. It also excluded nearby Springfield and Lima, which likewise had sizable black populations. Ohio's NAACP had issued a resolution denouncing Honda for both "anti–civil rights and anti-union activities." Moreover, blacks living in Columbus had been told that before they could be considered for jobs they must relocate within the hiring radius. Unwilling to risk moving and then not getting hired, they complained to the Equal Employment Opportunity Commission instead. The EEOC then discovered that although Honda was hiring a lot of women, it was excluding too many with small children and wasn't hiring enough physically big women to do the same jobs as big men.

Of equal concern was the fact that since the 1960s blacks had held one in four U.S. auto jobs, more than twice their percentage in the total work force, and now a trend was developing in the opposite direction. First Honda and then Nissan, Mitsubishi-Chrysler, Toyota, and Subaru-Isuzu had built or were building assembly plants in parts of rural Ohio, Tennessee, Illinois, Kentucky, and Indiana. There were far fewer blacks there than in the cities where most Big Three auto plants are located. Ford and General Motors might have transferred some of their production to plants in the rural heartland as well, but because of union contracts, they had had to bring their black employees along. To exacerbate matters, Japanese prime minister Yasuhiro Nakasone had in 1986 been quoted as saying, "In the United States, because there are a considerable number of blacks, the intellectual level is lower."

By 1986 nearly 200,000 Americans were working for Japanese-owned companies, and the number was expected to balloon in the years ahead. The Equal Employment Opportunity Commission needed a benchmark case to underscore the importance it attached to minority hiring. In June 1982, in the case of *Sumitomo Shoji* v. *Avigliani*, the Japanese had argued that a 1953 trade treaty permitted their U.S.-based companies to set their own employment policies. The U.S. Supreme Court said no, ruling unanimously that Japanese companies in the United States must comply with federal laws prohibiting job discrimination.

Inspiration for the Honda case is said to have come from a story that ran March 13, 1983, in the Cleveland *Plain Dealer*. Honda was the EEOC's target of choice because, as the first Japanese company to build an auto plant here, it was the most visible.

The *Plain Dealer* story told of a survey conducted by Dr.

Tony Hain, then a professor at the General Motors Institute (and later GM's director of strategic planning). Hain claimed to have interviewed executives from twenty of the three hundred Japanese firms with offices in the United States, among them Honda, Nissan, and Toyota:

> Hain said he was told few minorities were hired because the Japanese felt it most efficient to have a homogeneous work force which they believe has the same values and behavior.
>
> Japanese officials felt a commercial trade treaty signed more than two decades ago between Japan and the United States [still] protected them from equal employment opportunity laws.
>
> The Japanese felt when they come to the United States they know in order to be good corporate citizens they must hire Americans. But they will be damned if they will let Americans tell them which Americans to hire . . .
>
> The Japanese tend to hire young people because they find them more malleable and better oriented towards teamwork.

Jay Friedman, director of the EEOC's investigative unit, wouldn't tell me what the commission's inspiration had been in launching the Honda investigation. He did say that as a result of the Honda settlement, a standard had been set, a standard other Japanese companies would be required to follow.

Prior to the settlement, Honda enlarged its hiring radius to include Columbus, Lima, and Springfield, agreed to stop giving preference to applicants referred by its own associates, and began seeking references from black ministers in the area.

In Ohio, reaction to news of the settlement was muted. The story received more play than the company's $450,000 age-discrimination settlement of the year before, but not much more. The stories that appeared were mostly wire stories, and there was little, if any, editorial comment. Perhaps this was because the overriding concern in Ohio was (and still is) jobs, and Honda had been hiring while other auto companies were laying off. Or perhaps it was because the discrimination complaints had come from outside the company, not from within. State legislators had known about the complaints, but two months before settlement the state senate had approved sale of the Transportation Research Center to Honda by a vote of 33 to 1.

Ed Brown, a Honda associate from Norwood, seemed to speak for many Ohioans when he told me, "I think Honda knew exactly what they were doing when they hired who they did, when they put together their original work force. And what's wrong with that? They put up the money, didn't they? It was their investment, wasn't it?"

Brown had been a farmer and construction worker before hiring on at Honda. He still did a little of both to have enough money to send his two children through college.

One key to Honda's success has been an unwillingness to compromise on essentials—and a readiness to be flexible on almost everything else. Twenty percent of the company's work force is in production engineering or research and development, and 5 percent of its revenues are spent on R. and D. The man most think will soon be running the entire company was sent to manage the Ohio operation during the critical years of its expansion there.

Shoichiro Irimajiri came to Ohio in 1984 and stayed until the summer of 1988, when he returned to Japan to become director of worldwide manufacturing operations. Still boyish-looking at forty-eight, Irimajiri had previously helped run Honda research and development and been manager of the company's largest plant, at Suzuka. The first love of Irimajiri, as of Soichiro Honda, the company's founder, was racing, first motorcycles and then Grand Prix racing cars.

Irimajiri taught by example. At daily staff meetings he seldom talked about profits. If the quality and productivity were there, profits, he said, would take care of themselves. He spent much of his time out in the plant, "going to the spot." And he became very excited about what some at first considered little things, such as an associate's realization that he was walking seventy feet to pick up a part when, if the machine was moved, he could reduce the distance to fifty-five feet. Irimajiri grew stern when noting that the machinery used to build Accords in Ohio was more advanced than that used to build Accords in Japan, "yet their efficiency is nearly the equal to ours." He often said that productivity was not achieved by working harder, by speeding up the production line, or by buying new equipment as much as by streamlining each process by an accumulation of little things. And it was in improving the little things that each associate could make a contribution. Before leaving Ohio, Irimajiri said Honda's biggest challenge, now that it was getting big, would be to preserve the values it had had when it was small.

"Mr. Honda used to say, 'In a race competing for a split second, one tire length on the finish line will decide whether you are a winner or a loser. If you understand that, you cannot disregard even the slightest improvement.' "

Company officials determined early on that quality in Ohio must be equal to quality in Japan. Thus certain things could not be compromised. One was the need for continual training. "We can't exactly determine what your skills are," Al Kinzer would say. "But we can build a program geared to where we need you to be."

Another was cleanliness. Associates would wear all-white uniforms because white was the symbol of cleanliness. Wearing white, they would be more likely to keep their work stations clean. And there would be no radios. Associates would need all five senses to do their job the Honda way. At break areas there would be soft drinks and juices, but no food. And since associates could not smoke or drink coffee at work stations, their managers must not at their desks either.

It was this insistence on uniformity that triggered the company's first confrontation with the UAW.

The UAW had opened an office in Marysville shortly after the motorcycle plant went on stream in 1979. The union began trying to organize in earnest after the auto plant started production in November 1981. Weekly meetings were held to which workers were invited, and a first test of strength took place over whether union sympathizers could wear UAW paraphernalia with their uniforms.

The UAW contended that the right of employees to wear union insignia was a protected activity under the National Labor Relations Act. Shige Yoshida said no. Yoshida argued that the wearing of the blue UAW baseball-type cap, rather than the green-and-white Honda cap, was incompatible with the team concept and would detract from the quality image Honda wanted to convey. Visitors touring the plant who saw associates wearing different caps would not know what to think. In 1981 Honda lost the case at both regional and national levels of the National Labor Relations Board, but then, not satisfied, made a long-drawn-out appeal to the Sixth Circuit Court in Cincinnati.

A second test of strength occurred after the UAW succeeded in organizing the four boilermen in the auto plant. Yoshida refused to negotiate a contract, claiming this made no sense: a four-man unit was too small. Again the matter was referred to the National Labor Relations Board, again the NLRB ruled in the union's favor, and again, not satisfied, Honda appealed to the Sixth Circuit Court in Cincinnati.

Angered by what he considered stonewalling, Joe Tomasi, the UAW's regional director, and Hugh Smith, his organizer in Marysville, determined to fight back. Tomasi, a veteran member of the UAW's board of directors, was a World War II veteran who had "fought on all the bad islands" and been wounded on Okinawa.

In the early 1980s, in parts of Ohio, Japan was still the enemy. In the steel and auto country of the northeast, tires on Japanese cars had been slashed, rocks thrown through car dealers' windows. Tomasi asked his headquarters in Detroit to approve a battle plan. Solidarity House did so, although with some misgivings, it appears. Honda, after all, had been the most cooperative of the Japanese auto makers, the pacesetter in meeting clean air requirements, the one Japanese car company to build an assembly plant in the United States before being forced to.

Tomasi's plan was to hold an anti-Honda rally in front of the auto plant. Trade unionists from across the country would attend, as would UAW president Douglas Fraser. Following the rally, members would demonstrate in front of Honda dealerships in major cities. Stevedores on the West Coast were said to have agreed not to off-load Honda vehicles shipped in from Japan. The UAW had ordered thousands of green-and-white caps with the slogan "Boycott Honda" on them. The time was the spring of 1982.

Smith rented a field across from the auto plant (the farmer charged him a thousand dollars for one day's use), a large tent, two dozen portable toilets, and ordered hundreds of doughnuts and chicken dinners. But the night before the demonstration, Tomasi called Smith to say it was off. A week earlier, on instructions from Detroit, Tomasi had written Yoshida warning him of what was to come. Yoshida now had agreed to talk, to settle his company's differences with the union. Honda couldn't afford the bad publicity that would result from demonstrations and a boycott.

A series of meetings then took place between Tomasi and Yoshida at the Imperial Motel in Findlay, Ohio, Findlay being halfway between Tomasi's office in Toledo and Yoshida's desk in the motorcycle plant. Attending were Honda's labor attorney, Dan Minor, from the Columbus firm of Vorys, Sater, Seymour, and Pease; Richard Martin, an assistant to Fraser; and Gerry Lackey, Tomasi's attorney. On April 23, Fraser and Tomasi issued a joint press release. The Honda people saw and approved the release before it went out, but weren't signatories. "It wasn't necessary," Dan Minor told me. "We had nothing to add."

The release read:

> As a result of informal discussions between the UAW and Honda of America, both parties have agreed to announce that they have resolved all outstanding unfair labor practices. They are confident there will be no need to use the NLRB in the future to resolve disputes. Honda has restated its position of neutrality on the question of whether its associates wish to select a union as their bargaining agent. Honda notified its associates of the resolution of the boiler case and its continuing neutrality in matters of its associates' freedom of choice. Honda is optimistic that this relationship with the UAW will be a cooperative one. The UAW recognizes Honda's need to produce quality automobiles . . . and commends Honda for being the first Japanese company to produce automobiles in the United States.

On the same day *The New York Times* carried a story written by Clyde Farnsworth and datelined Washington that went much further. It said Honda "will no longer resist organizing efforts by the United Automobile Workers . . . The decision, which a Honda representative [in Washington] describes as 'the beginning of a new era of cooperation,' came after a UAW threat to boycott Honda's motorcycles and cars."

Three days later Honda's Al Kinzer was quoted in the Marysville *Journal-Tribune* as saying that local plant officials were "as surprised as anybody" to read the *New York Times* article.

"We have agreed with the union to resolve unfair labor practices . . . Where they [the *Times*] are getting all these other things we wonder. That's not what we meant by neutrality. We want to be in a situation whereby our associates can take their [own] choice regarding union representation."

Ignoring Kinzer's clarification, Tomasi and Smith proceeded as if the *Times*'s interpretation were the correct one. They assumed Honda not only would place no roadblocks in the path of UAW organizing attempts, but in fact would *encourage* such activity. To this day Tomasi contends this is what he and Yoshida agreed.

Events were to prove Tomasi naïve. Yoshida's interpretation of the agreement turned out to be very different. The company, while not openly fighting the union, as Nissan was to do, did absolutely nothing to be helpful either. It allowed— the union claims it somehow encouraged—an anti-union Associates Alliance to form. A "spontaneous" occurrence, Minor describes it.

Tomasi and Smith say this difference in interpretation, not tested until three years later, had a crucial effect on the way the UAW conducted its campaign. Union staffers from Detroit visited only infrequently and, when they did, kept a low profile. No mass meetings or rallies were held. Organizers worked out of a small office in a strip shopping center north of Marysville. And the ads the union ran in area newspapers used Honda, not UAW, terminology. Employees were not "workers" but "associates"; the UAW, a "quality union for a quality-minded work force."

By the summer of 1985 Smith calculated that a majority of Honda's workers had signed cards in favor of representation by the union. Given at least tacit support from the company, he felt it was time to act. Older employees were complaining about line speed, saying they were being pushed beyond their limits, and other issues had surfaced, too. Men with seniority complained of not having transfer rights. Others feared that more robots were coming and they would lose their jobs.

A stocky, gray-haired man with a patient, methodical air, Smith had become something of a father figure to some of the younger associates. A native of Coeburn, Virginia, he had lived in Ohio since 1952 and had for a time been president of the Ford local in Sandusky, where he still resided. He had helped organize the Volkswagen plant in Pennsylvania, where there also had been a neutrality pact between union and company. When it came time to organize the Volkswagen plant, management hadn't resisted.

By September 1985 Honda had announced another expansion. Smith knew he couldn't wait any longer. New employees would be harder to recruit than old. Earlier, the union had tried and failed to get the NLRB to declare Honda's maintenance workers a separate unit for organizing purposes. The company's position was that associates all received the same wages and benefits, and hence were interchangeable; maintenance workers often started on the assembly line and sometimes were reassigned there. There was no way to isolate the more sympathetic workers. There was no time to waste.

On October 24 Tomasi wrote Yoshida to say a majority of Honda's employees had signed cards saying they wanted to be members of the union. He asked that the company agree to let the union in without an election.

Yoshida refused. In a news release dated October 30, the company reported that it had rejected the union's request after "following the usual procedure of consulting its associates on major decisions." Honda had surveyed production and maintenance workers on all three shifts. Results showed that 73.2 percent of its employees wanted the company to reject the union's request for recognition without an election. A memo posted on company bulletin boards stated:

> In response to the letter from the UAW, HAM [Honda
> of America] should reject the UAW request and let the
> union ask for a secret election to resolve the issue. Agree
> strongly 58.1 percent; agree somewhat 15.1; disagree
> somewhat 11.8; disagree strongly 15.0.
>
> HAM associates have been pressured or harassed by
> UAW supporters into signing union cards. Agree
> strongly 13.1 percent; agree somewhat 31.3; disagree
> somewhat 22.8, disagree strongly 32.8.
>
> HAM associates who signed cards did so because
> they truly wanted the UAW to represent them. Agree
> strongly 17.6 percent; agree somewhat 29.6 percent;
> disagree somewhat 35.7; disagree strongly 17.1.

An independent observer then checked the cards and verified
that the union had at least the required 30 percent favoring
the union for an election to be called. The National Labor
Relations Board scheduled the election for December 19.

At this point the union shifted from a low-key, make-a-
few-contacts campaign to a high-energy blitz. Radio and
television ads charged Honda with increasing its line speed
and ignoring employee complaints. Reporters from major
newspapers and from Japan descended upon central Ohio
to cover the story. In Tokyo, an English-language account
read:

> The United Auto Workers (UAW) is now frontally
> challenging Honda's family-type way of management
> which unites the plant as one. It calls the Honda way
> "patriarchal despotism."
>
> The UAW offensive started from immediately after
> the work system was changed for the purpose of a large-
> scale model change. The parts to be handled and the
> work pace were changed, and the workers were confused.
> Especially, dissatisfaction appeared over the acceleration
> of the speed of the assembly line. The average age of
> the workers is only 27 years of age. The UAW is asking

"can you keep up with this pace, even when you grow older?" This appeal has elicited considerable sympathy.

There is a strong feeling of repulsion towards the union among conservative townspeople, however. Looking at the UAW, the eyes of the 8,500 people of the town of Marysville are even severer than the eyes of the Honda Plant workers themselves. This region, which is made up largely of corn and soybean fields, is so conservative that even supermarkets refrain from selling alcoholic drinks, including beer, on Sundays.

Honda's position was that it was neither for nor against the union, but that it would be up to its associates to decide. Meanwhile, however, many of these same associates, apparently on their own initiative, had taken it upon themselves to form a virulently anti-union Associates Alliance. Claiming support from businesses and individuals throughout Ohio (but none from Honda itself, and none has ever been proven), alliance members conducted an extraordinarily well financed media blitz of their own, with leaflets and billboards and full-page ads in local newspapers.

They talked a lot about Big Three plant closings. Their slogan was "We think for ourselves"; their battle cry, "Since 1979, one in four UAW members thrown out in the street." A cartoon showed a lean, fleet-footed Honda outdistancing a fat, cigar-smoking Detroit. The Detroit figure couldn't compete because it was anchored to a bulky, triangular-shaped rock labeled "UAW."

Kinzer says Honda remained scrupulously neutral. The company's concern was that there not be disharmony on the plant floor, either during or especially after the campaign. Both pro- and anti-union sympathizers were urged to use company bulletin boards in making their points. The company only interjected with information if there were errors in the memos posted by the pro or anti forces.

As the date for the election approached, the UAW conducted a survey of its own—a telephone survey. It showed the union to have less support than even the company had reported. And so, on December 16, three days before the election was to be held, the UAW filed unfair-labor-practice charges contending that Honda had illegally supported the Associates Alliance, illegally awarded increased benefits, and illegally intimidated its employees. The NLRB soon disagreed, ruling for the company. The UAW, which could then have asked that the election be rescheduled, called it quits instead.

"This is not an admission of defeat—far from it," Smith and Tomasi told their supporters. "But, for the moment, the confusion over unfair-labor-practice charges, the deliberate spreading of misinformation [by the Associates Alliance], and the rapid influx of new hires . . . create a poor climate for an election."

It may not have been an admission of defeat, but it was widely interpreted as such, and for a time the Associates Alliance campaigned to have an election anyway. Were there to be an election, the UAW would suffer an overwhelming defeat, alliance leaders argued. The alliance would then become the company union.

Honda did not encourage such thinking. "I don't know of any U.S. companies that have had much success with sweetheart or internal unions," Kinzer said. "Some exist, but if you examine them, you find that the company and union have a hard time figuring out how to deal with each other."

By concentrating on getting back to building cars, rather than on "teaching the UAW a lesson," Honda won for itself— in some circles at least—the reputation as an enlightened adversary, as a company that is hard to hate.

Not that Tomasi and Smith aren't bitter. Now retired, both Tomasi and former UAW president Fraser say the union lost credibility and momentum by throwing in the towel. Better to have fought and lost and then regrouped to come back and fight again. It was a mistake their successors have said won't be repeated at Nissan.

"Honda was too quick to respond to whatever problem we brought before them," says Smith. "We shouldn't have been so open with them. They had no pride. If something was wrong, and we said it was wrong, they right away went out and corrected it.

"Plus the people they've hired are so unquestioning. With so little experience. They don't think anybody other than the people they see every day can know very much. Let me give you an example. It was the damnedest thing. One day one of their Japanese supervisors slapped an American. Anywhere else, it would have caused a work stoppage. We talked with the Americans he worked with. And you know what they said? They said he probably deserved it." (The company's position on slapping—"or any other such socially unacceptable behavior"—is that slapping won't be tolerated. A Japanese found doing it will be sent back to Japan.)

"We were too much the friendly union across the street," says Tomasi. "We didn't go for the jugular."

The UAW sent Tennessee's Jim Turner in during the final phase of the Honda drive and later asked him to do a postmortem.

"If Honda keeps expanding, they may never be organized," he told me. "Everybody thinks he's got a shot at being a supervisor. And at least they give lip service to seniority."

Maybe so. But if rapid expansion has given associates the feeling that anyone who works hard enough can be promoted, it is causing problems, too.

In 1988 Kit Reynolds, director of Marysville's Mental Health Center, said she was getting an increasing number of referrals on Honda associates.

"They complain of headaches, of chronic back pain, of stomach aches. Their doctors have done a workup and found nothing wrong. Obviously, they're under a lot of stress, which they've internalized. German-Americans are like that. They're stoic. They don't complain. They need to talk."

Later that same year, Honda asked Bethesda Health Management Services of Cincinnati to create an employee development center. A key objective was to help associates cope with stress.

Yet, when Shoichiro Irimajiri returned to Japan, he was succeeded as head of the Ohio operation by Hiroyuki Yoshino. Yoshino brought with him a reputation as the world's fastest car builder. *Automotive News* said he had been "pushing out a new Honda every 41 seconds at the company's famous Suzuka plant."

With mighty Toyota gearing up in Kentucky to the south, the pace at Honda was having to quicken again.

8

Here to Stay

According to a Nissan spokesman, there are 33,275
new cars and trucks parked in cow pastures and
on the airfield around Smyrna.
—Nashville *Banner*, March 31, 1988

Jerry Benefield, who succeeded Marvin Runyon, is a stocky,
barrel-chested man of average height who looks a little like
a county sheriff. He owns a farm in Rutherford County, has
three daughters he dotes upon, and for a hobby raises
Tennessee walking horses.

In contrast to Runyon, whom many saw as speaking
from a prepared text, Benefield seems more relaxed. When
taping a speech for *Nissan Network News*, he sits on the edge
of his desk and talks extemporaneously. If he stumbles and
speaks ungrammatically, which he sometimes does, he will
usually say, "Let it go, anyway." Like Runyon, he arrives at
work in a chauffeur-driven limousine, but he seems more
down-to-earth.

Under Runyon, Benefield had been in charge of day-
to-day operations. As CEO, he still tries to visit some part of
the plant every day. On the shop floor, workers often stop
and ask him questions.

"I get reports on quality and productivity," he says. "I
don't have to check on these kinds of things. I go out to see
how the people are doing. Often, a general question masks
a personal question—about a promotion or safety problem

or whatever. I then go back to the man's supervisor and check it out. If it's a selfish question, I say, hey, you don't expect me to change company policy just for you, do you?"

Benefield was one of Runyon's first two hires, his manufacturing vice-president from the start. A Georgia native, graduate of Georgia Tech in industrial engineering, and eighteen-year Ford veteran, Benefield had risen through the ranks to become manager of Ford's Dearborn assembly plant. Both his father and grandfather had careers at Ford. Some thought Benefield would be a Runyon clone, but others were not so sure. Benefield was fifteen years younger, after all; sometimes he wore cowboy boots to work.

Jim Turner said men in positions like that have big egos and need to prove they can do something their predecessor couldn't. Turner would sit back and wait. He predicted that Benefield would become the union's biggest ally. In fact, Benefield did do a number of things Runyon hadn't done. But they weren't what Turner expected.

The UAW officially kicked off its organizing drive on January 19, 1988. The union's top brass from Detroit were in attendance, plus a half-dozen regional directors and an assortment of other officials. Union president Owen Bieber delivered the keynote address.

At fifty-eight, Bieber evokes the manner of an old-style trade unionist, but with a modern touch. Rolling and rhythmic in his delivery, he nevertheless manages to sound worldly.

He came to Smyrna with three Japanese joint ventures under contract, after all: NUMMI in California, Mazda-Ford in Michigan, and Diamond-Star in Illinois. His union, by relaxing its posture on work rules and agreeing to eliminate job classifications (originally put in to force employers to keep people on the payroll), had been able to blend its traditional protections with the Japanese concept of *kaizen*, or "continual improvement." At NUMMI, management had agreed not to lay off any workers without cutting executives' pay. At Diamond-Star, Bieber had said there was no incompatibility between UAW and Japanese approaches. Others on his staff had criticized Jerry Hammond and the Kentucky Building Trades Council for using the threat of a Pearl Harbor Day demonstration to force Toyota to hire union construction workers in 1986. Racism was a scourge Bieber's union had worked hard to purge, and the UAW prided itself on not being a Japan basher. What Bieber would say in Smyrna was essentially what John Junkerman had said in his *Progressive* article: namely, that Nissan's success could not be attributed to innovative Japanese techniques, but rather to the old-fashioned speedup.

Broad-shouldered and a giant of a man, Bieber shed his suit jacket before advancing to the podium. On the walls behind and around him were hung slogans that read: "Job Safety," "No more fear," "Put it in writing," "End sexual harassment," and "Together we can speak for ourselves."

"I may be wrong, but I don't think a backbreaking work pace is a sign of respect for employees," he said, to applause.

"And I don't think it's respectful of an employer to permit supervisors to engage in acts of blatant sexual harassment and then to defend those supervisors when they are challenged [more applause].

"I don't think it's enlightened to permit unsafe working conditions in a plant simply for the sake of pushing more production out the plant door [louder applause].

"Finally, I don't think an employer shows much respect for or confidence in its employees when it announces in advance that it will actively oppose the employees' right to organize their own union [cheers and loudest applause]."

Bieber said the UAW wasn't afraid to break with tradition when conditions warranted. NUMMI and the Mazda-Ford plant were places where American-style labor relations and Japanese-style work practices had blended very nicely.

President Reagan's Labor Department had gone so far as to tell the United Nations that NUMMI heralded a new era in collective bargaining.

At the close of the rally, Turner urged his in-plant organizing committee to get on with the task of signing cards. "The faster we do it, the better the chance we have of winning the election."

The union claimed that four hundred Nissan workers had attended the rally, but later acknowledged that some of those four hundred were visiting UAW officials. Reporters, though advised when the rally would be held, were not allowed to attend. "We wanted the Nissan people to have an experience, not an exposure," Turner explained.

Afterward, the campaign grew more spirited. Nissan made effective use of its television network in combating the union's assertions. Gail Neuman, Nissan's general counsel and vice-president for human resources, had once made a speech in which she said, "We have an in-house video system that reaches over a hundred locations by means of monitors we've put in every work area and in key locations in administration and the cafeterias. When it was installed, we knew it would help us communicate quickly and accurately with our employees. But none of us foresaw how valuable a communications tool it would become."

Turner's comment: "They're using the in-house video to combat our organizing drive. They have professional actors who play on the thing, and the news they put on is always negative news—about GM closing a plant or laying off people. They never show anything positive."

Throughout the campaign, Nissan portrayed General Motors as symbolizing just about everything that was wrong with the American automobile industry. One anti-union flyer listed sixteen GM plant closings, with dates and numbers of workers laid off. Another reprinted a story from *The New York Times* about a plant in Alabama where GM had let the UAW in without an election. "I think it's a crooked deal," a worker was quoted. "It's obvious the employees don't want a union here."

An anti-union committee, similar to the Associates Alliance at Honda, though with a lot less funding, formed. Its flyers carried some of the same cartoons, with the name Nissan substituted for Honda. Anti-union workers demonstrated at plant gates, waving American flags and brandishing signs that read: "Jim Turner go home."

Turner responded with printed brochures, released one a week for a time. Each carried the name and photograph of a disgruntled worker. "Don't let what happened to Richard Davidson happen to you," a typical one read.

> I was installing drive shafts which requires bending and lifting when two discs in my back bulged.
>
> The doctor the company sent me to just told me to go home and rest and gave me a corset to wear.
>
> Another doctor the company sent me to did the same thing, and the company wanted me to come back to work.
>
> I had surgery in November 1987 by a third doctor.
>
> After my injury I was put on light duty driving trucks off the line because I can't stand too long.
>
> The company overworks people. The work pace is just too fast. The people cannot work safely at that speed.
>
> I'm 26 years old and the thought of being like this the rest of my life makes me mad.

Somebody scratched "UAW" on the hood of a car coming off the line. Pro- and anti-union sympathizers each blamed the other. Turner offered a $1,000 reward for information leading to the arrest of the person responsible. But it was never collected.

Rutherford County newspapers ignored the campaign or, in limited coverage, tended to be anti-union. And so the union bought commercials on Smyrna's radio station, WSVT, and, in return, station owner Jack Bursack rebroadcast

Bieber's speech and interviewed Turner and others from the union.

Bursack is regarded as something of a maverick in Smyrna. He doesn't live there, but in a neighboring town. He is a burly man with a resonant voice and a background in police work. He had recently made application to upgrade his station from AM to FM. His interviews and the company's response offer an insight into what each side wanted the other to hear.

> BURSACK: Tell me, Jim, what has been happening since you kicked off your campaign?
>
> TURNER: People hurt on the job are being refused light duty . . . the company has contracted out the off-line jobs that people who are hurt would normally be entitled to . . . Ten minutes before it's time to go home, they'll come up to you and say you have to work overtime . . . Since we made an issue of it, they've started cleaning up their act on sexual harassment.

Bursack then puts questions to Charley Holt, who is twenty-nine and has been at Nissan since 1983. He is a quality assurance inspector, formerly a trim technician.

> BURSACK: What about this open-door policy we hear so much about?
>
> HOLT: I talked with Jerry Benefield once. I took a concern to him about an injury I had on the job. I was scheduled to transfer into another department. Which was going to make my job easier. Three days previous, my supervisor came down and said you're not going, no way. They were doing a rebalance [a changeover on the line from trucks to cars or vice versa]. I made arrangements to meet with Mr. Benefield.
>
> I went into his office, his real plush office. He had [country music singer] Faron Young playing in the background. His cowboy hat was on, his boots up on the

desk. I sat down and tried to talk about my livelihood to him.

BURSACK: Did you call him Jerry?

HOLT: No, I called him Mr. Benefield. I felt if I showed him the respect he was due he would do the same for me.

I expressed to him that due to my injury it was more or less imperative that I be able to transfer into this other area. If not, then I was going to be looking at another shoulder surgery.

The reply I got was more or less along the lines of "Well, if you can't hack it, get your jacket. That's what the policy is. That's the way it's gonna stand. We don't make exceptions." I kind of got the *que será será*.

I walked out of his office. I'll never forget that day.

Bursack soon started getting complaints from local advertisers. He denies that any of them pulled their advertising, but subsequently agreed that Jerry Benefield should also be interviewed—and by a different (and more sympathetic) talk show host. Benefield's interviewer turned out to be Jean Hurt, a local newspaper columnist and family friend. On the air, neither Hurt nor Benefield mentioned the UAW's organizing drive.

HURT: Jerry, how does management keep in touch with the cares and concerns of each employee?

BENEFIELD: Last night, I went back to work at nine forty-five and got with a group of employees who had invited me to meet with them at the start of their shift. It gave them an opportunity to ask any questions they wanted to ask. Then yesterday, during the day, I met with a focus group.

I have eight focus groups made up of eight employees each. They're randomly selected by computer from all over the company. Participants get to ask me questions and I get to ask them questions. We get to connect. Each of my vice-presidents does the same thing, each one of the plant managers, and each of the other managers, too. So over a period of a month, we come in direct contact, in a quiet forum, with a large number of employees.

HURT: Do you have a means in each department whereby someone somehow can get to top management to air a complaint?

BENEFIELD: Any employee in our company at any moment in time can get to anyone he or she wants to simply by asking. We have an open-door policy. I'll use myself as an example. My administrative assistant has instructions that if anybody calls and asks for an appointment she is to clear my schedule with God if she has to.

HURT: Jerry, how do you weed out the bellyachers from the true complainers?

BENEFIELD: We don't have too many bellyachers. Most of the people who come to see me have already been to see somebody else. Generally, they're the ones who have been unable to get their concerns satisfied. But you'd be surprised. I don't have that many who get to my office . . . We try to have every issue, every problem, every question answered at the lowest possible level. When you allow people to solve their own problems, they don't have to ask too many questions. They're capable and able and have the resources to take care of most things themselves.

HURT: The ideas that came over from Japan, how readily were they accepted? The exercise program, for example?

BENEFIELD: The exercise program is a big joke. We had some people who went to Japan and while there they participated in the morning exercise programs. And when they came back, on their own, some of them started doing them. But over a period of time, they all stopped. I don't know of any group that does them now. It never was company policy.

Asked about safety, Benefield noted that whereas other auto companies had been fined millions of dollars for failure to report accidents, Nissan had never been fined.

In the spring of 1988, Turner thought he saw his big opportunity. Plagued by huge inventories of cars and new trucks, Nissan had rented cow pastures and parts of an airfield around Smyrna, and over the next five months parked tens of thousands of vehicles there.

Because of the yen's rise in value against the dollar, and because there was still a 25 percent tariff on trucks imported from Japan, Nissan had found it more efficient to build in the United States all the trucks to be sold here. But by this time, Nissan was experiencing a worldwide sales slump. Most of its models were still the unimaginative "boxes on wheels" mentioned earlier, and the yen's rise in value had triggered price increases, which were also hurting sales. Smyrna-built vehicles were affected because many of their parts still came from Japan.

Turner and his organizers had experience with GM, and at GM big inventories mean layoffs and, if not layoffs, fear and uncertainty. It was the kind of atmosphere in which union organizers do best. It was during this period that the UAW got most of its cards signed. The UAW took visiting journalists on tours of the fields where the thousands of new vehicles were parked.

But Nissan didn't lay off any technicians or even any of its "temporary" contract employees. Instead, the company slowed line speed from 64 to 57 vehicles an hour and over the next several months gave fifteen hundred employees a week's extra training in safety, shop floor management, or communications.

Nissan's decision not to lay off despite huge inventory problems proved to be a watershed in the success of the Japanese auto makers in this country. Later when the recession hit, other Japanese auto makers and Japanese auto parts companies followed Nissan's example.

"We had said all along we'd do everything possible to avoid a layoff," said Rick Sommer, vice-president of manufacturing. "And yes, there were a few skeptics, and some anxiety inside the plant. But there seemed to be more uncertainty on the outside than within."

Jerry Benefield then did the something Marvin Runyon hadn't been able to do: he started announcing plant expansions.

The first hint of it came on January 17, 1988, two days before the UAW launched its organizing campaign. Benefield said Smyrna might assemble engines for Sentra model cars, and also make truck axles and plastic bumper parts. In May the possibility became reality, and in July a $31 million plant expansion began. Two months later, Benefield announced that Smyrna would supply panel parts for a minivan project Nissan and Ford would conduct jointly in Ohio. Nissan would design the vehicle, furnish panel parts, and build the power train; Ford would operate the plant.

By October, Smyrna's inventory problems had eased and the fields around Smyrna were empty again. Nissan then held another of its periodic all-day seminars for academics and business executives.

The seminar was pretty much what one might expect— a detailing of company strengths, a show-and-tell, a repeat of information already reported in various trade journals: Nissan has only five levels of management compared with twelve or fourteen at most Big Three plants. Its first objective is to produce the highest-quality vehicle sold in America. A second objective is to achieve a 10 percent improvement in productivity each year.

On this particular day, however, there seemed to be a subtext, a recurring theme which, in different ways, each speaker touched upon. If it had a name—and it wasn't given one—that name would have been "job security."

"We try to give each technician a hundred hours of training each year.

"Except for a few people in legal and advertising, we promote almost entirely from within.

"We have four hundred contract workers. They do our maintenance, security, and environmental control. They're here as a hedge in case we ever have to lay off. They give us the flexibility to put our regular people into their jobs if we ever need to.

"There hasn't been a single layoff in the history of this company."

Queried a few weeks earlier, Turner had conceded to the *Tennessean* that the majority of Nissan's 2,400 workers were still undecided about whether they wanted a union or not. He blamed fear of reprisals and the "company-backed" anti-union committee for slowing momentum. He predicted that the UAW would have 60 to 65 percent of the workers signed by the summer of 1989, but it was a far cry from his optimism of a few months before.

Turner told his people his cancer was in remission, but he was obviously wearing a colostomy bag now, and seemed less energetic.

In November, Benefield said Smyrna might add a second passenger car line, with the model still undetermined. In December, after a hiatus of more than two years, the company began hiring again. "Nissan sees 20,000 respond to 150 openings for workers," a headline in the Nashville *Banner* read. Then, on the anniversary of Bieber's keynote address, Benefield wrote Turner to say enough is enough:

"Your union has had more than a fair chance to organize our employees. There finally comes a time when you should put up or shut up. Our people are entitled to be left alone."

The organizing drive had become a divisive issue within the plant. "It's just a continual upheaval," Benefield wrote. Pro-union employees were trying to indoctrinate anti-union employees by badgering them at lunch or visiting them in their homes.

Turner didn't respond. He was sicker now. He had been on leave since the beginning of the month. His replacement, Jim Weaver, a veteran organizer from Atlanta, wrote back:

> We don't take suggestions from hostile company executives about when to file a petition . . . Our decisions are made by us in consultation with the workers active in the organizing drive. While our efforts are not designed as an endurance test, you will discover that we have a great deal of endurance as well as patience.
>
> When you were a resident of Michigan . . . Jim Turner was a resident of Tennessee along with 5,000 other UAW members. He continues to reside in Tennessee. We are at home here and have no intention of packing our bags and going anywhere else. We are here to stay.

After Japanese Emperor Hirohito died that same month, someone at Nissan briefly flew the plant's flag at half-mast. VFW members noticed and called Smyrna mayor Knox Ridley to protest. Ridley told the *Tennessean*, from his winter home in Florida, that "speaking personally, if not officially," he was upset.

At first, Nissan officials denied that the American flag had been lowered. But the next day, the *Tennessean* published a letter from Jerry Benefield that said:

> The day of the Emperor's death, the management at Nissan sent a letter of condolence to the Japanese consulate in New Orleans and also reaffirmed that the company would follow national protocol on the display of the American flag, which is the only flag flown at the Smyrna facility. On Saturday, because of miscommunication between Nissan and our contract security firm, the American flag in front of the facility flew for a brief

time at half mast. When the company discovered the
mistake, the flag was immediately returned to full mast.

Union members had taken pictures of the flag at half-mast,
but didn't use them. "We didn't need to," Turner said.
"Ridley and the VFW did our work for us." The union was
still reluctant to Japan-bash.

On April 3 Benefield announced that not only would
Smyrna build a third vehicle, but it would be doubling
production capacity to 440,000 units and adding 2,000 new
jobs. This hiring would begin in 1990.

On April 22 Jim Turner died of cancer in the Vanderbilt
University Medical Center in Nashville. He was buried in
the family plot in Crossville, Tennessee. Union officials Ben
Perkins and Maxey Irwin, with whom Turner had been
living, delivered the eulogies.

Steve Yokich, the UAW's senior vice-president (and
likely successor to Bieber), had been in Smyrna the week
before. Turner knew the members of his in-plant organizing
committee were burning out. Like Benefield, if for different
reasons, they, too, were anxious to have an election. At a
meeting at which Turner presided, Yokich told the members
that as soon as they obtained 168 more signed cards, the
union would file for an election.

On May 18 the UAW filed its petition.

9

Bridge over Troubled Waters

Tom Prather's leadership, and that of city council,
has made all the difference.
  —Alex M. Warren, Jr., senior vice-
    president, Toyota Motor Manufacturing
    Company, speaking about the easing of
    Toyota's adjustment problems

Although the furor created by the Martha Layne Collins
incentive package lasted well into the governorship of her
successor, Wallace Wilkinson, Toyota was fortunate in one
crucial respect. It had in Georgetown a mayor who not only
believed in the company, but wanted passionately for it to
expand further: to add an engine plant to its auto plant, a
truck plant to the engine plant, and one day a North
American headquarters, as well. He saw in Toyota's coming
a chance for Scott to become Kentucky's showcase county—
and for him, no doubt, an opportunity to further his own
political ambitions.

Tom Prather was often referred to as a "young old
man," from Georgetown, but not of it, not a good ol' boy
but someone with whom the good ol' boys could still feel
comfortable. There is an air of the Old South about him.
He never seems hurried. He makes a point and then circles
back to make his point again. Though he was scarcely thirty-

five at the time of our meeting, his hair was prematurely white.

"Ten years from now the Collins incentive package may look like a bargain," he told me.

The city council appointed Prather mayor in October 1986, ten months after Toyota announced it was coming to Scott County. Sam Pollock, the previous mayor, had resigned after suffering a stroke, brought on, it was said, by now having to work around the clock. The two part-time mayors before Pollock had been school bus drivers. After Toyota announced, the mayor's salary was raised from $7,200 to $29,800 a year.

Prather was thirty-three at the time and in his fifth term as a city councilman. Two former mayors, three other councilmen, and the city's finance director had wanted to succeed Pollock, but Prather got the nod. At the next election, he ran unopposed.

Prather had been captain of his college football team and voted the most likely to succeed. His grandfather had been Georgetown's four-term mayor, and one of his grandfather's campaign posters now hangs in the grandson's office. Until the early 1980s three generations of Prathers had owned the town's Chevrolet, Pontiac, and Buick dealership. After it was sold, Tom became a partner with his brother John in a Lexington bloodstock agency. The two bought and sold horses, but it wasn't enough of a challenge for Tom. He was divorced and was the primary parent for his son and daughter. The experience had matured him, he said. He wanted to be mayor because he knew that decisions made in the wake of the Toyota announcement would affect Georgetown for decades to come. "You either stay on top of it, or it rolls on over you. I'm determined that we're going to stay on top of it."

As soon as Toyota announced that its plant would be built in Scott County, county officials imposed on the company a one percent payroll and net profits tax. The tax was

imposed arbitrarily, and both Governor Collins and Toyota
considered this an unfriendly act.

"The governor told us, 'We'll provide for you. It won't
cost you anything.' But she didn't follow through," Charlie
Sutton, Scott County's judge executive, explained. The
county then refused to share any of its new tax money with
the city of Georgetown. That would be "inappropriate,"
Sutton said. The county was nearly bankrupt. It had bridges
to fix and roads to mend.

Sutton received Japanese visitor after Japanese visitor,
and call after call from Governor Collins's office, all pressing
him to reconsider.

"Toyota hadn't broken ground, hadn't invested any of
its own money yet. Everyone seemed afraid they would get
mad and go home. I nearly had a nervous breakdown, but
I stuck to my guns."

In addition to the tax, Sutton and former Georgetown
mayor Pollock drew up a $1.5 million "wish list," which
Sutton presented to Commerce Secretary Carroll Knicely. It
had everything from a helicopter to renovation of City Hall.
Knicely, his temper frayed, read Sutton the riot act.

Sutton is tall, tanned, and rawboned, with the look of
an outdoorsman. He has a background in police work and
was the first judge executive to support Wallace Wilkinson
as Collins's successor. He still lives in Scott County, but now
works for Wilkinson in Frankfort. He defends Wilkinson's
campaign against the Collins incentive package, saying, "The
Japanese don't understand American politics. Wallace
needed a big issue. His surveys showed that 118 of the 120
counties were against it."

The county's precipitate action not only caught Toyota
off guard, but left Georgetown in the lurch. City officials
were convinced (and accurately so) that it would be Georgetown, not the county, that would bear the heaviest burden
of increased police and fire protection and of extra class-
rooms for its schools. Collins had funded a four-lane highway

(named Cherry Blossom Way) from Georgetown to the plant site, but hadn't been able to find moneys to build the promised bypass around the town. Ambulances servicing Scott General Hospital were said to be experiencing delays as a result of the increased truck traffic.

It was in this mess that new mayor Tom Prather immersed himself. He started by having breakfast meetings with Alex Warren, soon to become one of Toyota's two senior Americans.

Warren, born in Augusta, Georgia, at twelve moved to Lexington, where his father was a Presbyterian minister. He received a B.A. and law degree from the University of Kentucky, and had worked for U.S. Steel, Rockwell International, and Leaseway Transportation. Working for Toyota in Georgetown (Warren would live in Lexington) was like coming home again, he said. Soft-spoken and seemingly egoless, Warren stood in sharp contrast to his predecessor, whom Prather had perceived as a hard-nosed negotiator.

Prather and Warren got along well from the start. From December 1986 to April 1987 they met once a week over breakfast in a private room at the Horse Park Inn, on the outskirts of Georgetown. They would arrive at seven-thirty and stay until ten, concentrating first on getting to know each other, then on understanding the needs and values of their separate constituencies. At first Warren brought Jeff Smith along. Smith had been Toyota's senior American before Warren and had defended the hard bargaining that had resulted in the Collins incentive package.

Prather saw Smith as machinelike, Warren as nuanced and more flexible. Prather's first concern was that Georgetown be able to retain its essential character. He had visited Marysville, Ohio, and been surprised to hear city officials there speak of "business as usual." But Marysville was not Georgetown, and Honda, with its four plants scattered across three counties, was not Toyota. Honda had come in with an initial investment of $35 million; Toyota's initial investment would be $800 million. Honda had built far enough from town so its impact would be minimal; Toyota's plant would be within sight of City Hall.

The two men's goal, as Warren describes it, was to pinpoint the pressures Georgetown was likely to face, then to determine which were real and which imagined.

"I knew that only ten families had relocated," Warren said. "And yet the school people were telling us their enrollment was up two hundred students. That's an average of twenty kids per family. I told Tom I was going to have to ask to see names.

"The same with traffic congestion. I had lived in Chicago and perhaps saw things a little differently. Here they had been used to pulling up in front of the store they wanted to shop in. Now they might have to park a block and a half away. There might be six or eight cars waiting at a stoplight instead of just the one."

Prather and Warren were meeting in secret. Others, however, were voicing their concern in newspaper stories.

"Residents are worried that the new growth will increase crime problems," said Barbara Tilford, a candidate for the city council.

"The reason we live in Georgetown is the small-town atmosphere. We want to maintain the same quality of life," said Steve Roberts, another council candidate.

"What's frightening to us is the fifty or sixty trucks coming through the center of town every morning," said Robert Snyder, chairman of the city-county planning commission.

Pressures began building for the city to annex the plant. If Georgetown annexed the plant, *both* city and county would receive the one percent payroll and net profits tax. Better a tax than the payment in lieu of taxation that reportedly the company favored; a payment in lieu of tax wouldn't grow as the company did.

Warren's reaction:

"I told Tom that if we were to be annexed—to pay city as well as county taxes—we needed to know how the money would be spent. Would there be better fire protection, a more professional police force, more long-term planning? I'd heard that they didn't buy a new fire truck until the old one broke down."

In April, four months after the two men started having breakfast meetings, Prather was able to announce that Toyota had *requested* it be annexed to the city. Georgetown's weekly newspaper of record reported:

> Toyota's request took Prather and the city council by surprise.
>   No one had been sure if the company would follow through on promises to help Georgetown.
>   "The pretty words had always been there and now the actions fit the words" [Prather was quoted].

Had both city and county been seen as forcing Toyota's hand, who knows what might have happened. Both Collins and Toyota had already lost face. Collins had had to admit she didn't know what was in her incentive package; Toyota had been forced to use union construction workers after starting to build its plant nonunion.

The skies were beginning to clear.

In June the Kentucky Supreme Court ruled 4–3 that the Collins incentive package was constitutional. At issue had been whether the state had the power to raise and spend money for the benefit of a private business. Proponents argued that the purchase and transfer of 1,600 acres, along with other inducements, were not a gift. Besides, the project was a *fait accompli*. And Kentucky would eventually receive fair market value through new tax revenues. Justices must "breathe life" into the 1891 constitution. The potential benefits to be derived were so great that the constitution must be judicially amended. The consequences that would flow from declaring the incentive package unconstitutional were unthinkable.

Those opposed argued that the true cost of the $125 million package could run as high as $350 million. Bonds used to finance the deal hadn't been counted in. "Pressure on the judiciary to find some way around the constitution has proved to be overwhelming," a dissenting judge wrote. "The court has caved in to pressure and strayed from its duty," said the *Herald-Leader*.

But the worst seemed to be over.

Once Toyota asked that its plant be annexed to the city, Prather fired his finance director and police chief and began making plans to convert the fire department from part- to full-time. "The good-ol'-boy network can't cut it anymore," he said. "We've got to do better."

Earlier, Toyota had invited Prather and his wife, Pat, and another man and wife of Prather's choosing to visit Japan and Toyota City. Prather picked Bill Hamilton, the new president of the chamber of commerce, and the four Kentuckians flew to Japan at the height of the cherry blossom season.

"We got the deep-red-carpet treatment," Prather told me: "fresh-cut flowers in our hotel rooms, lunch with Chairman Toyoda, dinner with President Toyoda, and a round of meetings with senior managing directors.

"In America, it's Hi, how are you? Now let's get down and do business. In Japan, it's Let's talk and get to know each other first. It got to be pretty wearing. I had to be on all the time. Over there, it's the ranking member who does most of the talking."

Prather found himself repeating the same anecdotes: about Scott County (not Bourbon County) being the place where bourbon was born, about his grandfather having invented the replaceable wheel, about Henry Ford then refusing to apply for a patent. Ford thought a car owner should repair the tire, rather than replace the wheel.

Prather was asked to speak before a large group of
executives, who included most of the men who run Toyota's
supplier companies. He told about his breakfast meetings
with Alex Warren. He urged a continuation of this close
communication. He suggested that if Toyota intended to
expand further, it consult with local officials in the planning
stage.

"We were just a couple small-town boys, off on a trip
with our wives. But we didn't act like Ma and Pa Kettle," he
said.

In November 1987 Toyota announced it would be adding five hundred workers to manufacture engines, axles,
and steering mechanisms. The $300 million expansion would
boost Toyota's investment in Scott County to $1.1 billion
and employment to 3,500. Securities analysts said the decision
reflected the weak dollar and continuing sentiment in Congress for legislation to restrict imports of auto parts. Toyota
then announced that, instead of Ohbayashi, it had chosen
Walbridge-Aldinger, a Michigan company, to be general
contractor for the engine plant. Securities analysts said
Toyota had selected an American company because U.S.
companies were having a hard time getting construction
work in Japan. But it also was another way of smoothing
relations with Jerry Hammond and the Kentucky Building
Trades Council.

Again, the worst seemed to be over.

But a few months later, Prather was hospitalized, first
following a water-skiing accident, then for blood clots in the
lung, finally for a slight stroke. One hand was partially
paralyzed, and his doctor urged him to slow down. This
proved easier to say than to do.

To professionalize the police department, Prather's new
chief, Craig Birdwhistell, had put in a new battery of tests
for promotions. He had also ordered new weapons for use
in the fight against crime, replacing the six-shot Smith &
Wesson revolver, which most of the men favored, with the

more modern fourteen-shot 9 mm Smith & Wesson semi-automatic pistol. Until then only six officers had guns furnished by the city; the rest were permitted to carry guns of their own.

Birdwhistell then raided eight of the town's suspected bootleggers and drug dealers. Using all his men to make the raids, he didn't advise them of what was in store until after they reported in for a mandatory evening training session. A few days later, Eddie Chesser, the veteran police chief whom Prather had fired, announced that he was running for mayor.

The pot continued to boil.

10

More Differences than Similarities

I don't like it. I think it's a little sneaky. In Japan, you don't see company presidents mixing with their workers. Executives have reserved parking spaces. Not everyone wears the same uniform.
—Ichiro Ogiso, Director of International Affairs, Japan Automobile Workers Union

Cross the Pacific Ocean and see how Honda, Nissan, and Toyota operate over there, and the picture starts to snap into focus.

There the differences among the three pacesetter Japanese auto makers become more apparent, their remarkable ability to adapt to change more obvious. I began to see why Honda has to keep running so hard, why the United States is critical to Honda's success, even survival—and far less so to Nissan's and Toyota's. I witnessed firsthand the price the Japanese are willing to pay to ensure their American operations don't falter. In Japan, workers do what they are told.

There, too, perhaps because they are in such a tiny minority, the few Americans who work for Japanese companies experience more culture shock: "No matter how hard I try, I am always corrected, almost never complimented," some say. "I was raised to be open, to share my feelings, but here I am expected to veil my emotions." "We sit side by side, in rows of facing desks, so close that our piles of memos and reports slide from one desk to another." "You learn never to speak in a loud voice, nor to expect the guy you had a great time with over the weekend to act the same in the office as he did at play. You're dealing with two different people." "And you learn not to bring your wife or girl friend to the office party, or any work function. She'll be embarrassed and confused, as will everyone else."

I began to understand, too, how agreeable and seductive living in the United States must seem.

At Honda headquarters, I met a man and a woman who, having lived in Ohio, now brief families going there to live. The two had "enjoyed America too much," they said. They told of the great difficulty they had had in readjusting on their return.

Honda's Japanese concede that a broad streak of conformism runs through the national psyche. Honda, however, prides itself on having managers who are more independent than those at other Japanese companies. Honda managers who wish to be even more independent volunteer to work in the United States. Seven of Honda's top nine officials have now served there.

The first thing I noticed, looking out the window of the airport bus driving in toward Tokyo, was that two thirds of the cars were white and nearly all the rest black or gray. The cars I saw were Toyotas, and then Nissans, scarcely any Hondas at all.

The next morning, when I went in search of a place to get a cup of coffee and piece of thick toast without their costing me a small fortune, I noticed that no one crosses the street against the light, not even when there are no cars coming. Then I realized that although the Japanese come in all shapes and sizes, they at first look alike because they all wear similar clothing. Street cleaners wear uniforms, schoolchildren wear uniforms, office ladies wear uniforms. Especially, the businessmen all look alike as they stand massed on street corners waiting for the light to change. They wear suits and ties in black or gray and carry black umbrellas. There are no suspenders showing, no bow ties, no striped or blue shirts. That night, after seven or eight, I see many of these same men, their ties askew now, clusters of them without women, laughing and talking, often singing, crowded into tiny restaurants with walls yellowed by cigarette smoke, the men all drinking beer, slurping noodles, eating yakitori chicken on a stick.

From my two previous visits, I remembered houses of wood, paper, and straw, but now everything seemed built of concrete, glass, and steel. Most neighborhoods had two- and three-story golf driving ranges, and from the street I often saw men standing on rooftops hitting golf balls into green nets. Tokyo subways are immaculate, devoid of graffiti, and easy to use. In restaurants, tipping is discouraged, since it cheapens the server and contributes to contentiousness. Ubiquitous vending machines sell everything from whiskey to toilet paper. And in department store windows most manikins have blond hair and blue eyes.

It all seemed uniformly strange and strangely uniform until I visited my three company headquarters. There, although the similarities remained, and at first the similarities seemed more prevalent than the differences, the differences started to emerge.

At each headquarters and on each floor of each head-quarters, an "office lady" was there to greet me. Always young, always bowing, always dressed like all the other office ladies, she would be wearing a blouse or smock with a name tag and a skirt that fell well below her knees. She would know my name, be there to guide me, to bring green tea, and later to help me find my way out.

Each headquarters had its own separate personality,
however. First, Honda:

In keeping with the image it tries to convey—more
international than Japanese, more youthful than tradition-
bound—Honda's headquarters is in the trendy, up-and-
coming Aoyama district, yet faces the residence of then
Crown Prince (now Emperor) Akihito. Until recently buildings in the area couldn't have windows facing the imperial
residence.

Honda's headquarters has windows, however, and according to a company brochure incorporates "various state-
of-the-art technologies" based on the company's philosophy
"of placing primary importance on space for the driver and
passengers while minimizing space used for mechanical
components." The Honda building has "the same thorough
approach to safety found in Honda cars: emergency stairways
at three corners giving at least two alternative directions of
escape in event of fire, stairwells reached via balconies open
to the outside, and balconies which serve to prevent fire
spreading upwards and eliminate the danger of falling glass
to pedestrians on the street below."

New-model cars and motorcycles are parked in the lobby,
but the place of honor is reserved for the company's Formula
One racing car, the model that recently won fifteen of sixteen
European Grand Prix racing events. Grand Prix auto racing
may not mean much to an American, or even to an older
Japanese, but to a European it does. And Europe is where
Honda hopes to sell its cars next.

In one corner of the lobby is a refreshment stand serving
California orange juice and rum-raisin ice cream; in another,
an office lady selling shirts and jackets bearing the Honda
racing logo. Upstairs, in the men's room that middle managers use, there are buttons and dials beside each of the
toilet stools. Touch one unknowingly and warm water gushes
forth.

Nissan's headquarters, on the other hand, seems more

European. Located in the Ginza district, Tokyo's Fifth Avenue, the executives talk about technological innovations and space-age robotics. After years of losing market share, the "hibernating elephant" has awakened, they say. At ground level, behind floor-to-ceiling windows, are displayed sleek new aerodynamically designed models called Sylvia, Maxima, and Prairie, said to symbolize the company's future.

Yutaka Kume, who became Nissan's president in 1985, seems less formidable and autocratic than the Takashi Ishihara whom David Halberstam described in *The Reckoning*. Yet the soft-spoken Kume, a former aircraft engineer and reader of classical poetry, is credited with steering Nissan's design engineers in a new direction. No longer are board members with mere accounting backgrounds permitted to suggest design changes. Whereas at Honda the top executives share desks side by side in one large, open room, Kume and Ishihara, now chairman, each have a floor to themselves.

Toyota, by all accounts the most conservative of the three, has its headquarters in Toyota City, two hundred miles to the southwest. Here flat terrain running toward hills in the distance reminds one of Kentucky. But there are no horse farms, or bootleggers presumably, and virtually everybody works in the automobile industry. Single men and women live in separate gray concrete dormitories, and the women have a 10 p.m. curfew. World headquarters is a low, buff-colored building, unpretentious in size and appearance.

Next to headquarters is an exhibition hall in which new-model cars are displayed. All are white. I am told not only that white is Japan's favorite car color (it won't fade, is easy to keep clean, makes the car look bigger, and has better resale value), but that Toyota makes five kinds of white: pure white, mica white, pearl white, super white, and super white number two. In an adjoining room are displayed features that appeal to the discriminating car buyer: air refiners to flush out cigarette smoke, sonar to warn the driver if he is backing too far, a TV beside the steering wheel programmed to display a map. The map becomes more detailed and specific as the driver nears his destination. Again, I am made aware of how great the differences between our two cultures are.

Japanese taxi drivers wear white cotton gloves and have a button they push to open the door when you're ready to get out. Their cabs have white cotton headrests for driver and passengers. In a traffic jam, the Japanese doesn't honk his horn or wave his arms, but remains remarkably passive. Most roads are two-lane, and outside Tokyo at least half are unpaved. Because houses and apartments in Japan are so small and the freeways, in the few places where there are freeways, so crowded, the Japanese man is said to spend nearly as much time in his car as he does in his home—particularly if he is determined to leave Tokyo on the weekend, as many now are. The car is one of the few places where he can relax, and thus must be kept spotlessly clean. If for Americans the car is still primarily a means of transportation, for the Japanese it is an extension of his living space.

Such differences are equally striking at company head-quarters.

All meetings take place in an impersonal conference room rather than a private office. The visitor is placed farthest from the door, his host facing him (except at Honda, where the visitor and his host sit side by side). There are always several Japanese, including an interpreter, present, and behind the visitor's back is a painting or a window his host can gaze at (or through) if he elects not to meet the visitor's eyes, as at first is usually the case. Calling cards are exchanged, and carefully studied, before anyone sits. An office lady serves green tea.

Most of the executives I met, perhaps all, understood English. This soon became apparent by the way their eyes lit up when a favorite subject was broached. Only Tetsuo Chino spoke English, however. Chino, as president of Honda

North America, divides his time between Tokyo and Southern California.

Several common themes emerged.

One was Europe and whether it will welcome the increased importation of Japanese cars. The concern was whether Washington will insist that cars built by Japanese auto makers in the United States should be considered American if exported from the States to the European Community.

Each company obviously hopes so, and none more than Honda. While Nissan already has a large plant in England (and Toyota and Honda have announced plans to build there), Toyota and especially Honda are gambling more on Washington's help. By 1991 Honda will be exporting 70,000 U.S.-made cars back to Asia, Chino said, 50,000 to Japan, and 20,000 to countries such as Taiwan and Korea.

"We will be helping you correct your unfavorable trade balance. We may be exporting more cars from the United States than your American car manufacturers do."

The Japanese see Europe as in roughly the same situation the United States was in the 1970s—ripe for a Japanese invasion. One difference is that Ford and General Motors have been rapidly expanding there since they know it is only a matter of time before the Japanese come. Moreover, the Europeans, while still able to compete in quality, are having problems because of increasing costs. Already the unprotected, non-car-making Irish, Danes, and Greeks buy 40 percent of their cars from Japan, while the French, Italians, and Spanish (who still have trade barriers) buy only 3 percent.

In Europe, Nissan is clearly in the lead. In 1981 it announced it was looking for a European site upon which to build cars, and England quickly emerged as the front-runner. The United Kingdom was already Nissan's number-one market in Europe. The Japanese learn English as a second language. And Margaret Thatcher needed a dynamic company to demonstrate that the British automobile industry wasn't headed for extinction. In 1984 Nissan announced it would build its plant in Sunderland, in the industrial Northeast, where virtually all companies are unionized, but where unemployment was running at 20 percent.

Nissan agreed that its plant would be unionized, but insisted on selecting the union and demanded that membership not be compulsory. While both company and union shy away from calling their agreement a no-strike situation, it nevertheless stipulates that there can be "no industrial action during negotiations, nor during subsequent mandatory conciliation or arbitration sessions." Nissan also insisted that workers be allowed maximum flexibility in moving from job to job, and that assembly-line workers be able to handle routine preventive maintenance and minor breakdowns.

As at Smyrna, several of the key executives in Britain are former Ford people. But, in a departure from the Tennessee pattern, a Japanese was named CEO and the plant operates on rotating shifts, a system the Japanese consider more democratic and effective. In the United Kingdom, Nissan builds the Bluebird (or Stanza), a compact-sized car, rather than the simpler-to-build truck or Sentra subcompact. And in Britain, which had suffered far more from the war with Germany than from the one with Japan, there is less squeamishness about praising the Japanese. Prince Charles has said Nissan is helping Britain's Northeast rise "like a phoenix from the ashes of an older industrial past."

Another subject of common interest at the three headquarters was Volkswagen.

The Japanese admire the Germans for their work habits, their craftsmanship, their respect for authority, and their resilience following a similar devastating defeat in World War II. Robert Cole, in an article published in the spring 1988 *California Management Review*, noted that Japanese companies looking for plant sites in the United States preferred locations where they could hire a German-American work force. The fact, however, that Volkswagen, a German car company, could establish a major American manufacturing presence, build cars here for nine years (1978–87), and then fail had given the Japanese much cause for concern.

What lessons were to be learned? How could a Japanese auto maker avoid a similar fate?

As mentioned in chapter 1, Shige Yoshida had studied Volkswagen's site selection and labor strategies and decided that Honda must do it another way. Robert Shook, in an authorized company biography, *Honda: An American Success Story*, reveals other details of the Honda study. He says it showed that

> while the American public had a love affair with the Beetle . . . Volkswagen mistakenly introduced the Rabbit before its engineers got all the bugs out. As a result, Rabbit owners were plagued with defects that often couldn't be repaired at Volkswagen shops. The cars had so many problems that even Volkswagen dealers began refusing them as trade-ins. While Volkswagen eventually came out with a better Rabbit, the damage had been done.

Zenzo Sonada, who oversees research and development at Nissan, saw VW's failure to design a car to meet the changing needs of the U.S. consumer as the critical problem.

Toyota, fresh from its success at NUMMI, saw it as a management problem. In Toyota City, in the training center where Americans stay while being exposed to the Toyota production system, there is a lounge, and in the lounge a library of American movies. One of these, prominently displayed, is *Gung Ho*, a spoof of what happens when a Japanese company takes over a unionized American auto plant. The plant is an old one, in a state very much like Pennsylvania, where Volkswagen had been.

Each company seemed confident that the Japanese could

meet the needs of the American consumer better than
Volkswagen, and at least as well as the Big Three. The
Japanese have closer ties to and more influence with their
suppliers, whose cooperation is needed to cut product development time. They have more familiarity with small-lot
production at a time when the American car market is
becoming niche-conscious, and in Japanese companies, manufacturing, research and development, and marketing work
together as a team. Turf battles are eliminated at the outset.

Still another question of common interest was what it
takes to become multinational.

Honda seemed to have given the subject the most
thought. It had been forced to do so.

Soichiro Honda has said that the ideal place for Honda
to have its world headquarters would be on a satellite circling
the globe. Land costs in Japan are so high that to expand
its Sayama plant, north of Tokyo, Honda has had to grow
vertically, by adding floors. And to save space, parts handling
has been refined to the point that trucks drive into the plant
and off-load parts at the very place on the line where they
will be needed next. Because Toyota and Nissan have a
monopoly on most car dealerships, Honda has had little
choice but to expand overseas. And because of its late start,
Honda is still developing a full product line. This deficiency
is less of a problem in the United States, where Honda has
earned a reputation for innovation, but is troublesome at
home, where the competition is more severe.

In its collective subconscious, Japan still seems to see
itself as a poor island nation, defeated in war, short on
natural resources, with a lingering feeling of vulnerability.
This may be what makes the Japanese run so hard to catch
up with (or stay ahead of) everyone else. If this is true, then
Honda—never truly welcome at home—must feel twice as
vulnerable, and believe it must run twice as hard. Honda
was the first of the Japanese auto makers to operate globally
with a North American headquarters coordinating both

manufacturing and sales. It is well on its way to having an independent research and development, product engineering, and product development presence in America, as well.

At Nissan, the goal is to have separate research and development facilities on three continents, in Japan, the United States, and Europe—with cars designed specifically for each market.

Toyota, the most conservative—and historically the most successful—has moved more slowly. Toyota has fewer executives with international experience than Honda or Nissan. In Toyota City, information has always been shared face to face within a limited circle of men who could finish each other's sentences. The fear was that if Toyota diverted too much of its attention overseas, its dominant market share at home could be nibbled away.

Besides, the company's experience in Kentucky was still mixed. Wallace Wilkinson, the Democrat who succeeded Martha Layne Collins as governor, had campaigned against the Toyota incentive package, and though in office for more than a year, Wilkinson had yet to visit Japan. Toyota's plans for further expansion in Kentucky were still on hold.

When I asked whether, if they had to do it over again, Toyota would still have picked Kentucky as its primary U.S. site, Kaneyoshi Kusunoki, in charge of the American operation, smiled and would only say ignorance had been bliss.

The sixty-three-year-old Kusunoki has been with Toyota for forty-one years. As a student, he planned a career in airplane engineering, but when World War II ended, the Japanese aircraft industry was devastated. He became a specialist in the automotive production system instead. "You might say I lost my wings," he remarks.

I asked him whether Toyota would allow its Kentucky plant to be unionized. Kusunoki said that would be a matter for Georgetown's employees to decide; the company would remain neutral. He added, however, that he was aware local management there did not favor a union. This factor would

be taken into consideration, as would the wishes of the
residents of Georgetown and Scott County.

Executives at each of the Japanese companies were
keenly aware of recent surveys showing that Americans were
becoming alarmed by the rising level of Japanese investment
in the United States. In different ways, each company appeared to be taking preventive measures.

Honda was increasing the percentage of blacks in its
work force and promising to export 70,000 U.S.-made cars
to help rectify our balance-of-trade deficit. Toyota had put
its expansion plans on hold and given large cash gifts to the
University of Kentucky and the city of Georgetown. Nissan
has agreed to a joint venture with Ford in Ohio and made
sacrifices in Japan so Smyrna would not have to lay off.

Nissan in Japan was having troubles of its own when Nissan
in Tennessee started experiencing inventory problems. In
Japan, sales were off, and the company was having to reduce
expenses drastically. Workers were staying on the job after
their shifts were done without extra pay. Managers were
squeezing extra years out of old equipment. But nothing
would really change until 1988, when the company's design
team began turning out newer, spiffier models.

Still, Nissan in Japan, with five manufacturing facilities,
had more ways of reducing expenses than Nissan in Tennessee did, with only one. And in Japan, workers were more
accustomed to doing what they were told. If the need arose,
they took forced vacations with partial pay, moved from
assembly line to supplier plants, and were transferred from
an assembly line making a weak model to another making a
stronger one. When Smyrna suffered inventory problems, it
was Nissan in Japan that took up the slack.

Haruo Ohno is manager of the Zama plant, twenty-one
miles southwest of Tokyo. He is also a member of the parent
company's board of directors. Small in stature, quick to smile,

he jokes about his name. "Whenever someone asks me something, my standard response is 'Oh no,' " he says.

Zama pioneered in the use of robots. It is the plant the company likes to show visitors (I was asked if I wanted to bring a camera). Four car models are built there, including the Sentra, with the majority sent overseas. Zama is, among other things, Smyrna's sister plant.

Thus, when Tennessee experienced inventory problems, when Smyrna had to park tens of thousands of cars and new trucks in cornfields and cow pastures, Ohno eliminated one of Zama's four assembly lines and transferred its workers, at great inconvenience to them and their families, to another plant.

"We take a special pride in our overseas operations," he told me. "We want for them to succeed."

11

Befriending the Machine

When a Japanese says as soon as possible, the
important word is "soon." How *soon* can it be done?
When an American says as soon as possible, the
emphasis seems to be on the "if possible."

— Kenichi Mizuo, Toyota Motor
Corporation, speaking about
his experiences at NUMMI

Auto plants in Japan look darker, more crowded, at first
glance less efficient than the newer plants the Japanese have
built in the United States. They aren't surrounded by empty
fields. Streets and roads around the plants are two-lane and
clogged with traffic. Workers arrive on bicycles, and inside,
there is said to be too little heat in winter and not enough
cool air in summer. You don't see as many robots installing
windshields, applying sealant, or painting car bodies as you
do in America. Ineffective older employees are not fired but
instead given "a seat by the window." There, with nothing
to do, the hope is they can be shamed into quitting.

But if these older plants seem less efficient than the
newer ones the Japanese have built in the United States, it
is usually an illusion.

Here the workers arrive early and stay late, and at
Toyota and Nissan they are often graduates of technical
high schools operated by the companies themselves. Parts
received from supplier companies are of near-perfect quality.

And all plants work rotating shifts, which means that, regardless of seniority, men work days one week and nights the next. With rotating shifts, experienced and inexperienced people work side by side, a critical factor at new-model time.

"In Ohio, we tried to rotate our shifts," Shige Yoshida told me. "We tried it in what we called a team training cycle, at a time when our work force was still small. We tried it for several months. Our associates said okay so long as the experiment was temporary. When we announced we wouldn't continue, they cheered. In Ohio, there's this belief that length of service gives you the right to determine what shift you work. It's what Al Kinzer calls the 'god of seniority.' "

"At Sayama," Kinzer added, "the average worker has nine to eleven years of experience. In Ohio, the average worker has only three or four. In Japan, he has gone through several model changes. It's hard to teach that kind of experience. We thought we could. We certainly tried. But it's like me telling you before you get married about all the little problems and difficulties you'll have."

Nevertheless, training remains crucial.

Honda, Nissan, and Toyota have already trained a lot of Americans: in Honda's case, mostly in Ohio; in Nissan's, mostly in Japan; in Toyota's, in both countries. And whereas the American sometimes sees the Japanese as unable to solve a problem without calling a committee meeting, the Japanese often sees the American as impulsive and not totally committed to the job. The Japanese go to great lengths to teach their approach to job performance as part of a total context, not something that can be learned piecemeal.

"You ask about something and an American will say, 'No problem,' or 'Knock on wood,' or 'I'm going to play it by ear,' " say Kenichi Mizuo and Isaho Ito, who have experience at NUMMI. "That's when the Japanese begins to be nervous. Japanese people are more pessimistic. They say, 'What if this happens? What if that?' "

Kaname Kasai, general manager of Honda's Sayama

number-two plant, who spent five years in Ohio, puts it
another way:

"Our Japanese associates have no very clear job descrip-
tions. Their skills overlap with one another. Each spots and
shores up the other's weakness. Americans, on the other
hand, think they must have a specific job description. They
say they need to know the *limit* of their responsibilities. At
the Marysville plant, I was a manager, but I would stoop to
clean up the workplace. Not because it was my job,. but to
show others. If there's a problem, the Japanese manager
goes to see for himself. The American will often insist that
the pertinent information be brought to his desk."

Nissan gives its non-Japanese employees a publication
called *Things You Want to Know about Nissan in Japan.* It notes,
for example, that

> in Japan, there is a tendency to regard paid holidays as
> a privilege, where workers in the West take their vacation
> as a right. The difference here is one of national
> character.
>   The rate of absenteeism is lower in Japan than it is
> in the West. This seems to arise from differences in work
> ethics directly and indirectly based on religious values
> . . . In Japan, it is felt that work is an integral part of a
> person's life, and consequently that it should be enjoy-
> able; this leads to independent efforts on the part of
> workers to improve their jobs and to upgrade the quality
> of their work . . . Since changing jobs is relatively rare
> in Japan the work that an individual does within the
> framework of a single company takes on a great deal of
> importance in his personal life.

Two American reporters, Holly Holland of the Louisville
Courier-Journal and Alezia Swazey of the Lexington *Herald-
Leader*, went to Japan in 1987 to observe and write about
Kentuckians training in Toyota City.

They noted that the Americans could accomplish only

about 80 percent of what the Japanese did in the same amount of time. They were impressed with how involved with their workers the Japanese managers are and with the emphasis on safety. They were astonished by what they saw on the plant floor.

> Large, dangling vents pump cold air into the plant, but they're not very effective [Holland wrote]. The pace, noise and close quarters charge the factory with heat and tension.
> At the end of a sequence of tasks, many workers *run* back to their starting positions. Their movements are so quick that it's sometimes difficult to see the parts as they pass through their hands.
> This is what Toyota calls "muda"—no wasted motion. Machines and robots don't know what it's like to pant, to stumble or to lose their grip. And so the workers learn to forget that, too.

The Japanese had posted signs designating certain walkways "Kentucky Road," "Lexington Drive," and "Scott Drive." They had learned phrases like: "I'm sorry, but I don't understand," and "Make yourself at home."

The two reporters noted that "the Japanese cook American food, but they don't understand that you eat at certain times of the day and eat certain things with certain other things. Potato salad sandwiches for breakfast do not have much appeal."

"And God is it awful," Holland quoted one Kentuckian. "At the plant, they all drink out of the same cup. They pass it around, and all drink from it. I don't know how they keep from getting all kinds of diseases."

At none of the companies do workers seem more loyal and less questioning than at Toyota. In Kentucky, Toyota has spent countless hours searching for compatible personalities, for people with just the right mix of aptitude and ambition. In Toyota City, they were already there. Far from the temptations of Tokyo, Toyota City is an auto maker's dream. Suppliers are located within a stone's throw of assembly plants, so close that at one I saw fewer than a dozen engines waiting to be installed in cars advancing down the line. With but three engines left on one truck bed, another truck arrived to take its place.

The Toyota production system features just-in-time delivery, small-lot production, and what Haruo Shimada (of Keio University) and John Paul MacDuffie (at MIT) call "human control."

Just-in-time delivery is what it says. Parts are delivered to the assembly line at the hour and in the exact quantity they are needed. Virtually no in-house inventory is maintained. There is no storage expense, and defects can be spotted and corrected immediately.

Small-lot (as distinguished from high-volume) production requires rapid communication between work stations. This acts to prevent defects or other problems from proliferating. For small-lot production to be effective, you have to make rapid die changes and machine setups.

Human control is what Toyota calls "giving wisdom to the machine." The Japanese believe machines have idiosyncrasies of their own and too often are not used to full capacity. Thus the assembly-line worker is encouraged to make subtle modifications to his machine to enable it to work at full potential. He is also given the primary responsibility for quality control and is encouraged to stop the assembly line if he spots a defect. To do this, he pulls an overhead rope, which lights up an *andon*, or electrical signboard. Colored lights alert the team leader and others to the problem, which is then quickly attended to. Such an action, if prolonged, can literally shut down the entire plant.

This vulnerability to plant shutdown is an important reason why Japanese auto makers in the United States have been so fussy about the people they hire and the companies they engage as parts suppliers. For in Japan, and perhaps especially at Toyota, the parts supplier is a part of the family. And Mother Toyota has many ways of making sure that her offspring remain loyal: by lending money or equipment; by giving guidance in design, accounting, or cost control; by loaning executives or workers.

After I visited Toyota City, I found it easier to understand why Honda and Nissan, with plants and parts suppliers more widely dispersed, their operations centered in and around crowded, chaotic Tokyo, were less intimidated at the thought of manufacturing overseas.

In November 1988, when I was in Japan, there were two groups of Americans training there: thirty team leaders from Ohio at Honda's Sayama plant, and seventeen Tennesseans in Nagoya, at one of Nissan's engine plants.

Steve Bump, thirty years old, a high-school graduate from Marysville, Ohio, has been with Honda since 1980. He has been promoted three times, is making his fifth trip to Japan, and is in charge of the thirty Americans being trained. His job is to be alert to any breakdowns in communications and to handle any personnel problems that might arise. Though soft-spoken, he is big and strong-looking.

Bump talked about the differences between work practices in Japan and back home. He noted wryly that in Japan overtime can be scheduled at the last minute and nobody complains. In Ohio he has to plan weeks in advance. He noted, too, that at Sayama, if somebody is away on vacation, he can still be, and often is, called back to work. Japanese supervisors are closer to their men. They drink beer and play sports with them, and because they know them better, they can be tougher, too. In Japan, Bump has seen Japanese supervisors slap their men. In Japan, too, every associate must participate in a quality circle. In Ohio fewer than three out of four participate in a quality circle, or in one of its substitutes; participation, though strongly encouraged, is still voluntary.

Honda was training two hundred American team leaders in Japan, some thirty at a time, many in preparation for assignments at the second auto plant. They stay in Japan for four weeks and get two weeks' training in Ohio at beginning and end. One of Bump's objectives was to show the Ohioans how closely Japanese team members interact, both among themselves and with workers from their supplier companies. Another was to demonstrate that when the Japanese run into a problem, they don't try to fix it in some quick, slapdash way, but rather trace it back to its origins. In this way, the problem, once corrected, is unlikely to occur again. Bump said that what the Ohioans pick up best on are all the little ways the Japanese have of making their jobs easier: by rigging the machine a bit differently, by inventing a new kind of tool, by fabricating a gizmo to stand or kneel on.

At thirty-seven, Dwight Woodlee is seven years older than Bump, and he has worked at Nissan since 1982. Unlike Bump, however, he is yet to be promoted, and is making his *first* trip to Japan. He is one of seventeen Tennesseans (fourteen technicians, two supervisors, and one operations manager) being trained to assemble engines.

He's here, he says, because at one of Jerry Benefield's recent focus group meetings several veteran technicians had asked why Nissan trained only supervisors in Japan.

A lanky, slow-talking native of Bell Buckle, a village southeast of Smyrna, Woodlee grew up on a farm and says farming was good preparation for his work at Nissan because "farming's not just a job, it's a way of life. You get up in the morning and do whatever needs to be done."

After high school, he studied electronics for a year at the Bell and Howell Institute in Atlanta, then served in the National Guard, ran a service-station repair shop, managed a motel for his uncle, and worked ten years as a machinist for Ford in Tennessee, where he was ultimately laid off. He wanted to train in Japan, he says, because he wanted to try something new. "Lots of people prefer to come in and do the same job every day, but not me."

Nissan had announced that Smyrna would soon assemble engines, and that a few veteran technicians would be sent for sixteen weeks' training in Japan. When they returned, their job would be to train others.

Before leaving home, Robert Preston, their group leader, urged the men to shave their beards and mustaches. The Japanese have trouble growing facial hair, he said; you don't want to put them on the defensive. Preston, who Woodlee said "can tell you to go to hell and make you enjoy the trip," is fifty years old and a veteran of General Motors' Cadillac Division. He started at Nissan in quality control and had already led several training missions to Japan. "Always be prompt," he told his charges. "For us ten-thirty can be ten minutes either way; but for a Japanese ten-thirty is ten-thirty. And take some gifts." Woodlee brought along Goo-Goo Clusters (Nashville's famous chocolate-covered coconut fill) and some bottles of Jack Daniel's whiskey.

The Tennesseans' host, the Aichi Machinery Company, had not trained a group of Americans before, but bent to the task. The Americans were lodged in a luxury hotel next to a McDonald's in downtown Nagoya and, at the plant, given a spacious room with many windows in which to hold meetings, change clothes, and relax. The Americans would work days, but not nights. Toshio Sugihara, nicknamed Suggi, would be their trainer.

Sugihara had already learned the English phrases he would need: "Turn on, turn off, maybe okay, no good, find out, does not meet standard." And he was adept at drawing quick sketches of what he could not express in words. He led the morning stretching, bending, and twisting exercises; urged the Americans not to walk with hands in their pockets (if you trip and fall, your face will be bruised), not to leave jackets unbuttoned (an unbuttoned jacket can be caught in machinery), and not to walk through large plant doors even if no vehicle is coming (you can never be sure).

The Tennesseans were from Smyrna's trim and chassis department—the department with the most union sympathizers. There, if something didn't fit, it could be twisted and bent until it did. Engine work, Woodlee soon discovered, required more precision.

He liked that at Aichi the assembly-line workers were responsible for quality control. At Smyrna, as at most Big Three plants, it was the quality assurance people who were. "If you know somebody is going to come along after, you're never quite as careful," he said.

He liked, too, that the Japanese approach seemed less complicated. In Smyrna, Nissan had state-of-the-art technology, which not everyone understood, which sometimes broke down, and which often took a long time to get fixed. The Japanese understood their machines better than the Americans did, knew them almost as you'd know another person. They had also figured out more ways to make their work simpler, more efficient, easier to do.

Woodlee learned not to say he was going to do something unless he really meant it, because the Japanese never did. Going to and from work, he and the others didn't all take the same bus, but tried to be less conspicuous. Like the Japanese, they changed into street clothes before leaving the plant.

"At home few of us bother to change after work," Woodlee told me. "We've got fancy locker rooms, modeled after the best in the industry, but we don't use them very often."

At first Woodlee compared the Aichi plant unfavorably

to the more modern Smyrna operation, but by the time he left, he wasn't so sure. He wondered if Smyrna didn't have too much advanced technology. A computer could be thrown off by a slight vibration or a temperature change. He determined to get to know his machinery better.

He now expected to be a team leader someday.

12

Needing Each Other

I went to the club for lunch, and guess what I saw.
On the bulletin board I saw a cartoon that showed
a Japanese bomber flying over the Middle West.
It was dropping Honda Accords and Gold Wing
motorcycles and the pilot was saying, "We're going
to win this one without firing a shot."
— A chamber of commerce official in
Marysville, Ohio, May 1988

Ultimately, the success of Japanese auto makers in the United
States will depend on how well they can blend their culture
with ours. Honda is taking the most risks in this regard.
Honda's key Japanese are staying for three, five, sometimes
seven years. Some are saying they may never go home.

When Honda's Japanese first started coming to Ohio, a
few families settled in Marysville, near the motorcycle plant,
but most chose to live in the northern Columbus suburbs of
Dublin and Worthington, thirty-eight miles away. These
early arrivals were mostly men who had left their families
behind. Honda leased blocks of apartments for them and
urged that they not attract undue attention to themselves by
going out in groups.

By then Dublin and Worthington were two of Columbus's fastest-growing suburbs, places where the sight of
newcomers arriving was a common occurrence. Columbus,
the home of Ohio State football, has often been called a

sports town without a big-league franchise. But because no one industry predominates, it has also come to be recession-proof. Populated by migrants from every county within a hundred miles, it still has a small-town, homogeneous feel.

Dublin and Worthington are different, however; more cosmopolitan. Dublin is home to Jack Nicklaus, the Columbus zoo, and a 130-acre office park. Worthington has brick sidewalks, a village green, and something of a New England flavor. Both had been attracting transients from someplace else soon on their way to somewhere new, people with scarcely the time or energy to notice a growing Japanese presence in their midst.

Once Honda built its auto plant next to the motorcycle plant, and its Japanese parts companies built factories nearby, dozens more Japanese would settle in the Dublin-Worthington area, many with families now.

Barbara Fumiko Richardson is the real estate agent who helped many of them find houses. A former Japan Air Lines stewardess married to Bradley Richardson, director of the Institute of Japanese Studies at Ohio State, she has lived in Columbus for twenty-three years. Prosperous and serene-looking, she drives a Mercedes now and specializes in higher-priced homes.

The Honda families preferred to buy new, she says. They didn't want a house that had been tramped through by strangers, nor one that had been lived in by a dog or cat. They didn't appreciate the broken-in feel some Americans cherish in an older home. Anything prewar in Japan is rarely attractive, and so much was destroyed during the war. Their dream house would have a cathedral ceiling, with floor-to-ceiling windows, and a foyer where shoes could be removed. Lots of light was critical, since because they have to study so much as children, the Japanese think of themselves as myopic. The husbands who arrived first were careful not to buy anything too expensive, anything that might set them apart from their Japanese co-workers. Most shopped in the

$125,000 range and made at least a 40 percent down payment. Hoping to play golf on the weekends, they bought houses with small yards that would require a minimum of upkeep. They did not bring much furniture with them. Japanese furniture is often too small for an American-size home.

By 1985 there were more than a hundred Japanese families in Dublin-Worthington, and several grocery stores there had begun stocking five-pound sacks of rice and the freshest of fish. Worthington was where the Japanese Saturday school was located, where the children received extra doses of mathematics, language, and social studies training so that when they returned to Japan they could still get into good schools. By 1985 Honda had created its first-of-a-kind family center there.

A one-story building next to the Brookside Country Club, the center has floor-to-ceiling windows as well as inside doors with clear glass panels, "Honda style," so anyone can look in or look out. The bulletin board is papered with notices of apartments for rent, houses for sale, and English classes to sign up for, and nearby is posted a list of expectant mothers, their doctors, and due dates. A lounge features a large television set and is scattered with Japanese fashion magazines. The library is filled with novels, detective stories, and videocassettes to supplement American school programs. And in a quiet corner is a place called the "closing room," used for getting through the complications of real estate transactions in two languages.

Koichiro Shinagawa is center director, a slim, energetic man who spends his mornings at Honda's headquarters near Marysville and his afternoons in Worthington or Sidney, where he supervises a second family center. His American nickname is "Coach."

The center's purpose is threefold, he says: to help new families cope with emergencies, to teach English, and to enable the women to enjoy their stay here. Because of the visas they hold, the Japanese wives can't seek employment, and thus need activities to fill their days. Shinagawa offers cooking and quilting classes and organizes trips to concerts and Broadway road shows. The road shows, he says, are five to seven times less expensive in Columbus than in Tokyo. He employs five interpreters to accompany the women on visits to hospitals and schools and to doctors' and dentists' offices. Shinagawa seemed to have thought of everything. Nothing was left to chance.

Yet by 1985 some of these Japanese women had lived in Ohio long enough to realize that Dublin's schools were overcrowded, that in a small town the neighbors might be friendlier and driving a car less intimidating. In a small town, too, it might be easier to have an American friend, the golf courses would be less crowded, and the children could still attend Saturday school in Columbus. For the Japanese mother, with a first car of her own, driving the children to Saturday school would be a chance to hone newly acquired driving skills. Some of the women were even saying the family center didn't do enough to encourage them to cope on their own. Honda, after all, was doing better here than anyone had expected it would. An engine plant was being built at Anna, and Anna was twice the commute from Columbus that the Marysville plants had been.

When you read a newspaper story about Honda of America, the dateline is usually "Marysville, Ohio." That is because the manufacturing headquarters is in the motorcycle plant, seven miles west of town. But even if Honda won't say so officially, Marysville is no longer at the hub of Honda's operations. Bellefontaine, twenty-nine miles farther north, is. Bellefontaine is now nearest to most of the assembly and supplier plants, and the town to which many of the new Japanese families are moving.

Governor Rhodes ruffled feathers when he bypassed Marysville's newspaper and chamber of commerce in negotiating

Honda's site location. He ruffled them further when he promised that Marysville's sewer system would be extended to the plant, and that Route 33 to the site would be widened from two lanes to four.

Rumors circulated that Rhodes had profited from sale of the land, since the site had been purchased from Ralph Stolle, the brother-in-law of Donald Hilliker, a former Rhodes business partner. Rhodes threatened to resign if anyone could prove he had made money on the deal, but although no one could, that wasn't the end of it. A group calling itself the Committee against Route 33 Expansion (CARE) was incensed that the governor's plan didn't include a steel-and-concrete divider. The increased traffic, they said, would pose a "death threat" to children getting on and off school buses. Billboards appeared with the slogan "Say No to Rhodes."

To make matters worse, *The Wall Street Journal* ran a story in 1982 headlined "Honda's U.S. Plant Brings Trouble, Not Prosperity, to Small Ohio Town":

> It was clear from the start that Marysville's waste-water treatment plant would have to be expanded to handle the 500,000 gallons of additional water that will flow each day from the Honda plant. The federal government will pick up some $6 million of the $8 million expense, but Marysville will have to pay the rest. That wasn't the way it was supposed to work, according to Mayor [Tom] Nuckles . . .
>
> "Nobody can afford to water their lawns anymore," a resident was quoted.
>
> "The only thing we're going to get out of this is jobs. And we're not sure we're going to get many of those," said another.
>
> There's the sense here that if Marysville had to have an auto plant, it would have preferred one built by General Motors or Ford.

No mention was made of the millions of dollars Honda was and would be paying in taxes each year to Marysville's school system.

Throughout the controversy, the company kept a low profile. It paid what it had agreed to pay for sewer-line extension. It didn't press the state to honor its commitment to widen Route 33 (in fact, it wasn't until six years later that a four-lane highway finally reached the plant site). It found a way to ship thousands of bushels of Union County corn back to Japan in the empty containers that had been used to bring in auto parts. And several Japanese settled in Marysville, including executive vice-president Shige Yoshida and his successor, Toshi Amino. Yoshida's daughter graduated from Marysville High School, and Amino and his wife, both Christians, joined Marysville's Methodist church. Mrs. Amino did volunteer work at the local hospital, and her husband went door to door for the United Way. Their first names are Toshikata and Satoko, but they asked neighbors to call them Toshi and Ruth.

But Marysville never truly warmed to the Japanese or reached out to Honda. Residents had to be prodded to create an international friendship center (after Bellefontaine did), and when that finally happened, the Protestant churches at first declined to participate. Mayor Tom Nuckles tells of receiving hate mail, and his wife, Patricia, of being accosted in the supermarket and criticized for helping "those people." Union County commissioners later seemed glad that Honda's second auto plant would be built not in Union but in Logan County instead.

"So far we haven't had to increase our police and fire protection," they told me. "Three discounters came in expecting a boom, but two have already gone out of business."

Once Honda built its engine plant at Anna and announced that a second auto plant would be built at East Liberty—and as more supplier plants built in the area—it became obvious that Bellefontaine would become the hub of the company's operations.

"Marysville is Honda, and Honda headquarters is Marysville. But Bellefontaine didn't complain when it didn't get any tax money," Toshi Amino would tell me. "They started a friendship center when there were just five or six Japanese families there. And the people who did it weren't just businessmen. We felt they did it because they wanted to help."

Toshi Amino has been with Honda for twenty years and spent half of them in the United States. Five feet tall and balding, he has been known to stand on a chair when introduced so the audience can see him better. A native of Kyoto, he was a Boy Scout and later became a scoutmaster. He says the scouting experience helped him do better the job he has now.

"In scouting, you're dealing with a gang of boys, and what's important is the teamwork. Nothing gets done because of threats. It's the same at Honda. In Tokyo, I had a line job in marketing, but I spent half my time in project team assignments. My closest friends are not necessarily the marketing people, but instead the engineering and research people I worked with on teams."

In California, Amino was vice-president in charge of motorcycle sales. In 1980, when sent to Ohio on temporary assignment, he asked what he was supposed to do. He was told, "Since you know so much about the United States, perhaps you will find something." Soon he became construction manager for the auto plant, then president (and construction manager) for Bellemar, the subsidiary next door that makes seats for the auto plant.

Amino tells how, while he was at Bellemar, a new Japanese engineer came to see him one day. The engineer had been one of the first to buy a house in Bellefontaine. He had two children, a boy who had just finished high school and a girl in the tenth grade, but neither could speak English very well. The boy wanted to attend college in the United States, but the father feared he would never be accepted. Amino picked up the phone and called Robert Carter, Bellefontaine's superintendent of schools.

"I told him the boy had finished high school, but still needed English tutoring. I wondered if Dr. Carter could help.

"Dr. Carter said sure.

"I asked when, knowing that in Japan for such a request to be granted would take weeks, maybe months. And then it would have to be a committee decision. In Japan, to make an exception to the rules is very serious.

"Dr. Carter said, 'How about tomorrow?' "

Carter says he doesn't remember much about the incident. What he does remember is that when he went to Japan a couple years later, as a guest of the Honda Foundation, Toshi Amino happened to be there, too, and made a point of taking him to meet his mother and brother in Kyoto.

Carter grew up on a farm south of Washington, Pennsylvania, and had come to Bellefontaine after serving as an assistant superintendent in Columbus. He had recently turned down an offer to be superintendent of a large Chicago-area school because he preferred to remain in Bellefontaine. He had been wounded in action while a combat engineer in Korea, and had spent a hundred days recovering in a Yokohama hospital, attended to by Japanese doctors and nurses.

"When the Honda families started moving into Bellefontaine, you would see the wives wandering about with dictionaries in their hands, looking lost," Carter remembers. "Their husbands were working eighty hours a week, trying to justify the confidence the company had placed in them. The wives had been left to cope on their own."

When it came time to pick a name for his seat parts

company, Amino called it Bellemar: Belle for Bellefontaine, Mar for Marysville. When the Honda Foundation added Bellefontaine to the list of communities where Japanese families lived and from which it would send an educator to Japan for a week's visit each year, Carter was the first to go. And when Bellefontaine became the first of these communities to start an international friendship center, Carter asked Amino for advice on how to do it.

"Don't promise too much," Amino said. "If anything, understate your objectives and put them in writing. Japanese people do not have this concept of volunteerism. They may be suspicious. Also, please treat all Japanese alike. They are in America now. Job and status differences should be left at the plant door."

Bellefontaine, a town of 14,000, is something of an island in west-central Ohio. Not yet connected by four-lane highway to a nearby city—to Columbus, Springfield, Lima, or Dayton—it has retained a certain innocence. Few rituals are more important than cutting the grass. You can pump gas without having to pay first. You still see decals on store windows that read "We hired a vet. We didn't forget."

"Ministers and school superintendents come back here to retire. If you're not accepted, it's your own fault," said Merrill Insley, Susan's father. "We're more of a Kiwanis than a Rotary town." (Rotarians are movers and shakers; Kiwanians can be managers at any level.)

The Bellefontaine *Examiner* has been owned by four generations of Hubbards. It runs pictures on page one of homecoming queens and every day lists traffic violations and other infractions. It seldom takes an editorial stand ("The town's too small. Everybody knows everybody else. We want to emphasize the positive," says Gene Marine, managing editor), but if it does, it's a doozy. When a store owner was gunned down in the presence of witnesses recently, and the grand jury returned an indictment of "involuntary manslaughter," the *Examiner* called the prosecutor weak, timid, and incompetent. He was routed at the next election.

Yet Bellefontaine has a certain sophistication and variety, too. Its library has a fax machine. Its mayor is an Italian-American Catholic who happens to be Republican. Indian Lake to the north, a modest ski resort to the east, and the Ohio Caverns to the south each year attract thousands of visitors. There are dozens of Amish in Belle Center and hundreds of Mennonites in nearby West Liberty, and West Liberty was one of the first midwestern communities to welcome refugees from Vietnam.

Bellefontaine was once a bustling railroad center. Four divisions of the Big Four (later the New York Central, and now Conrail) converged here, where the trains changed engines and their crews slept over in the forty-nine-bed YMCA. "We were known as the crossroads of America," says mayor Richard Vicario, who was a policeman then. "We had seventeen bars within six blocks of each other." But once the diesel replaced the steam engine and the federal government began building interstate highways, Bellefontaine's days as a railroad center were numbered. Other misfortunes followed. The Air Force built, operated, then shut down an early-warning radar station. Westinghouse and Rockwell International operated manufacturing plants that at their peak employed a thousand people—Westinghouse for thirty years, and Rockwell for twenty. But the land their plants stood on had been leased, and their general managers seldom stayed for more than two or three years. When in the early 1980s the recession hit, the plants closed down, citing the pressures of foreign competition. In 1982 Bellefontaine had to lay off police officers and firefighters and even turn off some of its streetlights to balance the city budget.

This was when Donald Hilliker, a friend and sometime business partner of Governor Rhodes, got into the act. Hilliker is a Bellefontaine native and perhaps its wealthiest citizen, although his business interests lie elsewhere now. He and Rhodes were stockholders in Wendy's International, and when Rhodes was out of office, the two had built motels in Atlanta, Chicago, and Orlando, before Disney World. Hilliker was troubled by Bellefontaine's declining fortunes, and both had heard stories about Marysville's lack of enthusiasm for Honda and the Japanese.

So one day Hilliker buttonholed Lee Dorsey, who ran the chamber of commerce. Dorsey was a former teacher and school principal who had grown up in East Liverpool, Ohio. His playmates had been the sons and daughters of steelworkers who still spoke broken English.

He remembers that "one morning Don Hilliker jumped me and said we've got to make a bunch of bumper stickers that say 'Bellefontaine loves Honda.' "

"I can't do it," Dorsey says he said. "We've got other industries here. They're not as big, but they've been here a lot longer. Honda's not even in Logan County. We do it for one, we've got to do it for all."

"That's a lot of crap," Dorsey says Hilliker told him. But Hilliker didn't argue. He went across the street to the Huntington Bank, where he was a director, and got the bank to pay for the bumper stickers instead. Soon "Bellefontaine loves Honda" stickers adorned hundreds of local car bumpers. After some delay and more discussion, Dorsey and Wilson Anderson, the local Ford dealer, convinced the chamber to buy space on billboards that made the same point, less forcefully.

The local Ford dealer might seem an unlikely person to promote Honda. But Anderson said Honda's arrival in the region had boosted purchasing power. He'd been selling Fords again as if they were going out of style. Besides, Honda didn't pressure its employees to buy the cars they had helped build the way Ford did. "When I worked at Ford, if an employee drove a foreign car, he had to park a mile away.

At Honda, if one of their employees goes to the Honda credit union to finance a Ford, there's no foot-dragging whatsoever."

The map the chamber of commerce put on its billboards showed Bellefontaine surrounded by two Honda plants and five of Honda's Japanese supplier companies. The Ford plant at Lima and Navistar's truck plant in Springfield were spotted in for good measure. The logo read: "Join Our Fine Industries; Locate Your Plant in Bellefontaine: The Center of the Action."

13

Everybody Wins

We found that the Japanese husband living alone
didn't eat properly, and that this affected his work
performance. He ate too much of what he wanted
to eat and not enough of what he needed. An
important duty of the Japanese wife is to ensure
that her husband eats a balanced meal.
>—Takesi Saito, at company headquarters in
Tokyo, citing one of the reasons Honda
started sending more families to Ohio

Honda had a problem that Toyota and Nissan didn't have.
It was still discriminated against in Japan and didn't have a
real presence in Europe yet, either. If the company was to
prosper, its future lay in the United States. But now Nissan
and Toyota were here, too, and if Honda was to stay ahead
of its two richer and most formidable competitors, it would
have to bring to America more Japanese, hundreds of them.
Their job would be to demonstrate, by example, the Honda
way, to ensure that the new engine and second auto plants
got built right, and to supervise model changes until enough
Americans could be trained.

For Honda, unlike Nissan and Toyota, was attempting
to do in America things it hadn't done in Japan. While
Nissan was manufacturing its simplest and easiest-to-build
car and truck models in Smyrna, and Toyota's NUMMI
and Georgetown plants were clones of its plants in Toyota

City, Honda was bringing to America a huge production engineering staff as well as combining seven engine-making operations—a feat it had never attempted before.

Thus the decision was made to send more Japanese to Ohio, and for much longer periods of time. The question was whether Ohio could absorb so many, or whether at some point the Ohioans might say enough is enough. Nissan had scarcely any Japanese in its Tennessee plant, and in Kentucky most of Toyota's Japanese were opting to live anonymously in the nearby city of Lexington. In Georgetown, Japanese walking down Main Street had been mooned by men driving by in a pickup truck. Besides, Lexington was wet and Georgetown dry.

The turning point came when Governor Celeste offered to sell the Transportation Research Center to Honda and Bellefontaine reached out to the Japanese.

Bellefontaine has scarcely 14,000 residents, but by 1990 there were fifty Japanese families living there. Contractors were building houses on speculation at last, and a real-estate agent was running ads in Japanese in the Bellefontaine *Examiner*.

How come? What was it about Bellefontaine and west-central Ohio that made them so special? Why wasn't there more resentment left over from World War II? It hadn't been that long, after all, since graffiti in the men's room at the motorcycle plant had read:

> Hondas built in Japan, tested in America.
> Atom bombs built in America, tested in Japan.

Most of the good feeling can be attributed to the ten thousand jobs that Honda has provided and the two to three thousand more its Japanese supplier companies have created. Not only do these jobs pay well, but they also seem to offer a high degree of job satisfaction.

John Stockdale's experience is a case in point. A Vietnam

veteran and a UAW shop steward at Rockwell International before hiring on at Honda, he at first had trouble adjusting.

"One of my mentors was a Japanese engineer. He used to walk up behind me. I still have a problem when somebody walks up behind me, but it's worse when it's an Asian who does it. But we talked it out, him and me, and it's not a problem anymore.

"I haven't felt so much a part of a team since I left the military. The Japanese aren't as creative as we are. They don't come up with as many new ideas. But they're lots smarter at taking a new idea and making it better. I don't have trouble keeping busy anymore. At my old job, if they didn't give me enough to do, I went over in a corner and read a book."

The Columbus *Dispatch* sets the agenda for most of central Ohio's smaller newspapers, and the *Dispatch* has been a Honda booster from the start. In 1987 it said in a lead editorial:

> Anyone who might have been skeptical about Honda's commitment to industrial expansion in Ohio may now move to the rear of the class . . . Honda's continued investment here sends a positive signal to other companies who may wish to take advantage of the state's work force and centralized location.

Furthermore, while Honda was creating thousands of new jobs, the town of Norwood, near Cincinnati, was suing General Motors in what it called an alimony proceeding. GM had been Norwood's largest employer, and at GM's request the city had just blocked off some of its streets to create an underpass. When GM announced it was closing its sixty-four-year-old plant, Norwood faced the loss of a quarter of its city budget. Townspeople were wearing black ribbons and armbands. And there had been similar, if less dramatic, shutdowns and demonstrations in other parts of the state.

And so in 1987, when the mayor of Wapakoneta, near
Anna, said he didn't care to do business with the Japanese
because they sank his ship in World War II, he soon became
Wapakoneta's ex-mayor. And in Xenia, when there was a
dispute over whether two sycamores and an aging ash on
the courthouse lawn should be replaced with buckeye or
Japanese snow pear trees, the snow pear trees won out.
When Lima's mayor complained that his city wasn't attracting
Japanese parts suppliers because Lima had unions and too
many black people, he didn't lose his job, but didn't win
many supporters either. And when the Bellefontaine *Examiner* received a rare letter critical of Honda or the Japanese,
it wasn't printed. It is rare anymore to find anyone in central
Ohio willing to criticize Honda. Those who do are usually
challenged.

The Springfield *News*, for example, ran a story in 1988
about the growing number of traffic deaths on Route 33.
William Denihan, Ohio's safety director, blamed them on
"the high number of employees at Honda and the way they
drive." Paying people a bonus to be on time is "counter-
productive," he said, because it "contributes to excessive
speed." (Honda pays a bonus of eighty to a hundred dollars
a month to employees with a perfect attendance record.) "It
would help if Honda would make its incentive program less
lucrative," the *News* editorialized.

The Bellefontaine *Examiner* lashed back in a rare editorial of its own. Rewarding associates for their good work
habits was not the problem, wrote David Wagner. The
problem was the state's slowness in four-laning Route 33.
"My thoroughly German grandmother was fond of the
admonition, 'If it's worth going to, it's worth getting there
on time.' If nowhere else, this ought to apply to one's place
of employment."

Yet none of this quite explains why Bellefontaine, and not
Sidney or Troy or some other town, would become Honda's

community of choice. Some of it had to do with the early creation of a friendship center, some to the initial response from Bellefontaine's school system, but most, perhaps, to the good chemistry that developed between American and Japanese women there.

"When I was growing up, if Mom was happy, the whole family was," said Honda's Susan Insley.

The friendship center was the brainchild of Tom Stout, pastor of the First United Presbyterian Church, and of Robert Carter, the superintendent of schools and one of Stout's ruling elders. They were soon joined by chamber of commerce executive Lee Dorsey and by Marilyn Miller, a veteran school board member. The Bellefontaine *Examiner* was also an early supporter, as were Ken Clark, minister at the Methodist church, and David Moreland, pastor of the Lutheran church.

But it was Marilyn Miller who was the pioneer. Her husband is an internist, and the couple had once lived in Haiti and Egypt as part of a Mennonite commitment to world service. Two of their children had taught English in China, and one was in El Salvador, documenting human rights violations. More of a doer than a talker, Miller volunteered for the center director's job.

She was paid $85 a week, assigned a budget of $12,000, and given a tiny office next to Lee Dorsey's at the chamber of commerce. She enlisted a corps of volunteers that included doctors' wives, lawyers' wives, and a number of former teachers. Most belonged to one of the mainstream churches or were Mennonites, and several were already serving as English tutors.

At first Miller tried to learn Japanese, but soon realized that, at fifty-three, she was too old ever to be very proficient. Besides, what was the point? The Japanese had told her they wanted to learn about America. Miller discovered that if she spoke slowly, and didn't use slang, the Japanese had little trouble understanding her. Their own language might be vague—"yes" didn't necessarily mean "yes," although "maybe" usually meant "no"—but they were skillful at reading her nonverbally, at sensing what was behind the words. Miller met with each wife upon arrival and then matched her with an American mother with children of roughly the same age. Soon each of the Japanese had an American friend who visited her periodically and to whom she could turn for help and advice.

Honda had given each family a handbook on how to behave. The assumption seemed to be that Americans, like Japanese, were all much the same.

> Be sure to write thank you notes on white stationery.
> Married couples say "we" and not "I."
> In the car, the VIP sits in the passenger seat in front.
> Make sure that your children wear different sets of clothes
> to school every day.

Miller found much of the advice impractical. She thought there was too much emphasis on gift giving. Americans helped people because they wanted to, not because they expected something in return. She sensed that what the Japanese women wanted was advice on how to avoid embarrassment. She and others came up with the following:

> Dandelions are not flowers to be admired, but weeds to
> be removed.
> Don't hang futons on balconies or decks to air (to us,
> this looks sloppy).
> Don't lock misbehaving children out of the house until
> they repent (neighbors won't understand).
> Encourage your husband to come home before dark so
> he doesn't have to cut the grass by the beam of his
> car lights.
> Don't let your children urinate outside where neighbors
> can see.

Drawing on experiences of loneliness she had felt when
living in Haiti and Egypt, Miller urged the Japanese women
not to be afraid to do anything an American might do: hire
a baby-sitter, attend a cooking class at the vocational center,
go downtown and have lunch with a friend. She wanted the
Japanese to be as free-spirited as young Mrs. Keiko Hirata.

"My husband wants me to look smart, to keep my Coca-
Cola bottle shape," Mrs. Hirata told me. "That's why I go to
the spa with my friend Cathy [Franklin]. To keep myself
proportioned. But Cathy doesn't go just for her husband's
sake. She goes because the exercise makes her feel good. I
want to be more like Cathy."

Miller succeeded to such a degree in making the Japa-
nese feel at home that three years later, when Koichiro
Shinagawa proposed that he create a family center in Belle-
fontaine like the one in Worthington, the Honda wives said
no. They were happy with things as they were, thank you.
They were delighted that they each had an American friend.
They preferred being able to socialize with the wives of
Japanese women from supplier companies, and not just
Honda wives. If Shinagawa were to create a center just for
them, they feared they might become isolated again.

After Miller resigned as center director (to go to India
with her husband to work for the Mennonites again), Toshi
Amino said in tribute, "We believed everything she told us."
Miller was succeeded by Nancy Saul, a woman twenty years
younger. "If Marilyn was a mother to the Japanese, Nancy
will be a sister," Lee Dorsey said.

Inevitably, there were changes in the way the center was
run. An interpreter was hired, the advisory board expanded
to include a Honda wife and one from AP Technoglass, the
largest Japanese supplier company. As more families moved
in, Saul found herself having to enlist a wider variety of host
families. She was running out of doctors' and lawyers' wives
and volunteers from mainstream churches.

Marianne Kesler is one of these newer hostesses. She

lives with her husband and four sons in a modest frame house near the center of town. Her husband teaches school and is a nondenominational minister who often conducts services at home.

Kesler has not one but two Japanese friends, though she tries not to see them together, she says. The Japanese seem to prefer it that way, since the pattern established had been for each woman to have an American friend all her own. Nor does Kesler plan some special activity when seeing one of her friends, as many of her predecessors had done. Often the woman will drop in for a peanut-butter-and-jelly lunch, or with her children after school. Sometimes she invites Kesler and her children to join her at the Honda plant pool.

Unless asked (and she seldom is), Kesler does not share any of her strongly held religious beliefs. She does, however, make an exception around Halloween, she told me. Japanese children like to dress up in masks and funny costumes, and Japanese parents like to have little children in strange outfits knocking at their door. It makes them feel part of the scene.

"I tell them I don't believe in trick-or-treating," Kesler said. "Our children don't dress up in devil costumes. They never wear masks that have blood dripping from their teeth."

In preparation for the *Examiner*'s Christmas issue, David Wagner recently asked several of the Japanese women if they would pose in kimonos in front of a Christmas tree. The *Examiner* had been running many pictures and stories about the Japanese, all sympathetic, most of them on page one: stories about plant expansions, pictures of women performing tea ceremonies, a photograph of Japanese children boarding a city school bus donated to drive them to Saturday school in Columbus. The Japanese had always cooperated before.

But this time there was hesitation, and silence, which by now Wagner knew meant something. Finally there was a tentative "yes, if . . ." Mrs. Keiko Namika said she would be happy to have her picture taken if she didn't have to wear a kimono. Kimonos took such a long time to put on, and not many women wore them anymore.

The picture that appeared, in color and on page one, was of Mrs. Namika, one of Marianne Kesler's friends. Her four small children were decorating the tree with folded paper ornaments. Their mother was wearing blue jeans and a red sweat shirt.

Bellefontaine's was the first school system in Ohio to hire a full-time person to teach English as a second language to the Japanese.

"We wanted someone straitlaced and structured, not a touchy-feely type," said Charles Kern, the assistant superintendent for curriculum.

Kern, like his boss, Bob Carter, had been to Japan as a guest of the Honda Foundation. One thing he learned was that Japanese boys are "pushed by Mom, doted on by Mom, usually almost spoiled by Mom." Another was that Japanese students have to study much harder, longer, and more intensely than American students do. After their regular school, most attend a cram school called *juku*. The last kind of teacher a young Japanese would need, Kern felt, would be someone "big on personality, but light on substance."

Kern is a structured, demanding sort of person himself. His parents are German-Americans, and he grew up in Cincinnati's "over-the-Rhine" district. The burnings of German-language books during World War I left scars that affected him and his family, as they did thousands of others of Ohio's German-Americans. It made them warier and more anxious to assimilate. Kern sees parallels between Ohio's German-Americans and the Honda Japanese who have come. Both are hardworking and resilient. Both believe the woman's place is in the home, taking care of the children. Both tend to overcompensate for some real or imagined deficiency.

The person Kern chose to be Bellefontaine's teacher of English as a second language was Susan Fisher. A native of Toledo, Fisher had spent four years teaching in New Zealand and was already tutoring several of the Japanese.

On a typical day, she gives English lessons to twenty-five children—one, two, sometimes four at a time. Her instruction is individualized, aimed not just at passing along words and phrases, but at how to cope. She teaches survival words: "recess, rest room, raise your hand, paper, pencil, slide, swings, jungle gym." Then she preteaches American holidays, so when Thanksgiving, Christmas, or Martin Luther King Day come around, they won't seem so strange. The younger the children, the quicker they learn, of course. But, regardless of age, Fisher says it often takes months, and sometimes longer, before Japanese children will ask a question, or volunteer something personal about themselves.

A part of her job is to brief other teachers on what to expect when a Japanese child enters the classroom. She notes that much of what we communicate is nonverbal. A student who comes late to class, sits in the back row, and never opens his mouth is still communicating. Many won't participate or put their hands up voluntarily, but will respond only when invited. They come from a culture where participation has to be initiated by the teacher. Some will not respond unless they are certain they know the right answer, since an incorrect answer means losing face. Some may nod their heads to signify "Yes, I know you are talking to me." But this does not necessarily mean "Yes, I understand." Some may smile when they don't agree or even when reprimanded. In their culture, a smile is a gesture of respect.

"In Japan, students are used to 'eating facts' to pass their examinations, to memorizing answers instead of coming up with ideas," says Fisher. "Just making conversation is hard for them. It's more than shyness or an inability to use the language well. It's a discomfort with spontaneity.

"When you ask an American child a question, we're told

that the average response time is three to five seconds. With a Japanese child, I've waited as long as a minute or more. They think about what they are going to say, translate, form, and organize it, then often scribe it on their hand—all before opening their mouths."

Fisher is careful not to give homework on Thursday or Friday for Monday because she knows the Japanese have stiff lessons to prepare for their Saturday school. She also consults with the private tutors their mothers engage. Some Japanese children have as many as five American tutors.

"In my mind," says Fisher, "I applaud when I see the girls curl their hair, apply lipstick, put on some jewelry— when I see them start to exercise a little independence. But I try not to say anything. I know if they change too much, they'll have a hard time when they go back to Japan."

At first Fisher called on each new mother, but that responsibility was soon taken over by the friendship center. Now she makes house calls only when there's a problem. And rather than drop in as she might with an American parent, she calls ahead or writes a note. She has found Japanese mothers to be more in awe of teachers than American mothers are, more anxious to impress. A cup of green tea always appears unsolicited, accompanied by special cookies or cakes.

Often the student has to act as interpreter for his or her mother, and this is sometimes hard on the mother. She always tries to cooperate, however. When it's hardest is when she is urged to have her child take some special initiative, to do something the regular teacher hasn't assigned. If the regular teacher is satisfied, the mother will question the wisdom of doing something out of the ordinary. She doesn't want her child to be different. She wants him or her to blend in.

Joe Vicario is a senior-high English teacher and former president of the local railroad workers' union. He has been a schoolteacher for thirty years and a Bellefontaine city

councilman for sixteen. He and Susan Fisher regularly
consult. Vicario says that at first the Japanese waited after
class every day until the American students had left the
room. Then they came up to his desk, thanked him, and
bowed deeply. Vicario had been instructed to bow in return—
although not so deeply, or the Japanese would be offended,
since they hold teachers in high regard. Vicario told me the
Japanese soon learned that they didn't need to bow to him.

"They are great at minding their own business," he said.
"There's never a discipline problem. They're not pushy in
any way."

Neither Vicario nor anyone else seems to see a doubling
or tripling of Bellefontaine's Japanese population as likely
to cause a problem. Japanese children account for less than
3 percent of the students, and though a disproportionate
number of them have been placed in gifted and enrichment
programs, most people see them as effective role models.

Listen to R. A. "Dutch" Wilde. He is the volunteer tennis
instructor at Mary Rutan Park. Every summer day a dozen
Japanese children, usually accompanied by their mothers,
show up for instruction.

"They're more intense than the American kids, more
focused," says Wilde. "They come to the courts more often,
and don't always have to compete. They get as much
satisfaction out of just practicing."

Others have been equally impressed.

"When I'm with my Japanese friend, time slows down,"
says Deb Ellis, responsible for school enrichment programs.
I ask what she means, and she says she isn't sure. She has to
think for a moment. Finally she says, "Maybe it's because I
can't speak Japanese and my friend can't speak English very
well that we communicate at a deeper level. We take walks.
We do things with our children together."

Wendy McVicker put it another way:

"They still value mothering, and this is refreshing to
me, a full-time mother in a society that doesn't seem to see

the point of mothers anymore. Tomoko was someone I could be with with my boisterous boys and not be constantly worrying that they were too loud or energetic. When I'm out with my children, I sometimes feel like someone with an unmentionable disease. The great thing about Tomoko was that she accepted children with all their chaos.

"Americans are so goal-oriented, so caught up in résumé building. We don't take time to appreciate life as it is. The Japanese notice so much. They pay attention to all the little things."

I didn't really understand what these Americans were talking about until I spent time with some of the Japanese women myself. I discovered that their children were always with them, the boys clamoring for attention, the girls turned out in bright dresses and headbands. Most lived in new houses with big yards in the northeast part of town, within walking distance of the park. And many ordered several varieties of fresh fish and special rice from the Noble Fish Company in Shaker Heights, Ohio, which made bimonthly deliveries. They all enjoyed talking about differences between their country and ours.

"Here I can wear anything I want," said young Mrs. Hirata. "I can wear clothes to emphasize my positive parts. In Japan, I have to stay fully covered. Nothing stands out."

"In Japan, the boys play with the boys, the girls with the girls," said Mrs. Saeko Hirano. "In America, the boys and girls play together. Even teenagers play hide-and-seek together. American children grow up slower, and I think that is good. The shy child does better here. American teachers are so encouraging. They praise even when what the child does is not exactly in the lesson. In Japan, it's always do this and do that."

"American women have freer minds," added Mrs. Yasuko Tsukamoto. "Japanese women grow up with so many traditions that hem them in. American women have jobs, have opinions, have their own way of living. And their husbands help them so much. They help with the children, go shopping with them, work in the yard. Japanese husbands don't have the time to do any of this."

"In Japan, our houses are so small, so cluttered and messy, sometimes our children, they write on the walls," said Mrs. Atsuko Hirobe. "But at least we don't let them watch television so much or make them stay downstairs in a dark place like a family room. We don't give them money for performing simple chores."

The Japanese women, I found, are drawn to clean streets and well-kept cemeteries, put off by too much food coloring and overfriendly teachers who insist on touching their children. They delight in one-on-one contact with Americans, but don't like to be taken along to large parties, where they feel as if they are on display.

Leaving one Japanese home, I discovered that it is Japanese custom to wave until the departing guest is out of sight. We waved goodbye from the porch step, from the driveway, from the street in front of her house. Looking back through my rearview mirror, I could see that this woman was still waving. I nearly ran into a tree.

Bellefontaine's experience with Honda and its supplier companies has been so positive that even the newspaper—once fearful of killing the goose laying the golden egg—has relaxed its policy of never saying anything that could be construed as negative about Japan and the Japanese. When Hirohito died, for example, the *Examiner*'s headline read: "Emperor Hirohito Succumbs at 87; Shadow of Dark Years Remained." More recently, the paper ran a front-page story about the growing incidence of *karoshi*, or early death from overwork, in Japan. At a recent workshop held at the vocational school for Americans desirous of working closer with the Japanese, a cartoon booklet titled *"Salaryman" in Japan* was given to participants.

Published by the Japan Travel Bureau, it notes that

" 'salaryman' is a word coined in Japan used to refer to all white collar workers. Salarymen are the driving force behind Japan's phenomenal postwar economic growth . . ." The salaryman works eighty hours a week, dresses like all other salarymen, thinks of his company as number one, when not working tries to play golf as often as possible, and uses holidays to catch up on his sleep.

You might think that after losing the railroad, radar base, and Westinghouse and Rockwell plants, Bellefontaine might be wary, but I found this seldom the case.

"Yes, there may be another fallout in the auto industry," said Lee Dorsey. "And yes, the plants around here could be affected. But we think Honda will be affected less than the others. The Honda people are always thinking several years down the road."

Car dealers have started calling their employees "associates." Doctors and dentists see people at night and on weekends now, since fewer of their patients are asking for time off work during the day. Clinics are paying more attention to back problems.

"I lost two of my best young people to Honda and learned from that," said Frieda Taylor, the owner of Gillespie Oil. "Even for assembly-line jobs, they want to know about the spouse. The spouse is the one who makes sure the worker gets up on time. Honda doesn't have near the absenteeism the rest of us have. Westinghouse pulled out, they told us, because they had the highest absentee rate in the country."

"I have many Honda people who come see me," adds Art Costin, M.D., a specialist in industrial medicine who took over the practice from his father. "They come with a broken leg or a back problem, and I get on the phone to Marsha Norman, the troubleshooter out there. Together we find a way to get the injured person right back on the job—back in some less strenuous activity he can do until he heals. Honda is very flexible that way, very unique. They don't want anyone to miss work.

"Do you think most of our other companies do this? No. Not even those without unions. They insist the employee be 100 percent before letting him come back to work.

"It's the same with carpal tunnel syndrome [wrist injuries from repetitive job motion]. Honda wants to know everything it can find out. Most of our other companies pretend the problem doesn't exist."

The old Rockwell plant sits behind a rusty chain-link fence in the northwest part of town. The paint has faded, its walls have a chalky look, and the parking lot has tufts of grass poking up through the cracks. Honda didn't elect to use this or any other empty or abandoned buildings when it came to Logan County. Instead, it built its own buildings and bought rather than leased the land.

For a place with lots of railroad tracks but few trains anymore, Bellefontaine and the Japanese seem to have struck a mutually advantageous partnership. As Mrs. Tsukamoto said, "The information about America is very misleading. It's about life on the East and West coasts, but not about life in the center. There are many stories about homosexuals and drugs and missing children—about America's not being safe anymore. But here people do not lock their doors when they go out. They do not even close their garage doors."

14

Settling In

In its impact, Toyota bashing can be equal to Japan bashing. We have to be very careful. Some things are permitted to smaller companies that are not permitted to Toyota—not just in the United States, but here in Japan as well.
> —Tsutomu Ohshima, executive vice-president, Toyota Motor Corporation, in an interview with the author, November 1988

After the furor caused by the unsuccessful attempt to build its plant nonunion and the flap over its incentive package had died down, Toyota tried to do everything right. It hired Kentuckians from each of the state's 120 counties, and more people from the minority population than the statewide average. It donated a million dollars so the city of Georgetown could have a community center. It announced it would create a day-care center for its employees. It encouraged the University of Kentucky to do another impact study. And when the time came for it to announce it was building its first car plant in Europe (in Burnaston, England), it made sure everyone knew that this time there was no incentive package involved.

"Welcome to the spirit of *kaizen*, the restless search for a better way—the Asian counterpart to American ingenuity," a company spokesman said.

Timed to coincide with the dedication of its Georgetown

plant, Toyota ran a nationwide series of magazine and
newspaper advertisements. Their aim was to show that
Toyota was moving ahead with America.

The lead ad showed a sensitive-looking young man
wearing a button-down shirt that carried the distinctive Polo
label. The copy read:

> Maybe he could have moved away to some big city
> somewhere and got a chance that way. But he didn't
> want to move.
>
> "I was born and raised in Lexington, Kentucky," [he
> is saying]. "And this is home. This is where I want to
> stay. I got a college degree in 1985, a B.A. in marketing,
> but there were no jobs. None that would give me a
> future."
>
> But then Toyota arrived.
>
> When we started hiring, he deluged us with five
> separate applications. That's how badly he wanted to
> work with us. When we finally met him, we were im-
> pressed with his drive. "My name's Rob Wehrle," he said.
> "And I'll take anything you've got. Just give me a chance.
> Let me show what I can do."

A second ad showed a man twenty years older. He is tanned,
muscular, neatly turned out in Toyota khaki and blue.

> "Listen, guys, I've got nothing to offer you."
>
> That's what Roger Lewis said when we first asked
> him to be inspection manager of our new auto plant in
> Georgetown, Kentucky—our master of quality control.
> He had years of experience in the auto industry, and a
> history of creative thinking. We knew he was our man.
> But he wasn't so sure.
>
> "When it comes to quality," he said, "I can't come
> close to what you do." He knew how good we were . . .
> he had been examining cars for years . . .
>
> "We're pretty good," we told him. "We admit that.

But you're pretty good, too. You've got things that we
don't have. What would happen if you—and others like
you—got together with us?"

A third ad showed a big door opening to reveal a glistening
white Camry.

This door leads to a different world.

It's one of the doors to our new billion dollar
automotive plant in Georgetown, Kentucky, just outside
of Lexington . . . The people in that world are mostly
Americans. They're independent, creative, impatient for
progress. But we're using techniques and thought pro-
cesses that were developed in another world—one driven
by patience, persistence and dependence on the group.

It makes for a nice mix: our American side teaching
our Japanese side how to step back, let go and fly with
big new ideas: while our Japanese side teaches our
American side how to slow down, focus and make those
ideas work . . .

Our business is making the best of both worlds.

Inspired by Alex Warren, the ads were one of several
initiatives launched in the spring, summer, and early fall of
1988 aimed at putting to rest all the bitterness and bad
publicity that seemed to have plagued Toyota in Kentucky
from the start.

Earlier, *The Wall Street Journal* had questioned Toyota's
practice of requiring hopefuls for entry-level jobs to take
fourteen hours of paper-and-pencil tests. "That's tremendous overkill," one consultant was quoted. Kentuckians had
been equally critical. Newspaper stories cited the batteries
of tests and complicated screening techniques and noted that
fewer than half of all Kentuckians had a high-school diploma
or its GED equivalent. The Louisville *Courier-Journal* reported that of 108,000 persons inquiring about jobs at
Toyota, fewer than half filled out an application form and

far fewer still took the required aptitude and dexterity tests. Of these, only 8,000 scored high enough to enter the assessment center at Kentucky State University in Frankfort.

Lexington and Louisville newspapers were far more aggressive and questioning than the Nashville *Tennessean* or *Banner*, or the Columbus, Ohio, *Dispatch* had been. Perhaps because of this, and the example these newspapers set, everything Toyota did still provoked the most intense scrutiny. When Toyoda Support Services of Fullerton, California, bought Georgetown's eighteen-hole country club, and a spokesman for Toyota Motor Manufacturing asserted there was no connection between the two companies, Kentucky newspapers were disbelieving. When the FBI dared to buy five Toyota Corollas for its agents to use, it was front-page news in *The New York Times*. And when *The Wall Street Journal* did another front-page story about the diminishing number of horse farms in the Kentucky Blue Grass, Toyota came in for a disproportionate share of the blame:

> Suddenly one farmer after another is selling or developing prime agricultural land that had been in families for generations. The buyers, for the most part, are real-estate developers, Japanese industrialists, and other latter-day carpetbaggers bent on making a fast buck.

Meanwhile, no one was saying anything bad about Honda.

Forbes magazine had published a cover story in January 1986 comparing Honda's auto plant near Marysville to American Motors' (now Chrysler's) Jeep plant in Toledo:

> Each plant builds roughly the same number of vehicles, but Jeep has twice as many workers . . . Both use enormous stamping machines to bend thin sheets of steel into side panels, hoods and trunk lids. But while at Honda the machines can change dies in minutes, that changeover at Jeep takes several hours . . . Honda spends

four per cent of its sales dollars on research and development; American Motors, only one per cent.

Business Week followed in April 1988 with a second cover story called "The Americanization of Honda." Pegged to the export of Ohio-made Accords back to Japan, the article made Honda seem as American as the Big Three.

It didn't seem fair. Toyota was Japan's leading car company, Honda a distant third or fourth. Toyota's initial investment in Kentucky was $800 million, Honda's in Ohio only $35 million. Toyota had gone out of its way to reassure the NAACP that it would hire plenty of blacks; Honda had a miserable record in minority hires.

"One advantage to coming last," Alex Warren told me, "is that Honda and Nissan have taught American parts suppliers what to expect. They have broken them in. A disadvantage is that our cars aren't as well known here, here in the heartland where the Big Three are strongest, too." Another disadvantage was that Toyota didn't have a charismatic leader like Shoichiro Irimajiri or Marvin Runyon with whom Americans could identify.

Conscious of the need to buttress its image, Toyota took the unusual step of holding a "first test car built" ceremony, even before its plant was dedicated. Team member John Wilson drove one of the eighty-five test cars, a shiny white Camry, through a huge paper curtain onto a blue-draped stage. Manufacturing president Kusunoki then announced that Georgetown was still in the running as site for Toyota's first American truck plant.

Two months later, in a gala four-day celebration, the auto plant was dedicated. On one day there was an open house for Georgetown and Scott County, which six thousand attended; on the next, an open house for all Kentuckians, which drew seventy thousand.

At the VIP ceremony, Lexington's philharmonic performed, and Martha Layne Collins and Greg Newby, a young

black speaking for team members, received standing ova-
tions. Collins told employees, "You've been everything I told
Toyota you would be." Newby said that after graduating
from high school, he had held two jobs and had been
unchallenged by both. Then along came Toyota. Toyota had
given him the opportunity to feel challenged. "Who could
ask for anything more?"

Fujio Cho, Warren's boss (and soon to be named CEO
of the Georgetown plant as well as a member of Toyota's
board of directors in Japan), then presented Georgetown's
mayor Tom Prather with ten new white Camrys. "You decide
how best to use them," Cho said.

But there were still complications.

Wallace Wilkinson, Collins's successor, had come to the
ceremony and said all the right things. But he had won the
governorship by campaigning against Toyota's incentive
package. He had said Kentucky was being "laughed at from
Tennessee to Tokyo," and that before giving away as much
as Collins had, he would have told Toyota to take its plant
elsewhere. Toyota wanted to believe that Wilkinson's statements had been campaign rhetoric. But a year had passed,
and Wilkinson still hadn't visited Japan.

Meanwhile, another University of Kentucky impact
study was released. It showed Scott County residents to be
even more disenchanted than before. Few found fault with
the Japanese as individuals—they were seen as hardworking,
family-oriented, and religious—but nearly 40 percent
thought Toyota might work its employees too hard, up from
just 12 percent the year before. Besides, tractor-trailers still
rumbled down Main Street. The question of whether the
bypass would be built around Georgetown was unresolved.
And Bill Hays, a member of the planning commission, was
refusing to vote anything more for Toyota until "somebody
does something about the belt line." Then, too, the UAW
had opened an office in a shopping center east of town. And
the *Herald-Leader* had run a cartoon that showed a sinking

battleship called the USS *Competitive Edge*, which looked suspiciously like the USS *Arizona*. It was being bombed by Japanese FSX fighter planes, and somebody on the ship's bridge was saying, "I knew they looked familiar. Didn't we help build them?"

In Japan, Toyota has the most elaborate dealer network, and the company vowed to replicate the best parts of that system over here—to give American dealers the technical assistance that Big Three companies couldn't do or hadn't done, to recruit black dealers, and to pay special attention to women. Recognizing that in the United States two thirds of new car purchases are made or influenced by women, Toyota saw women as deserving of particular attention.

John Miller is the only son of a man who spent a lifetime working on a Big Three assembly line. Today the son raises Thoroughbred horses and owns Toyota of Frankfort, the Kentucky dealership of which Toyota is proudest. Here are some of the reasons:

Miller's salesmen have their commissions reduced if there are any subsequent customer complaints. He gets his parts overnight from a distributor in Cincinnati. He has a drive-through oil change, and if other servicing requires more than an hour or two, he provides van service to downtown Frankfort and to Lexington, twenty-eight miles away. Each month, his people conduct a two-and-a-half-hour seminar for his new-car purchasers at which nothing is sold or promoted. Most attendees are women. Many have had bad experiences with mechanics who say, "Don't worry, honey, I'll take care of it," then present them with a three-hundred-dollar bill for repairs. The women learn how to change a tire, check the oil, and tell what could be wrong if there's a popping noise from the exhaust pipe or a clicking sound in the engine compartment.

J. D. Power and Associates, the authoritative automotive consultant, predicts that as the American car market becomes increasingly ever more competitive, customer service will be crucial.

In 1989 Tom Prather would win reelection as mayor of Georgetown, first in a tightly contested primary and then overwhelmingly in the general election, thus ensuring continuity in friendly local leadership. Still, Toyota would opt to consolidate rather than further expand.

It would concentrate on doing what it does best: building flawless automobiles. The line speed is slower and the layout appears to be simpler than at Nissan and Honda. And as at NUMMI, the Georgetown plant is a clone of a plant in Japan, in this case the Tsutsumi plant in Toyota City. Georgetown is assembling the Camry; Tsutsumi is assembling the Camry. The machinery is said to be the same, and the plant layout, too. It has been easy to train Kentuckians at Tsutsumi, then return them to Georgetown to work on the same equipment. The Camry is scheduled for a model change, but not for another year. Meanwhile, some two hundred Japanese are on hand to ensure that by then the Americans are totally indoctrinated.

Toyota has sixty Japanese permanently assigned in Georgetown (on three-year tours), plus two hundred to three hundred more on temporary duty. Plant president Cho says he expects to reduce the number of permanents to forty within two to three years.

Before announcing further plant expansions, Toyota seemed to be waiting to see what happened with the UAW's organizing campaign at Nissan, for the election of a new Kentucky governor.

Toyota had learned to be cautious. Robert Cobie, plant manager of AP Technoglass in Bellefontaine, Ohio, sells glass to both Honda and Toyota. Comparing the two recently, he said that when Toyota representatives come to call, there are always two people to deal with, one who presumably double-checks the other. With Honda, he says, there is invariably only one. Honda is in more of a hurry. Its philosophy is if an associate makes a mistake, he will learn faster—and probably not make it again.

Honda's more hurried approach would later get the company into some trouble. Toyota prides itself on never dropping a U.S. supplier once the two companies agree to do business. Honda's haste has occasionally resulted in a poor initial choice. Many in the national news media are looking for any chink in the Japanese armor, and the public relations fallout can be painful if a U.S. supplier is let go. Honda has had to learn that.

"For a Japanese company to take risks, the confidence has to be there," Carroll Knicely, Governor Collins's commerce secretary, told me in speaking about Toyota. "With the Japanese, decisions are made 75 percent on the basis of personal knowledge and trust, only 25 percent on business considerations."

15

Rolling the Dice

The difference between this campaign and other
UAW campaigns I've seen is that this one doesn't
have an issue.
                        —Jerry Benefield, May 1989

When the UAW filed for a representation election at Nissan,
the union claimed it had a clear majority of the company's
2,400 workers. Not the 70 percent it likes to have (since
there is invariably attrition between filing date and election),
nor the 60 to 65 percent Jim Turner had predicted it would
have—but a clear majority nonetheless.

Turner had known he had only a short time to live but
was refusing to quit; he kept insisting that his cancer was in
remission. He had known, too, that his in-plant organizing
committee was burning out; its members had been pressing
him to hold an election for months. Night-shift workers in
trim and chassis had made their own pro-union T-shirts,
after Turner advised them not to. They would become too
readily identifiable, would lose their effectiveness, he told
them. But they wouldn't listen.

Turner hadn't filed for an election yet because he had
hoped to get more cards signed—and because Solidarity
House in Detroit, its attention diverted, was engaged in a
war of its own. A radical group called New Directions
contended that the UAW had lost its way by becoming too
cozy with management. Worse: Victor Reuther, brother of

former UAW president Walter Reuther, had aligned himself
with the dissidents. Reuther had been quoted as saying that
if *he* were a Nissan employee, he would *not* vote for the
union.

Still, because Turner knew time was running out, he
went over the head of his boss, Ben Perkins, to Steve Yokich,
then head of organizing. Perkins had been arguing that not
only would the union lose, but it could lose big. The
company's failure to lay off when it had inventory problems
had hurt organizing efforts. So had Benefield's drumbeat of
announcements about future plant expansions. Perkins was
arguing against filing; Yokich was more receptive.

Yokich came to Smyrna and saw for himself the shape
the in-plant organizing committee was in—and how sick
Turner was, Turner who had led the drive to organize
Nissan from the start. If the union were to lose big, New
Directions and Victor Reuther would have to take some of
the blame. And if anyone could still rally the troops, it was
Turner. Yokich felt the union owed it to him to file.

And so Yokich told members of the in-plant organizing
committee, in Turner's presence, that if they got 168 more
signed cards, the UAW would file for its election. Privately,
he told Turner that even if they didn't get all 168 cards, he
should file anyway.

In fact, the union had little choice. Bulldozers were
already moving dirt for the first of Benefield's plant expansions. And because of the screening Nissan does of prospec-
tive job applicants, new employees would be harder to
organize than the old. The union didn't expect to win this
first election, anyway, I'd been told; it expected to do well,
but not win. Seldom does the UAW win a first election in a
plant with more than five hundred workers. Invariably it
takes a second effort, and often a third. By then company
promises made in the heat of the organizing campaign
haven't been fulfilled, and a sense of disillusionment has
set in.

News of the Yokich meeting leaked, and on April 28 *The New York Times* ran a front-page story saying the election was imminent. It would be the most important test to date of whether *all* the leading Japanese auto makers could remain nonunion—a classic confrontation. Besides, if *The New York Times* said it, it had to be true. Within three days, union headquarters in Smyrna received more than two hundred media inquiries. There could be no turning back.

Meanwhile, Jim Turner died, and Ben Perkins came in to run the campaign. The committee got fewer than half the 168 cards Yokich had challenged it to get. But on May 18 Perkins went ahead and filed for an election anyway.

Perkins is a forty-six-year-old black from West Virginia who in his younger days had helped organize an Army tank plant there. Smooth and articulate, he moved to Detroit and soon became the youngest staff member at Solidarity House. There he remained, moving up through civil rights and training departments until he became number two in national organizing under Steve Yokich.

Nissan's strategy was to have the election held as soon as possible, before the annual two-week summer shutdown, traditionally timed to include the Fourth of July. The union's strategy, which prevailed, was to hold the election on July 26–27, after the shutdown. Not only would this give organizers more time to make house calls, but the professionals among them could attend the UAW's triennial convention, being held in Anaheim, California, in mid-June. Their votes might be needed to neutralize the threat from radical dissidents there.

Perkins brought with him to Smyrna thirty professional organizers, five times the number involved in the Honda campaign. They made house calls in tandem with members of the in-plant organizing committee, with the locals wearing Nissan T-shirts so they would be immediately recognized. The locals answered questions on plant problems, the professionals on technical and larger issues. Perkins targeted 1,700 of the 2,400 in the potential bargaining unit for house calls, starting with the marginals, he said, then moving on to the hard-core company people. Only the 30 percent the union was absolutely sure of would go uncontacted.

The union led with the issue of plant safety. It contended that Nissan, by increasing its line speed and failing to observe proper precautions, had caused multiple injuries. It then scored a public relations bonanza when four pro-union employees demanded that the company release OSHA 200 logs, which contain a record of *all* injuries by name, date, and type—not just those resulting in a loss of eight or more workdays. The company refused, claiming that disclosure would violate its employees' privacy. But Tennessee's Occupational Health and Safety Administration disagreed and fined the company $5,000 for noncompliance. Nissan then appealed the ruling, a move that kept the logs sealed until after the election. The union contended, and most observers seemed to agree, that had this information been made public, Nissan's injury rate would have been much higher than what the company claimed. By mid-1992, the ruling was still being appealed.

Weeks before the election was held, Nissan held a news conference to announce that it would stop talking to the media until after the election (eight and a half weeks later, as it turned out). This decision was made against the advice of Nissan's public relations firm, which was owned by Sue Atkinson, Marvin Runyon's wife.

"We are going through a sensitive time," said Gail Neuman, the company's general counsel and vice-president for human resources. "It is important for us to concentrate our communications directly to our employees. The organizing campaign has caused disruption on the plant floor. Pro-union employees are refusing to help other workers unless they sign union cards."

Queried about the OSHA 200 logs, she said, "We will do whatever is necessary to comply with the law. Meanwhile,

we will be attempting to guard our employees' privacy."
(Members of the anti-union committee had cooperated by
filing suit against Nissan in an attempt to ensure that medical
records contained in the logs remained confidential.)

Asked why Nissan contracted out easy jobs rather than
giving them to workers with physical disabilities, Neuman
said, "We are committed to *never* [emphasis added] laying
off an employee. We work very, very hard on that issue. We
think that the maintenance buffer is a good one for us to
have. Notwithstanding that we have maintenance contracted
out, the fact is we do have many light jobs in the plant. We
frequently accommodate workers with restrictions because
of injuries."

Asked whether, if the union won the election, Nissan
would cut back on its expansion plans, she hedged.

"If our environment were to change in such a way that
we were unable to remain competitive, then, of course, we
would have to reassess investment plans. But that wouldn't
necessarily be the case, even if a union were elected here."

The OSHA 200 controversy had sparked a spate of pro-
union news stories. Even the pro-company Murfreesboro
Daily News Journal carried a page-one headline: "Refusal on
OSHA Logs Aiding UAW." *Business Week* gave nearly two
pages to the story. The bulk of it was devoted to worker
claims of grueling work pace, of supervisors telling assem-
blers to restrict their liquid intake, and to claims by a union
doctor that one in five Nissan workers had suffered an injury
in 1988. *The New York Times, The Wall Street Journal,* and CBS
News all predicted that the election would be close.

Ironically, the national media attention and pro-union
stories may have helped more than hurt the company. Nissan
had long contended that the union, not the company, was
the outsider—even though company headquarters was seven
thousand miles away. Nissan portrayed the union—on the
defensive because of declining membership—as more concerned with its national reputation than with legitimate

employee concerns. Layoffs and plant closings at GM were a continuing story on in-plant television monitors. So, too, was Victor Reuther's statement that if he were a Nissan employee, he wouldn't vote for the union. The company had had to park thousands of cars and new trucks on cornfields and cow pastures around Smyrna, but not a single technician, or even temporary worker, had been laid off. Nissan's message was that it was the company, not the union, that could guarantee job security.

In the months before the election—while the union was still agonizing over what to do—Nissan had been conducting focus group sessions with randomly selected employees that were aimed at exploring the single issue of worker-related injuries. By then it was obvious this would be the union's main campaign issue. The company wanted to know what employee perceptions were. Which were real? Which imaginary? Did workers really want team members without visible injuries to be given special preference? Should they be allowed not to have to rotate through the tougher jobs? What was fair?

Meanwhile, the anti-union committee was distributing buttons that read "Nissan, Love It or Leave It" and waving American flags during demonstrations at plant gates. Flyers reproduced headlines and news stories about Volkswagen, Mazda, and Chrysler:

> "VW Shuts Plant as Similar Cars Cut into Market"—Look what the UAW did for them.
> "The high number of injuries among workers at Mazda in Michigan raises fundamental questions"—Look what the UAW did for them.
> "OSHA fines Chrysler $1.5 million; largest penalty ever"—Where was the UAW's health and safety committee?

During the two weeks before shutdown and for a week thereafter, the company conducted roundtable discussions (the union called them "captive-audience sessions") for more than two thirds of its work force—for everyone, Gail Neuman told me later, except "the several dozen" known to be outspokenly pro-union. Employees were brought together in groups of twelve to fifteen, and seemingly selected at random (seldom with more than one person from any given team or unit). Certain employees were invited to attend more than once; all were shown a video, then urged to ask questions of the company representative there.

"If in the election next week, 1,201 workers vote for the union and 1,199 vote against, all 2,400 technicians will be represented by the union," the voice on the video intoned. "Even though Tennessee has a right-to-work law, the union would still represent all the employees . . . And you'd better believe that you're not likely to get much service from the union unless you're paying two hours' pay in union dues every month. You can't sit on the sidelines and say this election won't affect you."

This was the preamble, aimed at getting out the vote. Then came the sell.

"We've said from the beginning we didn't want a union. We're not friendly with the UAW like the Big Three auto makers have been. We didn't invite the UAW to organize our employees like NUMMI and Mazda did . . .

"So at Nissan you start knowing the company will not be easy in bargaining. You must also recognize that if Nissan employees voted for a union you will be sending a clear message to Nissan management. That message will be that Nissan employees prefer to be treated like UAW members. No more the one team with Nissan but two teams, the management team and the union team. Nissan employees would be telling management that they like the UAW's layoff policy better than they like Nissan's job security policy. It would be sending other messages to management about issues such as wages, benefits, and job rotation . . .

"This is a very important point. In negotiations, the union doesn't simply get to say we want to keep what we like and change what we don't like. All issues—the good as well as the bad—are put on the table.

"So start with a blank piece of paper."

Ben Perkins told me the blank piece of paper statement and what came next, the assertion that union members laid off at GM might well be given preference for jobs at Nissan, gave him the most grief. GM's Saturn plant was being built thirty miles away. There, laid-off union members were being given first hiring preference. Nissan was saying the same thing could happen at Smyrna.

"Filling two thousand new jobs [at Nissan]," the voice on the video went on, "hopefully with laid-off UAW members, instead of with your fellow Tennesseans, would be another important issue for the UAW. You must believe that laid-off GM and Ford workers with years of seniority with the UAW are a lot more important to the union than you are."

Finally the video voice turned to strikes and strike violence.

"Union organizers have told you a strike at Nissan would be very unlikely. In one of their handbills, they said that companies talk about strikes just to scare employees and that you shouldn't be concerned.

"[However,] that's a little different from what Owen Bieber is saying these days. At the UAW convention in California, just before shutdown, here's what Mr. Bieber had to say about strikes:

" 'Let me point out there are 817 occasions over the past three years that we have authorized strikes to obtain justice and fair treatment for our members.' "

Examples of strike violence in Toledo, Kansas City, Cleveland, and Hartford were cited.

Plant posters then hammered home the same message. "UAW Strikes: A Fact of Life," one title read. Underneath were newspaper headlines: "Skinned Dog Discovered Hanged near Picket Line"—Memphis *Press-Scimitar*; "Police Think Gunfire Related to Strike"—Springfield, Missouri, *Leader and Press*; "Sheriff's Deputies Clash with Strikers"— Gannett News Service.

Another plant poster entitled "Regardless of What the Union Says: This Is the Law" highlighted the quote: "Collective bargaining is potentially hazardous and as a result of such negotiations employees might possibly wind up with less benefits than before."

During shutdown, the company sent copies of the *Nissan News* to employees' homes. Inside were pictures and profiles of employees who had been union members before coming to Nissan and had bad experiences to tell. Also included was a list of questions to ask organizers:

How many UAW members have lost their jobs due to plant closing, layoffs, etc., since 1979?

How much money would the UAW hope to collect from Nissan employees if the union were to win the election on July 26–27?

Do UAW employees at GM, Ford, or Chrysler have leased vehicle programs? Why not?

Why do NUMMI employees, who are represented by the UAW, say their jobs are like "eight hours of calisthenics"?

Included, too, were stickers showing the UAW emblem with the Ghostbuster slash across it. "UAW Agents Respect My Privacy. Keep Away," the stickers said. Employees were urged to place these stickers on their doors and windows.

Outgunned, the union attempted to strike back. Informal polls showed its support to be waning. Cards signed when

the company was having inventory problems, and there was
a fear of layoffs, were proving worthless. Turner, unwilling
to admit he was dying, had failed to develop a strong second-
in-command.

Five days before the election, Perkins claimed to have
made thirteen hundred house calls, and said he would
complete the remaining four hundred before the vote was
taken. On July 23 he sent to black employees a letter from
the NAACP's Benjamin Hooks urging union support, then
a flyer to women employees purporting to show that women
were more likely to suffer injuries than men. In the final
days of the campaign the union contended that Nissan's
wage and benefits package was below that of the Big Three
auto makers. But in Tennessee, where the cost of living is
lower than in the North, it was an argument that didn't take.
The union then purchased thirty minutes on Nashville's
Channel 30, a Fox station, in an attempt to neutralize what
it called Nissan's disinformation campaign. It attacked the
form all employees are required to sign before being hired.
"I understand that my employment . . . is subject to such
rules, regulations, and personnel practices and policies, and
changes therein, as my employer may from time to time
adopt." The union said that unless the workers organized,
the company could do whatever it wanted, whenever it
wanted. Finally, even *kaizen*, the sacrosanct Japanese principle of continual improvement which the UAW had agreed
to at NUMMI, Mazda-Ford, and Diamond-Star, was attacked.
Carried to its extreme, *kaizen* equates to *kamikaze*, Maxey
Irwin said. Nissan's management would never be satisfied.
Its workers would burn out before any of them were old
enough to retire.

But it was not nearly enough. "The captive-audience
sessions were devastating," said Barbara Rahke, of the union's
national organizing team. "There was so much hype, so
much pressure and tension at the end. So many charges and
countercharges that anyone unsure, anyone who hadn't

made up his mind, didn't know *what* to believe. In situations like that, people tend to be conservative. They opt for the status quo. They don't want to to think that the people they work for, or the person who signs their paycheck, are dishonest. I'm certain that the company's union-busting consultant planned it that way." (The law firm advising Nissan on labor relations has long been Ogletree, Deakins, Nash, Smoak, and Stewart of Greenville, South Carolina, the same firm Toyota used before being forced to switch from nonunion to union construction workers. It ranks near the top of the AFL-CIO's blacklist of union-busting law firms, according to Virginia Diamond at the AFL-CIO.)

Community support for the UAW proved to be almost nonexistent. In Smyrna and Murfreesboro, business leaders stated categorically that a union victory would discourage new industry from coming in. Kiyoshi Kawahito, chairman of the Economics Department at Middle Tennessee State (and formerly head of the Japanese Saturday school), was bold enough to predict publicly that the union would lose, and lose big.

On July 27, when the votes were tallied, the company had won with nearly 70 percent of the vote, 1,622 to 718. All but 60 of the 2,400 workers who were eligible had gone to the polls.

At three in the morning, shortly after the results were announced, Jerry Benefield appeared. Surrounded by employees waving American flags and chanting "Team one, team one," he urged the winners to be humble, the vanquished to be good losers, and promised there would be no retaliation against those who had been union sympathizers. He backed away from earlier company statements that the organizing campaign had hurt production and caused dissension on the shop floor. "During the past thirty days we've produced the highest quality in this plant that we've ever produced," he said. He became testy only when challenged to defend his decision not to release the OSHA 200 logs. If the logs hadn't been requested by employees acting as agents of the union, at the height of an organizing campaign, there wouldn't have been a problem, he said.

Confident of victory, Nissan had neither slackened its line speed nor stopped working nine-hour days through the final stages of the campaign. Once the election was over, however, it went back to conducting focus group sessions on the single issue of work-related injuries.

UAW president Owen Bieber, in a prepared statement, had little to say: "All this election demonstrates is that when a company is . . . willing to use threat and misrepresentation to an unlimited extent, the company can delay, if not escape, its day of reckoning." Bieber said he would launch another organizing drive at Nissan after the mandatory one-year waiting period.

By then, however, Nissan's expansion would be under way. The company would be hiring two thousand more workers. The union, if it was to act, would have to move quickly. The larger question seemed to be whether Nissan's strident anti-unionism would leave a hard core of UAW support in the plant, impairing Nissan's competitiveness with other auto makers, and strengthening the union's resolve to regroup and try again.

In the aftermath of the election, Nissan executives received numerous invitations to speak from other companies anxious to learn how Nissan had been able to defeat the UAW so handily. Because they were anxious to heal wounds within the Smyrna plant, a Nissan spokesman said that all invitations were refused. The company's labor attorney, however, soon had a raft of new clients.

Commenting on the Nissan victory, Honda's labor attorney, Dan Minor, suggested that Nissan had been able to conduct such a "spirited" campaign because Smyrna's president was American, not Japanese.

16

Trying to Rise from the Ashes

The inescapable reality is that Japan-based multi-national companies have not come to terms with the multiracial and multicultural nature of American society.

—Owen Bieber in a speech at
Howard University, November 1989

For months after the defeat at Nissan, the UAW declined any but the tersest comment. Everything had gone wrong that could have gone wrong, and there was no point in rehashing. The AP photograph of workers at the Nissan plant waving American flags and wearing T-shirts that proclaimed "Union Free and Proud of It" had sent shock waves through union halls everywhere. For the Nissan election had been billed as critical to the UAW's efforts to organize *all* the Japanese transplants.

The UAW was still America's preeminent union, after all—uncorrupt, racially tolerant, the leader in the creation of a blue-collar middle class. Now, suddenly, it looked as if a large and fast-growing part of the American auto industry would remain nonunion. If so, the consequences would be huge. In the event of strikes at unionized Big Three and Big Three supplier plants, the Japanese would be able to move in and take up the slack.

Until the Nissan defeat—and despite an earlier setback at Honda—most people had thought the UAW was making headway in converting the Japanese to American labor philosophies. NUMMI was often cited as a stunning example of successful labor-management cooperation, as were the unionized Mazda-Ford and Mitsubishi-Chrysler joint ventures. As late as April 1989, U.S. Labor Secretary Elizabeth Dole had said, "NUMMI . . . has come to be considered the ideal management-labor partnership, a marriage said to be a *landmark* in America."

Now even NUMMI seemed in jeopardy. Things looked bleak.

But then Nissan fired one of the four union sympathizers that had asked to see the OSHA 200 logs, articles appeared in the Japanese press critical of Nissan's strident anti-unionism, and Jerry Benefield was quoted as saying Nissan was having trouble finding qualified workers to hire for its expansion program.

"We're getting a lot of hairdressers, a lot of waiters, a lot of people without industrial experience . . . people who can't fill out applications," he told the *Tennessean*.

The UAW began to regroup. Owen Bieber made a secret visit to Nashville to plan strategy. He agreed to hire the union supporter Nissan had fired, to keep open the union's meeting hall south of the plant, and to find ways to give associate membership to the seven hundred Nissan employees who had voted for the union. Associate membership provides discounts on insurance and other purchases. Returning to Detroit, Bieber then created a new department to handle relations with *all* Japanese auto makers. Dick Shoemaker, his administrative assistant and alter ego, was put in charge.

At six feet five, Owen Bieber is a giant of a man with bear-paw hands and a huge face, yet he struck me as oddly diffident. He tends to keep a low profile. From a German

Catholic family in Grand Rapids, he rose to union leadership in the region that includes Michigan's Upper Peninsula and the western half of the state. His region had few of the General Motors plants that historically have spawned dissent, but instead consisted primarily of small, independent parts suppliers. He is the first UAW president to preside over the union at a time when both membership and U.S. auto sales are in sharp decline.

His office is on the second floor of Solidarity House, the union's six-story headquarters on the banks of the Detroit River. Though a small conference table faces his desk, and there is an undisturbed view of the river through plate glass lining an entire side of the room, the office seems small for a man with responsibility for nearly a million auto workers. At first, when I met him, he seemed cautious, but soon gave vent to his emotions. He had just returned from Washington, where Congress had given a tumultuous welcome to Lech Walesa. Bieber had told associates that America's enthusiasm for unions in Eastern Europe was matched only by its low opinion of unions at home.

Fresh from a reading of *The Japan That Can Say "No,"* Akio Morita and Shintaro Ishihara's scathing attack on Americans for prejudice against Asians, and contention that Japan could alter the balance of power by selling microchips to the Soviets, Bieber sat at his conference table with his back to the river. He opened a file folder containing newspaper clippings from Japan and a flyer from Nissan's plant in England.

The flyer, signed by the plant's deputy managing director, urges workers who haven't done so to join the union. "There may be times when you need representation," it says. "The union offers legal representation free of charge. The union can provide a whole range of advice for your negotiators."

Bieber asked how Nissan could have such a policy in England and another so radically different in Tennessee.

The press clippings were from the *Nihon Keizai Shimbun*
and the *Japan Economic Journal.* By implication, they criticize
Nissan's anti-unionism:

> [If Japanese auto makers] intend to evolve into multi-
> national corporations, they must give up the farfetched
> goal of instituting Japanese labor-management relations
> overseas and respect local labor practices.
>   . . . Companies which succeed in maintaining good
> labor-management relations even when overproduction
> problems arise in host countries will be able to cope with
> any boycott movement. [From *Nihon Keizai Shimbun*, as
> translated in *The Japan Times*]

> . . . It would not be desirable for a Japanese firm to
> adopt a policy of formally declaring that it is up to the
> workers to decide whether they want to be unionized—
> while at the same time continuing its anti-union activities.
> [From the *Japan Economic Journal*]

Bieber noted that the Japanese press sometimes sounds more
pro-American than the American press. "The Japanese see
the company as one big happy family," he said. "When a
third of its employees are unhappy, something must be
wrong with the system."

He then chastises Honda and Toyota (in Kentucky) for
claiming to be neutral while doing everything possible to
keep the union out: Honda, by transferring employees back
and forth among its four plants so they will have to be
considered a single unit for organizing purposes; Toyota,
by requiring applicants for even assembly-line work to take
fifteen hours of written tests.

"Am I pissed off at Toyota?" he asked rhetorically. "You
bet I am. They had the opportunity to hire skilled, highly
qualified workers on furlough from Ford's plant in Louisville,
but chose not to."

* * *

Soon after, Bieber broke silence and for the first time spoke out against the rising tide of Japanese investment here. He asked listeners at Howard University to notice where the Japanese were building their plants, to observe whom they were hiring and not hiring, to watch whom Big Three companies were being forced to lay off, then to consider these things before purchasing a Japanese car.

The UAW is caught in a crisis not of its own making, at a critical juncture in its history. While not blameless in the decline of the Big Three auto makers, the key failures have obviously been management ones. Nobody asked the union whether to build large cars or small, or whether to reinvest or take profits. Given NUMMI's success, the argument can be made that the UAW has been readier to adapt to a world economy than most Big Three managers have.

Bieber said that by 1991, once Toyota's truck plant at NUMMI is up and running, the union will have pressure points that can be applied to convince Georgetown to stop resisting the union. But by 1991 Toyota's investment in Kentucky was many times larger than its investment in California has been. Now the UAW is too preoccupied with problems of holding on to the clout it still has at a downsizing GM to worry about organizing Japanese companies.

The UAW had been naïve in expecting the Japanese to play by the same rules that Big Three companies do. "America looks ten minutes ahead; Japan, ten years," Morita and Ishihara contend in *The Japan That Can Say "No."*

17

The Parts Revolution

We're selling to both Honda and Nissan, but not
very much. They're too demanding. More demanding than any of the American companies we
sell to. We're losing money, but it's good practice,
I suppose. The Big Three are becoming more
quality-conscious and we'll be ready for them.
　　　—The vice-president of a very large Ohio-based
auto parts company, October 1988

Dave Nelson smiles. He isn't surprised. He's heard that one
before. He says those kinds of people are going to have to
sharpen their thinking if they intend to remain Honda
suppliers.

The American auto parts industry is under as great
pressure from the Japanese as the Big Three—if not greater.
Less visible, more fragmented, and with little political clout,
many of these companies stand a good chance of going
under. For each time a Japanese manufacturer locates a
plant in the United States, its major suppliers usually are
not far behind.

Honda is a case in point. Because it was the first to build
assembly plants here, it was able to bring along many of its
supplier companies before anyone really noticed. Honda
made an early political decision to buy only American steel,
but for its engine and more complicated parts it still buys
mostly Japanese.

* * *

Dave Nelson has been Honda's purchasing vice-president since January 1988. An amiable man, he spends a lot of time on the speakers' circuit, where he has been known to say that one reason Honda hired him was because he spoke slowly enough for the Japanese to understand. In a more serious vein, he often talks about what it takes to be a Honda supplier:

"Parts or materials supplied to Honda must meet *Honda* specifications, not those of another company . . . In order to meet customer demand and bring our products to the marketplace quickly, Honda product development is accelerated at almost every stage. Our suppliers need to have the capability to meet extraordinary time demands in the development of prototypes and tooling and design changes."

Nelson, who grew up on a farm in Pike County, Indiana, was previously purchasing director for TRW, a Cleveland-based supplier of electrical components for the auto industry. He had been with TRW for thirty years, lived in four states, and held jobs in quality control, marketing, and manufacturing before moving into purchasing. He says that one difference between working for a Japanese company and working for an American one is that at an American company the philosophy is "If it ain't broke, don't fix it." At a Japanese company, everything has to be continually improved. The real reason Honda hired him, he thinks, was his varied work experience, all with the same company. When hiring Americans, the Japanese like generalists, not job jumpers. People who have held a variety of jobs with the same company are thought to be curious, adaptable, and good communicators. Nelson is nothing if not a good communicator.

A story he tells to illustrate Honda's purchasing philosophy goes like this:

"Some time ago, we were about to begin production of the four-door Civic. Through our doors came the president of an Indiana-based company who wanted to supply the jack for our Accord. At the time we were focused on finding suppliers for a number of stamped and related parts, and didn't offer him much encouragement.

"But instead of going away mad, he went back to his company more determined than ever. He went to a Honda dealer and purchased the jack then being used in the Accord. He studied every aspect of its design and function. He assessed his company's capability to manufacture a jack of equal or better quality. After several months he came through our doors again. This time he placed on our conference table the prototype and quotation for a jack which he declared superior in every way to the jack we were sourcing from Japan. And do you know what? He was right.

"Today his company is supplying the jack for every automobile produced at our Marysville plant—360,000 of them. And his jack, which bears the name Universal, is just that. It also is in the trunk of every Honda two-door Accord coupe being exported to Japan.

"There is more to the story. We were so impressed that we asked this Mr. Buck Ritenour if his company could also supply us with tool sets. He said he didn't make tool sets, but knew of somebody who did. So, on his recommendation, we contacted the Herbert E. Orr Company in Paulding, Ohio, and today it's the supplier of every tool set found in an Ohio-produced Accord or Civic."

Nelson's point is that with determination, a good research and development capability, and enough capital, any American parts company can become a Honda supplier.

Maybe so, but many dispute this. They say yes, Honda will buy simple, standardized parts from U.S. suppliers—steel, glass, wheels, tires, and trim—but for the more complicated components, for anything for the engine (or power train, as auto people like to call it), the company still buys mostly Japanese. Honda prides itself on being first and foremost an engine company.

In fact, Irimajiri himself has said, "At Honda, we have

preferred not to purchase the technology of others or to grow from external acquisitions . . . Over the short run, that presents some challenges in our efforts to source parts in the United States. We cannot accept 'over the shelf' parts."

Nelson has a staff of two hundred people (and, like all of Honda's key American executives, a Japanese counterpart to whom he reports). His goal is to boost the U.S. content of Accord and Civic automobiles to 75 percent by 1991, whether from American companies, from Japanese companies in the United States, or from joint ventures here.

Honda officials say two thirds of the parts now purchased from 160 Ohio firms are from American-owned companies. But when pressed, they acknowledge that the dollar volume from these is less than half the total. When asked whether Honda isn't buying far more from Japanese-owned companies in the United States than from American companies here, Toshi Amino stiffens and says the Japanese companies are providing the Americans with good jobs, aren't they? In 1988 Honda sponsored a workshop with the Mitsubishi Bank in Columbus to encourage more joint ventures between American companies and these Japanese suppliers. Jack Sizemore, the UAW's regional director for north and west-central Ohio, says that of more than one hundred unionized parts suppliers in his territory, only one has been able to sell directly to Honda.

Stan Smith is vice-president and general manager of J-P Industries, Bellefontaine's largest employer. J-P employs more than five hundred people and makes bearings and bushings for the auto industry. A nonunion plant, it has been a quality-one (highest-rating) Ford supplier since 1987.

Starting in 1986, Smith also tried to become a Honda supplier. He didn't approach Honda's manufacturing headquarters in Ohio, but its engine-making facility in Japan, since he was told this was the avenue he must pursue. He soon discovered that Honda's requirements were more exacting and complicated than Ford's, but persisted anyway. He kept sending blueprints and product samples, but never got to first base—not even after Honda built an engine plant at Anna, twenty-four miles away.

Instead, after Nissan announced in 1988 that it would assemble engines in Smyrna, he received visits from three teams of Nissan engineers. Nissan, which had announced a joint minivan project with Ford, had asked Ford to recommend potential parts suppliers. J-P was on the list. And although J-P is located four hundred miles north of Smyrna, in the heart of Honda country, it got the bid.

Nissan's philosophy, as explained by Bob Drake, its purchasing vice-president, is that once the company finds a supplier with compatible goals and enough research and development capability, it leaves the driving to him.

"If I give you the design and say 'Build me this motor,' my design might not be suited to your process," says Drake. "To meet my design requirements, you might have to retool, which increases my costs immediately.

"But if I say to you, I want you to design a windshield wiper motor that will fit into this space, and by the way, I want the wiper blade to be hidden when it's off and I want it to execute 4 million cycles—and one other thing, it needs to have holes in these exact locations so it will attach to the fire wall properly—when I do that, I've given you the black box with some pretty strict parameters. But I've left the design up to you—to be adapted to your process. You're the expert when it comes to making your process run efficiently."

Honda has a large and growing production engineering department. It also has lots of engineers in Dave Nelson's purchasing department. Nissan has far fewer staff engineers. Nissan intends instead to build upon its suppliers' expertise, says CEO Jerry Benefield.

As he geared up to meet the challenge of becoming a Nissan supplier, Stan Smith had his managers read a book called *The Goal: A Process of Ongoing Improvement* by Eliyahu

M. Goldratt and Jeff Cox. It tells the story of one Alex Rogo, plant manager in a fictitious town that sounds a little like Bellefontaine, "a place where there are plenty of railroad tracks, but not many trains anymore." Rogo's operation is a marginal one, and he has just three months to turn it around. He succeeds, of course, and how he does so is an Israeli variation on the Japanese themes of *kaizen* and just-in-time delivery techniques. The emphasis is on common sense rather than high-tech robotics. In a telling final chapter, Rogo tells a new disciple that without the *luxury* of continual pressure, his operation reverted to business as usual.

The need for constant pressure to be able to continually improve raises the question of whether American companies can adopt the Japanese system piecemeal and hope to keep up.

Capitol Plastics has been a Honda supplier for ten years. As soon as Honda announced it would be assembling vehicles in the United States, William Taylor, Capitol's owner, started bombarding Honda's office in Gardena, California, with price quotes and samples of molded plastic parts. His persistence paid off. Soon he had 20 percent, then finally 90 percent of the business.

Later, Honda asked Taylor to consider doing a joint venture with one of its Japanese supplier companies. Help was needed with hiring, purchasing, and community relations. No matter that the cash Taylor could contribute would be minuscule; Honda needed to blunt criticism that too many of its purchases were from Japanese companies in Ohio, rather than from the American companies there. Within a day after the deal was struck, Honda made sure it was announced in *Automotive News*.

"You never know quite what they're thinking," Bill Taylor says. "But you can be sure that they're thinking far down the road. They don't enter into negotiations with you unless they think of you as a potentially permanent partner.

Negotiations are a matter of continual refinement. Sometimes you don't know the final terms of what you're agreeing to until a day or two before you ship. The first price is never the final price. It's like a marriage. There has to be a lot of mutual trust."

Taylor is a friendly, unpretentious man to whom even first-line supervisors come for advice. He also is an important Chrysler supplier. He says once he signs his annual contract with Chrysler, he seldom hears from them until a year later. Not so with Honda. With Honda, scarcely a day goes by without someone from their plant in his or someone from his plant in theirs, or one of them calling him on the telephone. "They don't call one of my assistants, they call me," he sighs. "Schedules change. Part refinements need to be made. They must think that by calling me they'll get quicker results."

Toyota's hope had been that no supplier would locate more than "half a shift away." In Japan, its suppliers are within bicycling distance of its assembly plants, and Toyota had dreamed of replicating this same system over here. It hasn't been able to everywhere, obviously, but one place where it has is with Johnson Controls.

Johnson Controls is located on the south side of Georgetown and makes seats for the Camry. Without a contract in hand, without an agreed-upon unit price, without even a handshake agreement, it invested $9 million, expecting to earn the right to supply Toyota with all its needs. As at Capitol Plastics, the American executives there considered the final contract award a mere formality. For Johnson had supplied NUMMI, and an atmosphere of mutual trust had developed—that was all that mattered.

Johnson delivers seats in lots of sixty at a time, in more than twenty different styles, trucking them across town every hour or so, ready for insertion on the assembly line, as in Toyota City. The only inventory maintained, either at Johnson or at the auto plant, is in the truck or on a conveyer that simulates the inside of a truck.

Plant walls are dotted with pictures and charts—visual aids so that even a casual visitor can know what is going on: before-and-after pictures of improvements made, photos of who is in which quality circle, suppliers rated by quality and delivery performance, a chart showing scrap rate by part, absenteeism against previous year and month. Moreover, Johnson uses the same board of codes and colored lights that Toyota uses to alert team leaders to where and why the assembly line has stopped.

Not everything is modeled after Toyota, however. Employees don't wear uniforms, nor do managers sit at desks in blocks of four. Instead, they have separate offices. "Offices give our people the chance to think and concentrate," says Don Buchenberger, who supervises manufacturing. He gives his closest attention to hiring.

"It used to take us one or two days to hire someone. Now it takes three or four weeks. Each candidate is interviewed by five people, who then compare notes. If anyone has doubts, the applicant isn't hired. We check references carefully. Our work tends to be very repetitive. We can't have someone who's likely to become bored. We want to know if the candidate can be motivated to seek continuous improvement. And to share his or her ideas with others. Ours is a team operation. Anything we can do to cut costs and improve quality, we want to do. In this day and age, it would be easy for a Japanese company to build a competing plant over here. We don't want that."

Johnson's slogan for the nineties is "Exceeding customers' expectations." The company is nonunion, as are the vast majority of parts companies supplying the Japanese. In fact, a fast-increasing number of both Japanese *and* American parts companies are nonunion now.

The UAW has organized scarcely any of the nearly three hundred Japanese parts companies that have come to

the United States. Nor, with its attention diverted by business
with General Motors, Ford, and Chrysler, and unsuccessful
efforts to organize Nissan, has the union had the time or
energy to try very hard. With their emphasis on just-in-time
delivery, it seems unlikely that Japanese auto makers will
buy from a unionized parts dealer unless they have no other
choice. In the event of a work stoppage, the just-in-time
system breaks down. Then, too, the Japanese (and American
parts suppliers before them) have built small plants, most
staffed with fewer than two hundred people, in parts of rural
Ohio, Indiana, Tennessee, and Kentucky. Such plants are
quick to put up and quicker still to pull down in the event
of a UAW organizing attempt.

"If there's a light at the end of the tunnel, it's a speeding
train," UAW vice-president Odessa Komer recently told
Automotive News in reference to the decline in union membership among auto parts suppliers. "I don't know of a plant
we have that does work for the Japanese. They keep working
at it and putting bids in, but none are even close."

Candace Howe, the UAW's former staff economist, wrote
in a paper titled "The Future Is Now, and It's Going All
Wrong":

> The quality of the interstate highway system and the
> deregulation of trucking have increased the economic
> feasibility of sourcing beyond Michigan. Regions to the
> south have become more attractive for their proximity
> and lower wage labor. The Dana Corporation alone [a
> Toledo-based maker of engine and transmission parts]
> has closed 30 union plants and opened 40 to 50 [smaller]
> non-union ones.

Several of the union leaders and parts company executives
I talked with told of neutrality pacts negotiated that trade
concessions at headquarters plants in the North for an

agreement not to organize these new, smaller plants in the Lower Midwest and Upper South.

The early decision by auto makers in Japan to subcontract components rather than expand in-house capacity to meet new demand stands out as one of their most significant departures from American practice. Subcontracting carried the risk of poor quality until the Japanese solved the problem by controlling their suppliers by dispatching executives, extending long-term contracts, buying the entire output of factories, and providing loans of money or equipment.

A similar pattern is now developing in the United States. The Big Three are buying an ever-larger share of their parts on long-term contract from a decreasing number of technically sophisticated "first-tier" suppliers. These integrate the parts they make into subsystems or modules with other components purchased from smaller, lower-tier, and still-lower-wage suppliers. In reducing the number of direct suppliers, the Big Three are able to improve quality and reliability of delivery.

The question is whether they will be able to do this as effectively as the Japanese have done.

Ford recently put out the word that it wouldn't be buying from Japanese parts companies new to the United States unless what they had to offer was "clearly superior technologically" to what Ford's current suppliers could offer. A significant price advantage would no longer be enough.

"This doesn't mean we won't be buying from Nippodenso or other Japanese companies that have long supplied us," Clint Lauer, Ford's vice-president for purchasing, told me. "Our policy is not anti-Japanese but, rather, pro–existing supplier. We are trying to protect our existing North American supplier base, which includes Mexico and Canada. These people have invested to produce large numbers of units. It is not in our long-term interest to see them destroyed."

Nissan executives in Tokyo told me they thought an important reason Ford wanted to do a joint minivan project was so it could learn how better to manage its parts people. Others have been equally anxious to learn from the Japanese.

Walt Dennis is president of H-F Industries in Columbus, Ohio. H-F is a leading provider of seat fabric to Bellemar, a first-tier Honda supplier.

"I went to Japan and visited the cottage industry where women make the fabric for seat covers," Dennis told me. "They do a lot of things we can't do: pay old people less than the young, hire people with physical or mental problems and pay them less, too, pay women less. But we've been able to adopt some of their methods. We have a clean room that's swept every night. There's no radio, no talking, nobody goes to the bathroom except during breaks. Productivity has improved dramatically. We've created a new mind-set."

The American parts suppliers who seem to do best with the Japanese are those who answer their own phones and are willing to work nights and weekends, if need be, those able to contribute new ideas that the Japanese can then hone and refine, those willing to sacrifice quarterly earnings for market-share gains.

Likewise, the heartland towns most successful in attracting Japanese auto-parts companies seem to be those likely to provide continuing support after the initial courting period. In 1987 Bradley Richardson and Reiko Tsuzuki of Ohio State's Institute for Japanese Studies visited most of the places in Ohio where the Japanese had built plants.

"The Japanese enormously value regular demonstrations of interest and commitment, whether symbolic or substantive," they wrote. "Japanese business decisions are very long-term oriented. Japanese companies look for a secure, supportive environment. Wives are one of the single most vulnerable aspects . . . How Japanese students can best be served is another vexing problem. Generally, the bigger the community, the lower the active interest in the Japanese."

18

We, Not I

Interruptions are what we're here for. I can't close
my door and say Darlene, hold my calls, anymore.
There's no time to do paper work.
—Gary Dodd, a senior executive at Toyota
Motor Manufacturing, Georgetown,
Kentucky

Working for a Japanese company isn't for everyone. Sometimes it requires more patience than an American is prepared
to give.

Gary Dodd worked at Ashland Oil for eighteen years
before joining Toyota. At Ashland, he had drawn up the
agenda for senior staff meetings, and the focus was usually
on heavy subjects such as whether to spend $3 million to
drill a hole for oil in some quadrant of the gulf, or whether
to acquire an insurance company. At Toyota, he has the
same assignment, but here the focus is on the day-to-day,
the specific, sometimes on very tiny, operational details.

"In American companies, the buzzword is 'time management,'" he told me. "Every upper-middle executive takes
a course in time management. At Toyota, there's no such
thing. You're out in this huge open space, available to anyone
and everyone who wants to talk to you. You have to always
be ready to deal with what's going on right now.

"At Ashland, everything was very structured with respect
to who does what, when, and how. The decision making was

very rapid. We made course corrections, as necessary, as we
went along.

"At Toyota, we are very slow to make decisions. So many
people have to be involved, the more the better, it seems.
Ideas are then massaged by the group. Implementation then
is very rapid, however—with scarcely any course corrections."

In Tennessee, the state-funded Japan Center in Murfreesboro gathers and distributes material explaining the Japanese
to the Americans and the Americans to the Japanese. Tennessee has a more diverse group of Japanese companies than
Ohio or Kentucky, and thus the demand for such information is particularly strong. One of the most popular of the
Japan Center's offerings is a two-page handout that contrasts
American and Japanese business practices:

> In American companies, decisions are usually made at
> the top, more attention is paid to training specialists than
> generalists, organizational changes are often sudden and
> abrupt, and there is more of an emphasis on win-lose
> than win-win.
>   In Japanese companies, questionnaires and surveys
> are more frequently used, managers are often rewarded
> for being methodical and meticulous rather than decisive,
> decisions are made by consensus, and there is more
> competition between groups than between individuals.

Honda in Ohio employs many more Japanese nationals than
its competitors, and there special arrangements have been
made to ensure that the Americans and the Japanese understand one another.

At eight every morning, Scott Whitlock chairs an hour-
long production meeting of managers and senior engineers.
Participants sit in a large semicircle and include twelve
Japanese men and thirty-eight Americans, of whom twelve
are women. Earphones are provided for simultaneous trans-

lation, as at the UN, and at the back of the room a woman
sits at a computer and transcribes a summary of what is
said—as it's being said. Seconds later, her summary appears
in English on two five-by-five-foot wall screens for anyone
who might have missed something.

After the briefest of introductions, Whitlock asks for
reports, and it is the Americans, not the Japanese, who talk.
They speak of problems, not accomplishments. They report
in microscopic detail every flaw that has occurred during
the two shifts in the twenty-four hours since they met last.
Accidents or injuries, if any, are cited first, then problems
in production or quality.

Whitlock doesn't ask questions. He doesn't need to,
because as part of each report the manager or technician
explains, again often in microscopic detail, what he or she
has done (or is about to do) to prevent a similar situation
from ever occurring again. There is no finger pointing. No
one is blamed for not doing his job. Often, someone from
another department or supplier company will be thanked
for offering crucial help.

Near the end of the session, the three Japanese vice-
presidents, who sit directly across from Whitlock, comment
on what they have heard. They speak in broken English, but
they don't mince any words. Their remarks are sharp and
to the point. The emphasis is not on what's been achieved
but rather on what's still left to be done.

The general topic this particular morning is how to
improve the percentage of cars coming off the line that can
be straight-shipped (that is, sent directly on to dealers)
without touch-up repairs. The percentage had reached 80;
the new goal will be 85.

The production meeting is over by nine. Every day at
nine-thirty then, Whitlock and other managers from the
motorcycle plant, first and second auto plants, engine plant,
purchasing, finance, and corporate planning meet in a nearby
conference room.

There are twenty people present, twelve Japanese and
eight Americans, nineteen men and one woman (Susan
Insley). They sit around a rectangular table, with each
American beside his or her Japanese counterpart. As in the
production meeting, it is the Americans who do most of the
talking. The meeting is conducted in slow English, with the
Americans omitting every "a," "an," and "the" in their
sentences and taking care to pronounce "ing" endings clearly.
They use an overhead projector and often a freestanding
bulletin board to make their points. The bulletin board has
a row of buttons on its upper right side and doubles as a
facsimile machine. Anything written on it can be reproduced
in seconds for distribution to the people around the table,
and often is. The Japanese have few problems with written
English, I am told; it is the spoken English that sometimes
gives them problems. Company president Hiroyuki Yoshino,
who takes thrice-weekly English lessons, has urged his Japanese associates to spend as much time studying English as
they do playing golf.

Comparing staff meetings at Honda with staff meetings
at the law firm of Vorys, Sater, Seymour, and Pease, where
Insley and Whitlock were partners before, Insley says that
at Honda you seldom hear the word "I"; it's always "we."

"At Vorys, the direction was set by our two senior
partners, who did 70 percent of the talking. Here everyone
is asked his opinion, even if it isn't volunteered. Mr. Yoshino,
like Mr. Iri [Irimajiri] before him, seldom talks more than 5
to 10 percent of the time. And when he makes a decision,
it's never a question of cutting the baby in half but rather a
synthesis of all that has gone before."

When in Japan, I asked at each of the three companies if
there was anything they had learned from their experience
in America that they had brought back for use in Japan.
Only at Honda could anyone recall anything specific. There
Kaname Kasai, manager of the Sayama number-two plant,

said Mr. Iri had said that as Honda grew larger, it would need to do a better job of systematizing its procedures. Scott Whitlock, he said, was helping the company to do just that.

Whitlock grew up in Aurora, Illinois, where his father managed "the largest Caterpillar plant outside of Peoria" and his mother was a lawyer. A graduate of Denison University and Harvard Law School, Whitlock practiced law for seventeen and a half years before joining Honda. Like a lot of the Americans the Japanese seem to hire, Whitlock has a gift for making complex things simple, for asking questions a foreigner might not think to ask, for being good at implementation. He says that as auto plant manager he has more freedom than his father had. He claims his Japanese counterparts understand 80 to 85 percent of what he says and 95 percent of what he means.

Still, others at Honda say they wish the Japanese would work harder on their communication skills. "Americans are more direct, say what we mean, are less inclined to beat around the bush," I sometimes was told.

In her doctoral dissertation on Japanese companies in Ohio, sociologist Kinko Ito devotes more space to communication problems than to anything else.

Japanese culture fosters the ability to understand without words, she says. The Japanese shy away from too much directness. They do not like to come right out and say what they are thinking. Having lived packed together in one small part of a not very large island, they have learned not to be confrontational. The Japanese language contains superbly vague phrases that take on different meanings depending on tone of voice and facial expression. Japanese put the emphasis on hearing within a total context: taking into account the occasion, the speaker's personality and status, one's relationship to him, his manner of delivery, posture, hand gestures, and so on. Americans at Japanese companies are uncomfortable with vagueness and impatient with ambiguity, Ito says. They say the Japanese are afraid to call a spade a spade.

On the other hand, I found many Americans at Honda who prefer working for the Japanese to the Americans they had worked for before. They like the identical uniforms, say it is easier to talk to their boss (and their boss's boss) when everyone looks the same. They like being busy all the time and being asked what they think. They like not having to worry about laundering their clothes.

Honda's operation has more of a Japanese flavor than Nissan's, or even Toyota's. You see more Japanese visitors in the lobby, wall signs in Japanese, fewer attempts to prove this is an American, not a Japanese, company. Purchasing vice-president Dave Nelson tells of flying to Tokyo in sport shirt and slacks, and feeling uncomfortable. Looking around, he saw that his Japanese colleagues were all wearing dark suits and dark ties. Others speak of unwritten rules and rituals:

Japanese always wear their caps out on the shop floor, but not in the office.

They change out of their uniforms before leaving the plant.

They never sit on the edge of their desks, or speak in a loud voice.

All read everything they can get their hands on about Honda and the auto industry, and stay informed.

As more Japanese families came to Ohio, at first for three years, now sometimes for five or seven, Honda began urging them to settle in scattered small towns instead of clustering in one of Columbus's northern suburbs. It was felt they would learn more about America that way. Irimajiri even considered setting up—but didn't establish—a special fund from which the Japanese could draw if they entertained Americans in their homes.

Still, many cultural barriers remain. John McVicker,

who headed the English program at Honda's Anna plant, gives an example.

One of his students was a Japanese middle manager who had a gift for languages. He could have been an excellent English speaker, but chose not to be. Instead, with the arrival of additional Japanese at the engine plant (at last count some three hundred), he chose to eat regularly at one of the Japanese cafeteria tables, instead of with the Americans, as he had previously. McVicker asked why, and urged him not to, saying that by doing so, he was missing an opportunity.

"John," the man finally said, "I can't afford to stick out. The other Japanese will think I am showing off. They will think I'm trying to prove I can fit in better than they can here."

Some Americans have learned, too, that if they have a personal problem with their Japanese supervisor or counterpart, they shouldn't mention it at work, but rather invite him out for a drink and discuss it then. Others say if one Japanese does it, it's a good bet that all will, that Japanese don't think different is better, but rather that likeness is best. Some also question Honda's practice of paying first-level employees all the same regardless of their beginning job skills. In Japan, those who do particularly well get a small performance bonus. Toyota has started paying a small performance bonus to American workers as well.

In Kentucky, Toyota encourages the Americans who are stronger to carry, when necessary, the weaker members of the team.

"Americans tend to have a clear-cut sense of individual responsibility, but when it comes to teamwork and helping each other, I see some difference between the Americans and Japanese," says Kaneyoshi Kusunoki.

Americans exaggerate too much, adds "Nate" Furata, Toyota's trainer there. He has told the Americans who report to him that he won't read their memos until they stop using words like "never," "ever," "always," "very," and "tremendous."

"The Japanese start with a different set of rules and logic," says Bruce Henke, a lawyer at Vorys, Sater in Columbus who represents twenty of Honda's Ohio-based Japanese supplier companies. "There are times when no matter how illogical it seems, they will pick a plant site that is frankly lousy. They like a certain stand of trees or they say the countryside reminds them of something back home. Then, to make matters worse, when you are right in the middle of negotiations, they will say they want to make the announcement on such and such a day because this is a lucky day in Japan or when their president wants to come to the United States. We lose our bargaining power, but they don't seem to care."

The Japanese say that by coming to our heartland, they are helping us recover what we say we have lost—our work ethic, our pride in craftsmanship, a sense of community. They don't see their success here as Japan winning and us losing but rather as a win-win for both.

19

Better Jobs Back Home

The transplants are murdering all of us—all of the
Big Three.
> —Lee Iacocca, speaking to reporters
> in Washington, November 1989

It has often been our experience in racing that
when one team is successful, the rules will be
changed . . . We have never said that was unfair;
every rule change has given us the opportunity to
be challenged and to learn again.
> —Shoichiro Irimajiri

As the 1980s drew to a close, it became obvious that the Big
Three—having again underestimated the Japanese, by opting for short-term profits over market share—faced a threat
to their very survival. Detroit had used too few of its profits
from the quota-protected years to develop new products,
and now the Japanese were challenging even Cadillac and
Lincoln. Prediction after prediction of a turnaround in GM's
and Chrysler's fortunes had fallen short. The transplants, a
by-product of the trade restrictions Detroit had battled so
hard to get in the early 1980s, now stood poised to increase
their output dramatically in an already crowded car market.
The transplants had come to the American heartland lured
by financial incentives from state and local governments, the
effect of which was to further heighten their advantage over
existing Big Three plants. The naïve notion that the Japanese

would reduce their car shipments to the United States once they started to build cars here had proved wrong.

In 1989 the Honda Accord was America's number-one selling car, the first time ever for a foreign car maker. Of the top four car models sold in the United States, four were Japanese, six of the top ten in customer satisfaction. Jerry Knight, writing in *The Washington Post*, called the Honda Accord "America's dream car":

> Two kids, a cat or a dog, cable TV, a health club, a home in the suburbs and a Honda in the driveway. It doesn't get any better than that for most Americans.
> The car in the driveway would have been a 1957 Chevy once, or a 1965 Mustang, but last year, 362,707 American families bought a new Accord. That's 14,000 more than bought a Ford Taurus and almost 30,000 more than bought a Ford Escort, America's best-selling car in 1987 and 1988.

By the end of the decade, Honda was no longer denying reports that it was seriously considering moving its corporate headquarters from Tokyo to Columbus, Ohio. "But this will probably not occur this year or even the year after," a company spokesman said. In 1992, following a spate of Japan (and Honda) bashing, the idea was put on hold

By mid-1990, the glut in U.S. and world auto production had arrived. Fixed sticker prices had vanished, and incentive programs, normally the domain of domestic manufacturers, were becoming the domain of Japanese auto makers, as well. Now even the best-selling of the Japanese cars, the Hondas and Toyotas, which had been so well regarded that their manufacturers could dispense with the rebates and other inducements to which American car makers had turned, were having to respond. Their dealers were finally scrambling to become salesmen instead of mere order takers. Incentives were introduced, and distribution fine-tuned. City dealers that had been getting too many models with manual transmission—which drivers in stop-and-go traffic disliked— were now getting only the models they requested.

But as Ford and the other Big Three auto makers improved quality to levels approaching those of the Japanese, the Japanese raised their standards, too. A totally revamped Honda Accord was introduced, and there was talk of product turnarounds in thirty to thirty-six months instead of four years, as now. Each year a new-model Accord, Civic, or Prelude would be introduced. In 1990 Honda would bring onto the market its first station wagon—designed and built in the U.S.A.

The Japanese are nothing if not competitive, and especially so among themselves. Honda's early success in penetrating the American market had spurred Nissan and Toyota to do likewise. As niche products became more important to competitive success, the Japanese built sports and luxury car models in quantities of fewer than a hundred thousand units, a practice at odds with America's mass-marketing tradition. Toyota and Mazda soon followed Honda in predicting they would soon be exporting American-made cars back to Japan.

While in the old days Japan's Ministry of International Trade and Industry (MITI) could tell a Japanese auto maker what to do, MITI's influence seemed to be waning. MITI had been trying to discourage Japanese auto makers from adding capacity in Japan for fear that if demand there slackened, companies with excess capacity would step up their exports, creating new trade frictions with the United States. The Japanese auto makers now seemed to be ignoring MITI's advice.

What would the future bring? What did it all mean? In an era of too many cars chasing too few buyers, of stable rather than rising prices, the American consumer could not help but benefit. In such an atmosphere, it was hard to imagine Washington bailing out Detroit again. With nine assembly plants in six states and Canada, the Japanese were

creating tens of thousands of new jobs while the Big Three
were eliminating even more. While the Big Three had been
building small cars overseas and buying more of their parts
there, too, the Japanese had been bringing their parts
suppliers to the United States with them.

In 1988 J. D. Power and Associates noted in an Asian
Image Study that the Japanese car makers were losing their
price advantage. Power predicted that over the next several
years they could lose their quality advantage, too, as the Big
Three continued to improve performance. Then the battle-
ground could shift to marketing and advertising strategies,
where the more creative Americans might have an advantage.
To keep the initiative, the leading Japanese companies would
move upscale (Honda already with Acura, Toyota with Lexus,
Nissan with Infiniti), Power predicted.

By the end of the decade, all this was happening, with
the exception of the hoped-for U.S. superiority in advertising
and marketing strategies. Honda was running full-page ads
noting that Acura had ranked first in customer satisfaction
the last three years. Toyota introduced its Lexus by filling a
wineglass with water, placing it atop a $35,000 sedan, ele-
vating the rear wheels so it wouldn't zoom away, then
gunning the engine to 157 miles an hour; the water in the
wineglass didn't even ripple.

Nissan went a step further. Its Infiniti ads at first neither
included a picture of the car nor said anything about
performance. Instead, commercials featured shots of a field
of pussy willows or of rain falling on a pond, as an announcer
talked about the harmony between man and nature. What
is luxury? he asked. Is luxury something that gives you
satisfaction? Is luxury something that impresses you? "It is
Japanese by nature that luxury should evoke a sense of
simplicity, beauty, and tranquillity." Despite the success of
Sony television sets and other high-quality products, few
Japanese companies had ever dared to play on their overseas
origins when advertising in the United States. Not so Nissan.

These flagship models will be the test vehicles for production techniques likely to spread throughout Japanese factories in the 1990s. Since Toyota's Lexus and Nissan's Infiniti recently eclipsed Honda's Acura in the J. D. Power customer satisfaction index, Honda has reemphasized quality, "to go deeper rather than wider" in the words of former Honda of America manufacturing president, Hiroyuki Yoshino.

In still another attempt to boost sales, Japanese car makers in the late 1980s were reviving the horsepower race of the 1960s. Honda, which had made its name with inexpensive, no-nonsense family cars, introduced a $60,000 sports car that looks like a Ferrari. Nissan said it would import a sports car with twice the horsepower of the Datsun 240Z, its star in years past. In the 1980s, in the wake of two energy crises, it had seemed unpatriotic to flaunt power. But now, with cheap fuel and a need to push sales, fast cars were coming back. The horsepower race was another way of symbolizing Japanese determination to challenge U.S. and German luxury car makers. Capability at high speeds translates into superb performance in the low and middle ranges, the Japanese say.

What, if anything, could stop the Japanese march toward dominance of the American automotive industry?

"A unified national strategy," Ford's Clint Lauer says. "It makes no sense for some in Washington to complain about the rising tide of Japanese investment while state governors are saying come on in, the water's fine."

Ford is the one American car company the Japanese fear and respect. Nissan's Smyrna and U.K. plants are staffed with former Ford executives. Toyota tried unsuccessfully several times to negotiate a joint venture with Ford before being approached by GM. News of Ford successes often finds its way onto Honda bulletin boards.

In 1992, Ford and Chrysler threw their support behind a proposal from Dan Rostenkowski, chairman of the House Ways and Means Committee, that would count vehicles built by Japanese companies in the United States as part of a cap or upper limit on future Japanese vehicle sales. So far, Japanese car exports to the United States are limited by the Japanese government, but sales of Japanese cars made in the U.S. and Canadian factories are unrestricted. It seems doubtful that such restrictions will become law. That the possibility exists, however, is enough to force a company like Honda to put on hold any plans to diversify its narrow product line with a U.S. minivan or light truck plant.

Ford's performance over the last decade, during which it went from near failure to become the strongest of the Big Three auto makers, proved that an American company could reinvent itself. The Japanese say the principles which Ford's former CEO Donald Petersen espouses are like Japanese principles:

"Focus on products instead of profits, and the latter will naturally follow.

"Give your people a say in running the show, and a share of the rewards as well.

"Be consistent."

Ford, likewise, is in greatest favor at UAW headquarters. When in late 1989 Harold "Red" Polling was tapped to become Ford's new chairman and CEO, he stated: "We have no plans to close any plants . . . I think we're probably in a better position than our domestic competitors . . . As demand declines, we are able to adjust by cutting back on overtime in most cases and therefore not have to go through layoffs."

Union leaders say that when members don't have to worry about job security, they are far more productive and flexible, less fearful of change.

But how well the Japanese succeed in continuing to gain market share will depend less on what Ford does than on more basic things: better design, retaining the quality edge, on whether the American Big Three again opt for short-term profits over market share gains, and on remaining nonunion. The three leading Japanese auto makers believe that to retain the quality edge, they must keep the union out. Today, only 3 percent of the UAW's 900,000 members are at Japanese-owned factories in the United States.

After failing to organize Honda in 1985, the UAW still thought that first Nissan and then Toyota would be organized, and that then Honda would fall. Because of what the union had done to make NUMMI a success, the UAW believed that Toyota would not resist unionization at its Kentucky plant. After all, Toyota chairman Eiji Toyoda had said, "The UAW, as a union representing auto workers in the United States, is an influential organization and to ignore it would be difficult."

But within days of the UAW's Nissan defeat, Toyota's position hardened. On August 7, 1989, Fujio Cho, Toyota's CEO in Kentucky, told *Automotive News*:

> Basically, we believe this is a problem the employees have to decide for themselves. But we are not going to take a pro-union stand, either. At this time, we believe our human relations and personnel policies are being well received by the employees. They can talk to us directly. We haven't heard of anything that would require a third party like the UAW to come in.

At the Georgetown plant, anti-union "truth teams" were then allowed (the UAW says encouraged) to form.

Subaru-Isuzu in Indiana had also promised to be neutral, saying it would be up to its employees to decide. After the Nissan victory, it, too, toughened its stance.

"We do not believe a third party such as a union is necessary," said a spokesman. "Our company relies upon team cooperation. We feel this team approach at Subaru-Isuzu makes any third-party intervention unnecessary."

Neither Toyota nor even Nissan appear to fear organizing attempts. Both have doubled or are about to double capacity at their Kentucky and Tennessee plants, and each will soon have 6,000 workers there. In most circumstances, such large numbers would seem to make such a plant easier to organize, especially at Nissan where a legacy of bitterness remains from the UAW's unsuccessful organizing attempt, and because there is a unionized work force at GM's Saturn plant nearby.

But Nissan's work force is Tennessean, and Saturn's work force is from out-of-state. Many of the Saturn workers still fly home on weekends. Moreover, at Nissan, where you once heard the phrase "seniority is a UAW word," seniority practices have been introduced. With a new mid-size car soon to be built, every employee will have the opportunity to change jobs—and be retrained for the new job—on the basis of seniority.

There still remains the question whether the Japanese government will want Japanese auto makers to be seen as having helped to destroy America's preeminent labor union. The Japanese aren't so secure that they don't need to be perceived as good U.S. corporate citizens, especially now with polls showing that many Americans perceive Japan to be our greatest threat. Toyota, as the largest company in Japan's largest industry, has said it must be careful what it does because, "in its impact, Toyota bashing can be equal to Japan bashing." Honda also remains very concerned about its image: because of its poor record in minority hires, because of the large number of Japanese nationals working in its Ohio plants, and because of its current problems with the U.S. customs service.

A foreign company's failure to Americanize its executive ranks is sure to be of continuing interest to our national media, especially since Europeans seem to do a better job of this than do the Japanese. In the last two years, Honda has halved the number of Japanese working in its Ohio plants (to 345), and reduced the number of Japanese families living in various Ohio towns. Honda also now has forty Americans on long-term assignment in Japan. In comparison with Toyota and especially Nissan, however, it still has a ways to go. Honda appears to fear too rapid Americanization, in part because American executives tend to put shareholders' interests—rather than associates' and customers' interests—first.

On both the question of the Americanization of executives and embracing some sort of union, Honda can be expected to keep its options open. Tetsuo Chino, then president of Honda North America, remarked to me that in Italy Fiat had been able to work out a sophisticated accommodation with its unions, the implication being that such an arrangement is not out of the question here. Bridgestone, which acquired Firestone in 1983, has been highly successful making tires with a unionized work force in La Vergne, Tennessee, a few miles up the road from Nissan in Smyrna. And Jerry Hammond, the Kentuckian who used the threat of a Pearl Harbor Day demonstration to force Toyota to build its plant union, now sits on the board of Bluegrass Tomorrow with Alex Warren, a former adversary. Hammond's union brothers are currently building an $800 million expansion on Toyota's Georgetown, Kentucky site.

Even Nissan agreed to have a union at its car plant in England. But as Peter Wickens, the plant's personnel director, notes in *The Road to Nissan: Flexibility, Quality, Teamwork*, the company had no choice. There are over two thousand manufacturing companies with more than five hundred employees in the United Kingdom, he says, and of these only twenty can be described as nonunion. Of the twenty, most are in the high-technology sector, employing large numbers of highly skilled graduates or of women engaged in light assembly work. Had Nissan attempted to operate a plant nonunion, it would have been interpreted as a declaration of war.

In the United States, strike threats and seniority issues have been the major stumbling blocks between the Japanese and the UAW. A just-in-time inventory system makes the Japanese especially vulnerable to work stoppages. And the Japanese feel they must retain the right to select the most qualified worker for a given job.

The Japanese also remain vulnerable on the civil rights front because of where they have located their factories. As the Big Three shut down more plants, resulting in disproportionately heavy unemployment of urban blacks, this might still trigger a backlash leading to boycotts or legislation to curtail foreign investment. In the spring of 1992, when Chrysler dedicated its new Jefferson plant in downtown Detroit, *Automotive News*, in a lead editorial, took the Japanese to task for not paying the "social costs" of doing business here. "While the Big Three auto makers have long been leaders in employing minorities at high wages, helping to create a black middle class, the transplants (and Saturn Corp.) have been sucking some jobs out of the city and transplanting them in the countryside where no pressing need for them exists." Benjamin Hooks, the retiring executive director of the NAACP was quoted as saying, "My priority is to get the brothers and sisters I represent to buy this (American) product. We have been biting the hand that feeds us, and feeding the hand that bites us."

Whether the outgoing executive director of the NAACP has the clout necessary to get many blacks to stop buying Japanese cars is another question. Moreover, if Honda and Toyota fail to Americanize their managerial and engineering staffs fast enough, pressure could be brought on the State Department to restrict the number of work visas granted.

Critics contend that the transplants still rely to an unfair degree on imported parts. A common misperception of visitors to Honda's auto plant is that it is a "knockdown operation," says Susan Insley. "They think we import the kit, then put it together over here. The fact is some Japanese transplants in the United States already use more parts made in America than some Big Three plants do." In some instances, this may be true, but it seems equally true that the Japanese transplants are still either importing most of their *more complicated* parts or buying them from Japanese supplier companies that have built new plants here. These transplant supplier companies import some of their components, add value to them, and then ship to the auto maker. Honda came to the United States first, does the most actual manufacturing here, and is the most vertically integrated. Thus, Honda—and not Toyota yet—still poses the greatest threat to the Big Three, and particularly to Chrysler. Consequently it is Honda that has been catching most of the recent flak.

There is the contention that the Japanese are repatriating huge profits, yet hardly any transplants are more than marginally profitable. Far more money has been invested in plant expansions than is being sent back to Japan. Critics, however, see operating at or near a loss as a thinly disguised strategy to gain market share, and hence, tantamount to dumping.

Fearful that with the Cold War at an end the United States will need a new enemy, the Japanese Government has urged its auto makers to concentrate on profit improvement rather than market share gains. The objective is to lessen political tension by giving the American Big Three a chance to recoup. Japanese car prices are now pegged higher than "normal" and car exports from Japan have been "voluntarily" reduced 800,000 units or 5 per cent below 1991 levels. Like GM and Chrysler, Nissan and even Toyota have said they are considering elimination of some of their smaller, less profitable car lines.

This calculated retreat coincides with a temporary collapse in the Japanese stock market, and a downturn in the Japanese economy, that has made the cost of borrowing money for capital investment far more expensive. Although the American Big Three, and especially Ford, have the most to gain from the Japanese retreat, the American consumer could wind up paying more for both Japanese *and* American cars.

Among Japanese auto makers, Honda stands to be hurt the most since the slowdown will give Nissan and Toyota, with their plant expansions already underway, a chance to catch up. Honda has been having its troubles lately.

In 1992, the U.S. Customs Service ruled that Civics made in Canada could not be imported into the United States duty-free because they did not contain 50 percent or more North American content. The ruling seemed politically inspired since Civic engines are manufactured in Ohio. The Canadian government vigorously protested, saying the United States was endangering the Free Trade Agreement by making new rules on the fly. Rather than wait to appeal, Honda also protested vigorously, but to no avail.

Subsequently, Shoichiro Irimajiri, who had fathered Honda's Ohio expansion before returning to Tokyo to become a member of his company's ruling troika, resigned, citing stress and depression.

Now the key questions seem to be:

Will Honda tire of always having to run faster to stay ahead of its Japanese competitors? Honda has fewer friends in the Japanese government than Toyota and Nissan. And, unlike Toyota and Nissan, Honda has steadfastly refused to consider a joint venture with a member of the American Big Three, a decision which makes it more vulnerable politically in the United States.

Which of the three leading Japanese auto makers will ultimately be able to design the best cars for the American consumer? Honda still has the lead, but Toyota has deeper pockets and a newly designed, hot-selling Camry.

Will the transplants be penalized for buying most of their complicated parts from Japanese supplier companies in the United States—rather than from U.S.-owned companies? Presumably not. The transplant supplier companies are already selling significant quantities of parts to the American Big Three.

Will the perception continue to grow that the reason for GM's and Chrysler's difficulties is far more the fault of their own management weaknesses than of Japanese competition or the UAW? And, if so, with what consequences?

W. Edwards Deming says "management is responsible for 85 percent of all problems."

In an era when the Big Three are building cars in Japan, Mexico, and Korea for sale in the United States, while the Japanese are building increasing numbers of cars in the United States for sale in the United States (80 percent of the Honda Accords sold in the United States last year were made in Ohio), who is to say which is a foreign car and which domestic?

Will "eight-hour aerobics" burn out American workers before they are old enough to retire? Or by giving assembly-line workers real responsibility and a say in how their jobs are to be done, have the Japanese found a better way to manage?

The New York Times recently ran a front-page story saying that in the last year 20,000 American manufacturing executives and engineers had visited Toyota's Kentucky plant. The visitors were convinced that what they would find there would change the American way of mass production. A partner at Arthur Andersen said, "Virtually every U.S. manufacturer is trying some element of the Toyota system."

David Cole, who heads the automotive research institute in Ann Arbor (and whose father was once president of GM), concedes that the bone and muscle of the American auto industry may be moving south, but asserts that the brains never will. When asked what, if anything, the Big Three can do to stop losing market share, he responded emotionally.

"Let me draw you a picture," he said. "One afternoon, Gloria Steinem goes out and buys a Toyota Camry. That night she dreams that not a single female hand touched that car as it was being built."

The problem with Cole's parable is that although women are prohibited from working on the assembly line in Japan, most Camrys sold in the United States will soon be built in Kentucky. And in Georgetown, more women work on the assembly line than at most Big Three plants.

Nissan's Jerry Benefield predicts that when Nissan, Honda, and Toyota establish their North American headquarters, it won't be in Detroit or anywhere close.

"Why should they do that?" he asks. "In Detroit, they'd be a minority player. They'd never get the attention or protection that other auto makers get."

In May 1989 even Hoot McInerney, president of Detroit's largest automobile dealership, acknowledged on the front page of *Crain's Detroit Business* that "the stigma of buying a foreign car in Detroit is eroding now."

Maryann Keller, a securities analyst with Furman, Selz in New York, still thinks the American Big Three will continue to lose market share, but no longer flatly predicts that they will, as she did two years ago. Married to Jay Chai, a Korean who helped negotiate Toyota's joint venture with General Motors, Keller has made countless trips to Detroit and Japan. She is published in trade journals on both sides of the Pacific and is the expert source most often quoted by our national media. She thinks Big Three market share losses will be less than they were in the 1980s, given the fact that the Japanese now have to pay as much to borrow money as the rest of the world's auto makers.

The 1990s will be tougher, she says. We'll see more competition among Japanese companies, more emphasis on profitability. Few Japanese auto makers are doing well now, as economic problems in Japan have depressed profits at home. The Japanese still have the new plants and much younger work forces. They don't have the same pensions and medical benefits to pay, but their cost of doing business has risen, and local content issues have become more important.

Given the current concern over the U.S. trade deficit with Japan, it is unlikely Honda, Toyota, and Nissan will continue to expand here as aggressively as they have in the past.

There are, however, a number of things to remember

about the Japanese: They understate their objectives. They keep their options open. They are forever cutting costs. They believe not only in giving the customer what he wants but in exceeding his expectations. And they go to extraordinary lengths to avoid laying anyone off. (That's why they all have a layer of "temporary" workers doing housekeeping, security, and other routine tasks—as a cushion.) Sacrifices will be (and have already been) made in Japan before belt-tightening is ever asked of the more vulnerable American plants. No matter that the American plants are less profitable. America (and to a degree, Europe) is the future for the Japanese auto industry.

The Japanese will do whatever it takes to succeed here. Worried about the mounting hostility to Japan's huge investment in the United States, the Japanese government previously offered Japanese companies large tax deductions if they would give money to American hospitals, schools, and other nonprofit institutions. The government has since ordered car makers to raise prices and reduce exports to the United States.

As the recent recession deepened and our presidential election campaign heated up, anti-Japanese sentiment grew more virulent. Newspapers and magazines devoted an extraordinary amount of space to the fiftieth anniversary of the Pearl Harbor attack. President Bush took the CEOs of the American Big Three to Japan with him, and afterwards Lee Iacocca charged that Japan was "stiffing" the United States on trade matters while a Japanese politician called Americans lazy. The trip fueled at least a temporary "Buy American" frenzy.

But in a country of such diversity as ours, fast becoming more so, the singling out of a particular nation or ethnic group for bruising seems likely to further increase divisiveness and erode national unity. Once one group becomes fair game for attack, it becomes hard not to single out others.

The UAW, which has had good reason to resent the anti-union behavior of Honda, Toyota, and especially Nissan, has refrained from Japan bashing for this very reason.

It is no certainty that central Ohio, northern Kentucky, and middle Tennessee will replace Detroit as the center of the American automobile industry, but it remains a possibility. Thanks to Honda, Ohio still leads the nation in auto parts production and is the number-two car maker, with the prospect of more capacity to come. Until recently, Toyota appeared to have put its plans for further expansion on hold. But, late in 1989, it announced it would be *at least* doubling its North American production by 1995.

In 1990, Toyota announced an $800 million expansion on its Georgetown, Kentucky site. Community relations had continued to improve. The bypass road around the town, long mired in controversy, was finally being built. Horse farms had become internationalized. IBM has sold its giant typewriter plant in nearby Lexington. Toyota was now middle Kentucky's largest employer and could command more respect. Former Governor Wallace Wilkinson finally went to Toyota City and offered whatever it might take to keep Toyota from building its new plant in Indiana or Tennessee. Toyota chose Kentucky again, but this time refused an incentive package. Unlike their American counterparts, the Japanese have an uncanny ability to learn from their mistakes.

During the 1940s and 1950s, hundreds of thousands of men and women abandoned towns and small cities in the Lower Midwest and Upper South to find work in Detroit. Detroit was the Arsenal of Democracy. Its productive capacity was prodigious. What was good for General Motors was good for America, we all believed.

Today another generation is finding better jobs in the auto industry without having to leave home.

Detroit and the Big Three are now working to catch up.

Afterword

I decided to write this book in the late spring of 1987, after a visit to Mount Vernon, the town I grew up in. It is a county seat of 14,000 that once had won an All-American City award. But like a lot of Ohio towns, it had stopped growing. Its leading industry had pulled up stakes and moved to Houston, leaving little more than a skeleton behind. The interstate had passed it by, thanks in part to store owners who feared that if a superhighway came too close, the townspeople would shop in Columbus. Few of the people I remembered from high school still remained.

I hadn't been back in a while, and when I saw some of the townspeople, and even farmers, driving Japanese cars and trucks, I was surprised. I couldn't remember anyone driving anything but American before. I heard, too, that city fathers had tried to attract a Japanese auto parts plant. They failed, I was later to learn, because Mount Vernon already had a small parts plant (with a UAW work force), because the farmer whose land the Japanese wanted to buy wouldn't sell, and because Main Street was felt to be still too much of a dividing line between white collar and blue.

I became curious, and my curiosity grew stronger when I discovered that in nearby towns there were people with no more than a high-school education making $30,000 a year to start at Honda. I looked further and found a similar phenomenon in the parts of Tennessee and Kentucky to

which Nissan and Toyota had come. The people being hired
were predominantly of German,. English, and Scots-Irish
descent and had lived in these places for many generations.
These, I learned to my surprise, were Americans the Japanese perceived to be the most like they were.

One year in college, I had had a Japanese roommate.
He visited my home and later, when I was in the Navy, I
took a month's leave and visited his. In Ohio, he was surprised
to see how big the houses and yards were. What he liked
best were all the tall trees. In Japan, we traveled together,
up and down the narrow part of his country that isn't
mountainous. In South America and West Africa, where I
was later to live, I could be stranded and scarcely see anyone
for days at a time. Not so in Japan. Over the next hill, or
around the next corner, there was always another inn or
pachinko parlor. I remember wondering how so many people
could live in such harmony together.

I had once written an article about two refugee families,
one Vietnamese, the other Hmong, who had resettled in the
Philadelphia area. I tracked them for nearly a year and
learned to pay more attention to what they did than to what
they said. I found that sensitive subjects had to be backed
into or circled before they could be approached directly, if
ever. I found that they had smuggled in forbidden herbs
for use as medicines, and even convinced immigration officials that a second wife was a cousin or aunt. They concentrated on reinforcing the old so they would have strength
enough to embrace the new. I remembered that when living
overseas, I had unconsciously done similar things. I wondered how an island people like the Japanese could transfer
such a large part of their most important industry to another
continent without resorting to similar devices.

I started by visiting the towns where the three leading
car companies had built their plants. I talked with Americans
who worked on their assembly lines, with union organizers
and with teachers who had Japanese children in their class-

rooms, with parts suppliers and township trustees. At first, except at Nissan, company executives were unwilling to talk to me. Honda had somebody writing an official biography. Toyota, having suffered an avalanche of bad publicity, was gun-shy.

But I persisted. I kept going back to the same towns, kept talking with some of the same Americans, and with others they recommended. Gradually the company executives became curious. Finally they were willing to talk. Later I went to Japan and they invited me to visit their headquarters and assembly plants there.

The Japanese liked that I didn't have a hypothesis I was trying to prove. The fact that I was looking at three companies instead of just one put things in a different perspective. None wanted to be outdone by the other.

A number of people were especially gracious in sharing their insights or in suggesting approaches I might not have thought of on my own. In this regard, I want to thank Toshi Amino, Pamela Bradley, Kiyoshi "Nate" Furata, Phyllis Genther, Mrs. Atsuko Hirobe, Frank Joyce, Maryann Keller, Andrew Pfeiffenberger, Marvin Runyon, David Wagner, and Toshiaki Yasuda.

Naoki Tanaka and Hiroshi Tsuzuki of Television Tokyo Channel 12 and Bradley Martin, Tokyo Bureau Chief for *Newsweek* (and a friend from days when we were reporters on the Charlotte *Observer*), helped to educate me in how Japanese see Americans, as did my onetime college roommate Dr. Tokio Suzuki, now a professor of engineering at Keio University.

Special thanks to Mary Fogg at Nissan, Tom Shoupe at Honda, and Mark Neff at Toyota, who did everything from running down details to setting up many of my appointments. I could not have accomplished what I did without their good-natured help and patience. John Shook at Toyota, Masumi Toba at Nissan, and Bret Anderson at Honda assisted me while I was in Japan, as did Yvette D'Arcy with Nissan in London, England.

Librarians at the public library in Bellefontaine, Ohio, Newcastle, England, at the Nashville *Tennessean*, and at the Columbus *Dispatch* were particularly helpful, as was the newsroom staff of the Bellefontaine *Examiner*.

I am grateful to Walter James Miller, who read my manuscript and suggested many helpful improvements in phrase and construction, and to Jack Finefrock, who did the same with regard to certain matters of tone and substance. My agent and friend, John Ware, was a staunch and enthusiastic supporter from the start. Jonathan Galassi, my editor, gently prodded when I needed to be prodded and helped me to realize I knew more than I thought I did. Elaine Chubb at Farrar, Straus asked countless, caring questions. And Mitsuro Tomita, my editor at Kodansha, helped me to sharpen my focus. Special thanks to Tina Isaac, my editor at Kodansha America, for her enthusiasm and conviction that the first edition of *Jump Start* was ahead of the curve. Responsibility for the book's contents, however, is solely mine.

I did my research and writing while living in Gambier, Ohio, the home of Kenyon College. It proved to be an ideal spot for such an endeavor, not least because of its long association with Junzo Shono, the celebrated Japanese novelist and short-story writer. The fact that I was "from Gambier," about which Shono has written two books of fiction, helped to open several doors in Japan. "Do you live near the upside-down tree?" and "Do you know the living Buddha?" were questions I was asked. Special thanks to Kirk Emmert, who proposed that I be made an affiliated scholar at Kenyon, and to Peter Rutkoff, who convened a group of professors against whose sensibilities I was able to test early findings.

In addition to those mentioned above, I interviewed and wish to thank Hiro Adachi, Satoko Amino, Wilson

Anderson, Karla Jean Andrews, Sue Atkinson, James R. Baldwin, Daniel Behrens, Jerry Benefield, Owen Bieber, William Boozer, Ed Brown, Don Buchenberger, Ernest B. Bumgarner, Steve Bump, Jack Bursack, Ron Butler, Robert Carter, Richard Celeste, William J. Chambliss, Tetsuo Chino, Fujio Cho, Jane C. Clark, David Cole, Robert Cole, Martha Layne Collins, Art Costin, James C. Cotham III, Ewing Crawfis, John F. Creamer, Cris Crissinger, Gary Damesworth, Richard Davidson, Walt Dennis, Clarence M. Ditlow III, Gary W. Dodd, D. Michael Dodge, Lee Dorsey, Robert Drake, James Duerk, Julie M. Eliason, Deb Ellis, Donald Ephlin, Herbert E. Everss, Jennie Farkas, Clyde Farnsworth, Robert Y. Farrington, Harry N. Faulkner, Michael S. Flynn, Helen Fogel, Douglas Fraser, Jay Friedman, James T. Goode, Keith Greer, John F. Gregory III, Bill Hamilton, Jerry Hammond, John H. Hammond, Jr., Fred H. Harris, Miyuki T. Hashimoto, Emil Hassan, Sam Heltman, Bruce Hencke, Stephen Herzenberg, James Higgins, James Hilliker, Saeko Hirano, Keiko Hirata, Barbara Holcomb, Ted Holmes, Charley Holt, Richard B. Hoppe, Candace Howe, Tom Hubbard, Donald T. Iannone, Merrill Insley, Susan Insley, Glenn Irwin, Maxey Irwin, Isaho Ito, Kinko Ito, Carl Johnson, Heather S. Jones, John Junkerman, Michael J. Kane, Eikichi Kasai, Kaname Kasai, Kiyoshi Kawahito, Harold Keck, Charles R. Kern, Marianne Kesler, Al Kinzer, Carroll Knicely, Bobby Knuth, Kasiwa Kudo, Yutaka Kume, Kaneyoshi Kusunoki, Peter Laarman, Paul Lantis, Clint Lauer, Dave Lavelle, Lisa Learner, John M. Lippert, Louis Lockhart, Dan Luria, George Lusby, Candy McCampbell, John Paul MacDuffie, Smack McFarland, Susan Macknight, Walter K. McPherson, John McVicker, Wendy McVicker, Bonnie Manning, Gene Marine, Stan Marshall, Kaeki Matsumoto, John Miller, Marilyn Miller, Dan Minor, Kenichi Mizuo, Jerry Moder, Steve Mooney, David Moreland, Janice Moreland, Ben Moyer, James Musselman, Ralph Nader, Keiko Namika, Dave Nelson, Gail Neuman, Akira Noro, Patricia Nuckles,

Tom Nuckles, Brian O'Neill, Ichiro Ogiso, Haruo Ohno, Tsutomu Ohshima, Jane Allen Offut, William Osos, George Patterson, Ben Perkins, Tom Prather, Lynn Pratt, Mark F. Pratt, Robert Preston, Barbara Rahke, Michael Reichert, Kit Reynolds, James A. Rhodes, Bradley Richardson, Barbara Fumiko Richardson, Knox Ridley, Max Robinson, Takesi Saito, Kazuya Sato, Nancy Saul, Cathy Schulze (Carrigan), Byron Scott, Carmen Scott, Jack Scott, Esther Millon Seeman, Harley Shaiken, Koichiro Shinagawa, Richard G. Sims, David J. Slaybaugh, Hugh Smith, Stan Smith, Rick Sommer, Zenzo Sonada, John Stockdale, Tom Stout, R. A. "Rudy" Sturma, Toshio Sugihara, Charlie Sutton, Sheilah Sympson, Freda Taylor, William Taylor, Ginny Tenpenny, Peggy Thompson, Joe Tomasi, Motosuke Tominanga, Yasuko Tsukamoto, Reiko Tsuzuki, Jim Turner, Joe Vicario, Richard Vicario, Lou Vito, Carole Wagner, Jerry C. Waldrop, Alex M. Warren, Jr., Thomas Waters, R. A. "Dutch" Wilde, Howard F. Wise, Scott Whitlock, Gene Wolford, Betty Wolstenholme, Dwight Woodlee, Shige Yoshida, Bill Young.

There were several people, scarcely more than a handful, who asked that their names not be mentioned. Nearly everyone I approached agreed to talk, although in a few cases it took more than a year.

Bibliography

The coming of the Japanese auto makers to the American heartland is such a recent phenomenon that little has been written on the subject. I relied primarily on personal interviews and observations, but also used the following for background and reference:

Alexander, Lamar. *Friends: Japanese and Tennesseans*. Tokyo: Kodansha, 1986.

Cole, Robert E. *Japanese Blue Collar: The Changing Tradition*. Berkeley and Los Angeles: University of California Press, 1973.

Collins, Robert J. *Max Danger: The Adventures of an Expat in Tokyo*. New York: Charles E. Tuttle Company, 1987.

Cusumano, Michael A. *The Japanese Automobile Industry: Technology and Management at Nissan and Toyota*. Cambridge, Mass., and London: Harvard University Press, 1985.

Fallows, James. *More Like Us: Making America Great Again*. Boston: Houghton Mifflin Company, 1989.

Feldman, Richard, and Betzold, Michael. *End of the Line: Autoworkers and the American Dream*. New York: Weidenfeld & Nicolson, 1988.

Halberstam, David. *The Reckoning*. New York: William Morrow and Company, 1986.

Iacocca, Lee. *Iacocca: An Autobiography*. New York: Bantam Books, 1984.

Ito, Kinko. "Organizational Adaptation of Japanese Companies in the United States." Presented in partial fulfillment of the requirements for a doctor of philosophy degree at Ohio State University, 1987.

Keller, Maryann. *Rude Awakening: The Rise, Fall, and Struggle for Recovery of General Motors.* New York: William Morrow and Company, 1989.

Lacey, Robert. *Ford: The Men and the Machine.* New York: Ballantine Books, 1986.

————. *Nissan in Tennessee.* Smyrna, Tenn.: Nissan Motor Manufacturing Corporation, U.S.A., 1983.

Morita, Akio, and Ishihara, Shintaro. *The Japan That Can Say "No."* Tokyo: Kobunsha Kappa-Holmes, 1989.

Richardson, Bradley M., and Uedo, Taizo. *Business and Society in Japan: Fundamentals for Business.* New York: Praeger, 1981.

Sakiya, Tetsuo. *Honda Motor: The Men, the Management, the Machines.* Tokyo and New York: Kodansha, 1982.

————. *"Salaryman" in Japan.* Tokyo: Japan Travel Bureau, 1987.

Shimada, Haruo, and MacDuffie, John Paul. *Industrial Relations and "Humanware": Japanese Investments in Automobile Manufacturing in the United States.* Cambridge, Mass.: Massachusetts Institute of Technology, 1986.

Shook, Robert L. *Honda: An American Success Story.* New York: Prentice Hall Press, 1988.

Tasker, Peter. *The Japanese: Portrait of a Nation.* New York: New American Library, 1987.

Tolchin, Martin and Susan. *Buying into America: How Foreign Money Is Changing the Face of Our Nation.* New York: New York Times Books, 1988.

Toyoda, Eiji. *Toyota: Fifty Years in Motion: An Autobiography by the Chairman.* Tokyo and New York: Kodansha, 1985.

————. *Toyota: A History of the First Fifty Years.* Toyota City: Toyota Motor Corporation, 1988.

Wickens, Peter. *The Road to Nissan: Flexibility, Quality, Teamwork.* London: Macmillan Publishing Co., 1987.

Index

About the Author

David Gelsanliter, native of a small town in the Ohio heartland, is a former foreign service officer and the former general manager of the *Philadelphia Inquirer* and the *Philadelphia Daily News*. A journalist and fiction writer now living in Dallas, David is currently finishing a book about the Honda of the American newspaper industry to be published in 1993.